DATE DUE

GRAHAM SMITH

WHEN JIM CROW MET JOHN BULL

BLACK AMERICAN SOLDIERS IN WORLD WAR II BRITAIN

St. Martin's Press
New York

© Graham A. Smith, 1987
This edition published by arrangement with I. B. Tauris & Co Ltd,
London

First published in the United States of America in 1988

Printed in Great Britain

ISBN 0–312–01596–8

Library of Congress Cataloguing-in-Publication Data applied for

CONTENTS

To LEON, ANN and JODY

ACKNOWLEDGEMENTS

This study has been over ten years in the making and it is impossible to thank all the librarians and archivists who have helped me in Britain and America. I must however pay special tribute to Mike Miller, Charles Shaughnassy and Morris MacGregor in Washington DC. Thanks too to the Eleanor Roosevelt Institute for a research grant and to Bruce and Joyce for endless hospitality. In Britain I owe special thanks to Dr Mary Ellison of Keele University for help and encouragement and my patient editor Iradj Bagherzade. I am grateful to the Controller of Her Majesty's Stationery Office for permission to reproduce Crown Copyright material. Finally, I am grateful to Joan Malin, my typist, and my wife, Gerry. Both have lived with this project for a long time.

Preface

A t about twenty past eleven on the evening of Friday, 5 May 1944, as the Allied war effort was gearing up for the D-Day landings, a 33-year-old English woman and her husband were lying in bed at their home in Combe Down, a quiet suburb of the city of Bath. As they were dropping off to sleep they heard a knocking at the window of their living-room. Looking out of the bedroom window, the woman saw a black American soldier standing by the wall below. 'I'm lost,' the GI said. 'I've come to find my brother, but I haven't found him. I've got to get back to Bristol tonight. Could you tell me of any transport or buses to get me there?'

The woman put on her underwear and went downstairs. She lit the gas and invited him in. 'I thought I could explain it better inside,' she said later. The GI then asked if she could put him on the right road. 'I suppose I could,' she replied. Putting a coat over her nightdress she walked up the road with the man and directed him down the hill to his destination. Now he knew the way the soldier insisted on escorting the woman part of her way back home. Twenty minutes later her husband, wondering where she had got to, had begun to walk towards the station in search of her. Half-way down the road he heard someone rushing towards him in the dark. It was his wife.

In a state of some distress the woman explained that the black GI had pulled a knife on her and threatened to kill her. He had pushed her against a wall and had forced her to have sex.

The husband took his wife to a first-aid post and the police were called. By now it was after 1.00 a.m. and, while they were on the way to the doctor's, the woman recognized the black soldier about half a mile from where the incident took place. Leroy Henry, the accused GI, denied being involved and had no knife on him, but he was handed over to the US military authorities. He was seen by American police investigators twice before 2.30 a.m. on the Saturday morning at Bath police station where he had been taken. At 4.30 on the afternoon of 6 May, he was transferred to a military police station. There Henry signed a statement that he had been drinking most of the previous evening, had returned to camp at 10.30 p.m., and then gone out again, effectively absent without leave. From there his account tallied with almost everything the woman had said. Leroy Henry admitted the assault.

The drama unfolded exactly three weeks later when Henry, a 30-year-old American Army technician, went on trial for rape at an American Army court martial in Wiltshire. It seemed a pretty clear-cut case.

The doctor who had examined the woman found bruises and superficial cuts on both legs below the knee, though there was nothing on her thighs or abdomen. There was evidence of recent sex but no evidence of a struggle, though the doctor was quick to point out that he had 'known cases where the woman was so terrified that she was incapable of struggling'. Events took an unexpected turn, however, when Henry volunteered to take the stand.

The American asserted that the statement had been extracted from him under duress. During his interrogation he had been made to stand for long periods, he had been sworn at and kicked and fainted from cold and hunger. 'A police investigator wrote just what he wanted to write down,' Henry claimed; 'God dam, you will sign,' he was told. Henry's version of that night's events was much more mundane. He had met the woman twice before — in April and then again a couple of days before the alleged rape. He'd had sex with her on both of these occasions and had paid her £1 each time. On the evening in question he'd met her at 8.30 p.m. and arranged a date for later after she'd told him how to get to her home. The quarrel arose over money and this, he argued, had led to the allegation of rape. The woman had demanded £2 this time and he had refused to pay.

The woman denied Henry's story though she admitted she would go to the pub alone sometimes, and that her husband was on war duty some evenings. Even the prosecuting counsel, an American officer, found the whole situation somewhat bizarre, though it was put down to the quaint habits of the natives:

> The action of the woman in getting out of bed and walking off with a dark strange soldier is rather odd, but in our relations with the English they do things that we don't do, and many of us will be able to teach our wives lessons. English wives do everything possible to help their husbands.

The end of the trial came abruptly. After a short recess the American colonel acting as the president of the court turned to Henry: 'We find you guilty and sentence you by the unanimous vote of every member present to be hanged by the neck till dead.'

Despite the public preoccupation with the anticipated opening of the Second Front (now only a few weeks away), many Britons were gripped by the Henry case. It also occupied the attention of the Foreign Office and the American Embassy in London; there were questions in the House, and petitions to General Eisenhower about what was seen as a gross miscarriage of justice. Many found it totally incongruous in the midst of a multitude of incongruities that a black American could be tried by an American court under American law, and sentenced to death for a crime that was not a capital offence in Britain. Some were confronted sharply with the extensive powers that Parliament had granted to the US Forces in 1942, and were acutely aware that they only knew about the Henry trial because Anthony Eden had insisted that when British civilians were involved American courts martial had to be held in public.

Others, more conservative, like Home Secretary Herbert Morrison and Secretary for War, P. J. Grigg, had argued as soon as black GIs arrived in Britain in May 1942 that their sexual contacts would lead to trouble, as would the British sympathy for them.

The issues raised by the Leroy Henry trial were part of a whole package of problems that came with the racially segregated American Army to Britain during the Second World War. Over 130,000 black GIs spent some time in the country, parts of which resembled Mississippi as the racial segregation practised by the American command first took hold in the West Country and East Anglia, and then spread elsewhere. As the British Cabinet wrestled with the question of how to cope with this unsolicited complication, official committees in London toyed with the idea of spreading authorized rumour campaigns, or setting up separate social facilities for blacks and whites after the American fashion. Jim Crow had hardly met John Bull before 1942. Their 3-year-long acquaintanceship produced some of the most dramatic and hitherto unknown episodes of the war.

1

Prologue: The Great War Black Americans in Europe

When the Japanese attacked the United States Pacific Fleet early on Sunday morning, 7 December 1941, the day that President Roosevelt said would 'live in infamy', black American families must have viewed the prospect of war with mixed feelings. This particularly applied to those families with members who had served in the Great War, and specifically to those who had served their time overseas in France. While the black soldier enjoyed a unique freedom and equality there, the humiliation he suffered at the hands of his white compatriots is clearly on record. Black participation in World II was to mirror this dilemma. This time, however, overseas service was to take place in countries such as Britain which had seen few black men.

In many ways the experiences of black soldiers in World War I, brief though they were, were a glimpse of what was to come in the 1940s. Important too was the perception of the black role in the war by whites and blacks when hostilities ceased in 1918. Some of the whites who were the younger generals and field-grade officers of World War I were the senior commanders in World War II. Denied promotion in the Army, their black compatriots in the earlier conflict became leading spokesmen and civil rights activists in the 1940s. The wars were close enough in time to provide a continuum of experience for both races.

The purpose of this book is to study the impact of the black American soldiers on Britain in the Second World War, but an examination of service overseas in the Great War, and of British attitudes particularly, is revealing. Many of the same hopes, fears and anxieties were to emerge a quarter of a century later in much the same form; to use a cinematic cliché, 'only the names had changed'.

After the United States of America declared war on Germany on 2 April 1917 full mobilization of American troops took some time, and some soldiers did not reach the front until the war was nearly over. As far as black troops were concerned they were to fight and work in 'jim crow' units, segregated on racial grounds from their white compatriots. By now the term 'jim crow' meant the total and almost absolute separation of the races from cradle to grave, particularly, though not exclusively, in the southern states of the USA. It derived from Thomas D. Rice, a white-minstrel show performer who in 1828 copied a dance routine called *Jump Jim Crow* from an old black man. Rice popularized the dance all over the country and even brought it to London in 1836. Much later in the century jim crow became a generic name for blacks and then by extension was used to describe the segregation laws which were a feature of life in the South in the decades after 1877.

Segregation in any case had been the policy of the United States Army for the duration of the Union. If jim crow was the familiar pattern of civilian life for most blacks there was no indication that their military experiences were going to be any different. The Secretary of War, Newton D. Baker, like his successor Henry Stimson in the Second World War, did not see the Army as a place for social experiment. Baker, a southerner by birth and family background, had made his name as a reform mayor of Cleveland, but he held the view that the War Department could not 'undertake at this time to settle the so-called race question'. He did assure the National Association for the Advancement of Colored people (NAACP) though that black soldiers would be 'justly treated'.[1]

Strangely enough the four black regular army regiments – the 9th and 10th Cavalry and the 24th and 25th Infantry – were not sent to France. Two all-black infantry divisions were formed for combat duties in France – the 92nd and 93rd. The 92nd Infantry Division was formed in November 1917 largely from draftees, and Major General Charles C. Ballou was placed in command. The 93rd was formed in January 1918 from a basis of National Guard units and consisted of four infantry regiments, the 369th, 370th, 371st and 372nd.

After meeting with the French general Henri Pétain on 15 January 1918, General John J. Pershing ('Black Jack' as he was nicknamed while serving with a black cavalry regiment in Cuba during the Spanish–American war), the Commander-in-Chief of the American Expeditionary Forces in France, consigned the 93rd Division to the French Army as replacements for some of their units. Each of the 93rd's regiments could be regrouped if needed. As Pershing later noted: 'Unfortunately, they soon became identified with the French and there was no opportunity to assemble them as an American division. Very much to my regret these regiments never served with us, but it was gratifying later to hear of their being highly commended by the French'.[2] In fact those blacks who fought with the French enjoyed equality with whites on a scale most had not previously encountered and this was to have repercussions when they were to return to the United States making demands as 'uppity niggers'.

Much of what little publicity there was about black troops in the Great War related to these combat divisions, but by far the vast majority of blacks in the Army were actually in noncombat service organizations – 338,000 out of a total black personnel of 380,000. Of the 200,000 blacks sent to France about 160,000 were in the services of supply. These 'labourers in uniform', as some called themselves, performed arduous, unglamorous but essential tasks as road builders, grave diggers, general labourers and as dock workers in Bordeaux where punishments included sleeping on cracked limestone rocks and being doused every morning with an ice-cold shower. Black organizations complained that black troops were being under-used and were not getting a fair share of favourable publicity. The Army was concerned at this and Pershing suggested later to the War Department that the name 'Labor Battalion' be changed to the more 'dignified' title of 'Services of Supply'.[3]

The memory of this lingered on arousing the anger of the President in 1942 when some of the first American black troops to land in the British Isles (in Northern Ireland) were described as labourers by the press. Franklin Roosevelt wrote with some petulance to Elmer Davis, the head of the Office of War Information, on 17 June 1942: 'This is your No. 1 headache. The Army people are dumb when it comes to a matter of information that Negro troops landing in Ireland are for "service supply". In other words, it is the same old story of publicizing the fact during the World War that the Negro troops were sent to France as "labor battalions".'[4] As a result a directive was swiftly passed on to the commanding generals in the field. They were not to publicize noncombatant troops as such but just to label them '"negro troops" . . . being cognizant of the adverse effect of publicizing most Negro troops serving in World War I as labor battalions.'[5]

Though the vast majority of the blacks were service troops such publicity as there was about them concentrated on those in the combat units. What is not in doubt is that by far the most controversial aspect of the black American presence overseas in the Great War was the question of relationships with the civilian and (to a lesser extent) the military population in the countries where the soldiers were serving. This was also to become an overriding concern in the Second World War, particularly as far as Britain was concerned. The problem usually focused on relationships between black men and white women. Thus the US authorities issued regulations intended to make such contacts impossible. Not surprisingly this heightened the bitterness felt by the black soldier.

The black experience in France in the First World War was very like that in Britain in the Second – certainly in one respect. Any instructions issued by the American authorities to effect the segregation of the black Americans from the whites tended to be ignored by the French. Unlike

Britain though, where in later years there were many officials who were willing to connive at the American attitude, in France there were angry protests from some sections of the government.

Two black American women, Addie Hunton and Kathryn Johnson, who served in France during the Great War, have told how as soon as they arrived in Brest they encountered not only American prejudices 'carried across the seas', but also 'a continued and subtle effort to inject this same prejudice into the heart of the hitherto unprejudiced Frenchman'.[6] There were frequent examples of attempts by the US authorities to curtail contact of the black soldiers with the French. The men of the 92nd did initially have some freedom to visit the local towns in France and mix with the people but this soon ended. A battalion of the 367th Infantry was billeted in July 1918 in Rengenville in the Vosges and the men were ordered to stay out of French homes. On 4 July, during Independence Day celebrations in the local town, a white officer saw fit to instruct white troops and local citizens in the inferiority of the black soldiers and warned against black Americans mixing with white women.[7] Some time later in September 1918 at Revigny, the French owner of a *foyer du soldat* stated that she had been told by the American authorities to place black and white diners in separate rooms.[8] Again an official instruction by Lieutenant Ernest Samusson was issued to the town mayors of the Meuse department. This warned about the local populace's relations with the 371st Infantry Regiment of the 93rd Division, and hinted at white American fears:

It is requested that the civil authorities concerned take steps to co-operate toward the prevention of these harmful relationships by enlightening the residents in the villages concerned of the gravity of the situation and by warning them of the inevitable results.

The question is of great importance to the French people and even more so to the American towns, the population of which will be affected later when the troops return to the United States. It therefore becomes necessary for both the colored and white races that undue mixing of these two be circumspectly prevented.[9]

Black officers evidently fared little better then the men in the ranks. In October 1918 thirty-three artillery lieutenants arrived in St-Nazaire, eventually to enter the French Artillery School near Varnes. The French Military Mission was told how the Americans wanted these black officers to be treated. They were to receive 'no more attention than was required in the performance of their military duties; that to show them social courtesies not only would be dangerous, but that it would be an insult to the American people.'[10]

The most controversial order on segregation issued in France during the Great War (and in many ways closely resembling some official instructions in Britain in the 1940s) was a document of 7 August 1918, issued by the Chief of the French Mission at the headquarters of the American Expeditionary Force, Colonel J. A. Linard. Though intended for French officers and written by a Frenchman, there can be little doubt that the document was issued with US support and possibly with Pershing's authority. Entitled 'Confidential: Au sujet des Troupes Noires Americaines', the document's purpose was to instruct the French in the white American attitude to the 'colour question'. There was concern at the 'familiarity and indulgence' with which the French were treating the black soldier. The black man, it continued, was 'an inferior being' and his 'vices' were a 'constant menace'. Hence, Linard announced: 'We must prevent the rise of any pronounced degree of intimacy between French officers and black officers . . . . We must not eat with them, must not shake hands or seek to talk or meet with them outside of the requirements of military service . . . . Make a point of keeping the native cantonment population from "spoiling" the Negroes'.[11]

The fears of the white American officials were transparent enough. One of these was of equal concern back in the USA – the overriding dread of sex relations between black men and white women; such relations, it was hoped, could be avoided through rigid segregation. Hence the US Army saw fit to issue instructions on this matter. From the Le Mans area in Mienne on 26 December 1918 came an order from Brigadier General Erwin that one of the duties of the military was to 'prevent enlisted men from addressing or holding conversations with the women inhabitants of the town.' A few months later an order issued to the black 804th Pioneer Infantry on 20 March 1918 was even more blunt. These enlisted men were not to talk 'or be in company' with white women regardless of what these women might feel.[12] The basis of this fear was the belief that whatever freedom the black soldier enjoyed while serving overseas in the Great War would lead to demands for the same kind of treatment on his return to the USA. Major General Charles C. Ballou thought that social equality, which was the 'dominant idea with many', would cause many blacks to be 'very much set up by this new and agreeable condition'.[13]

Despite the vehemence of American instructions, and their regularity, the French populace ignored the white American view and afforded the black soldier an equality he had not known before. W. E. B. Du Bois, the black academic, argued in *The Crisis*, the journal of the nascent NAACP, that in 'a thousand delicate ways the French expressed their silent disapprobation. . . . A new, radical Negro spirit had been born in France, which leaves us older radicals far behind. Thousands of young black men have offered their lives for the Lilies of France and they return ready to offer them again for the Sun-flower of Afro-America'.[14] William N. Colson, an ex-officer of the 367th Infantry, told the story of the black soldier returning home past the Statue of Liberty. When asked why he snapped a salute at it, he replied, 'Because France gave it'.[15]

The reaction of some French officials to the instruction issued by Linard in August 1918 left no doubt as to the strength of their views on the racial question. According to Du Bois the document began to circulate amongst prefects but when the French Ministry heard about this it ordered copies to be collected and burned.[16] The document was read in the French National Assembly almost a year after its publication, and it was disapproved of by many members, one of whom listed examples of the mistreatment of black soldiers by white Americans. French citizens similarly befriended the black soldier. Furthermore, despite all the prohibitions, it was reported that there were about 1,000–2,000 marriages between black Americans and French women, including, according to Colson, 'a surprisingly fair percentage . . . among women of culture and refinement', and this in itself fostered some of the white fears.[17]

The question of sex and morality was always at the forefront in the perception of the problem of the American black soldiers in France, and there were some aspects of this that were certainly to recur when blacks were again overseas a quarter of a century later, particularly in Britain. The most important of the concerns were whether black women should be sent to comfort black men, as well as the incidence of rape and venereal disease amongst the black troops. Involved with these problems were the apocryphal stories of black sexuality that British newspapers, too, were not immune from publishing. The London *Daily Herald*, a left-wing paper, said about the Great War that 'whenever there are black troops who have been long distant from their own womenfolk there follows a ghastly outbreak of prostitution, rape and syphilis'.[18] The US military authorities did not squarely face the problem of providing female company for black soldiers. So when blacks were not allowed to associate with 'decent' white women overseas they sought out the lowest red-light areas which often led to a relatively higher incidence of venereal disease among black troops than among their white compatriots. In fact the problem of venereal disease amongst all American soldiers in France was a serious one to which the Army authorities gave much attention. At one stage in 1918 the French President offered to establish licensed brothels for the visiting Americans though Secretary Baker's advice when he saw Clemenceau's letter was, 'For God's sake . . . don't show this to the President [Wilson] or he'll stop the war!'[19]

One of the difficulties for black soldiers in France was that they saw few women of their own race. The YWCA

camps in France with their female volunteers were rigidly
segregated and some white women refused outright to
serve blacks. There were few black women volunteers and ·
only when the black soldiers had the job of burying the
war-dead at Romagne were black women workers used, in
the hope that their companionship might stop the men
rebelling against this soul-destroying assignment. The Red
Cross (still segregated overseas 25 years later) did treat
blacks well in hospitals, but Surgeon General William C.
Gorgas, an Alabaman whose father had been a high-
ranking officer in the Confederate Army, refused permission for black nurses to go to France.

The rape issue during the war years was shrouded in
mystery. Major General James C. Harbord, the Commander of the Services of Supply in which most blacks served,
was very concerned about black relationships with white
women, claiming after the war that a number of blacks had
been hanged for rape. Investigation of this charge proves it
to be untrue. Only one member of the 92nd Division was
convicted of rape in all of their six months service in
France. The Judge Advocate General of the Services of
Supply himself admitted that the rape stories seemed not
to be 'substantiated'.[20] Stephen Graham, a young British
author who travelled widely in Russia and the United
States, wrote about black America in 1920. On the rape
issue he is worth quoting in full:

> The rape legend was imported, and every effort was made to
> infect the French male with race prejudice. Happily the
> propaganda failed. For one thing, Puritanism does not easily
> take root in a French heart, and for another, the French
> have no instinctive horror of Negroes. Possibly the rape
> legend even made the Negro a little ornamental from the
> point of view of amour. . . . As everyone knows who served in
> the ranks, women of easy virtue were extremely plentiful
> and complaisant. The need might easily have been to protect
> the Negro from the women rather than the women from the
> Negro. The fact is simply that the Negro walking with a
> white woman is to the southern American White as a red rag
> to a bull.[21]

Many white Americans, however, did not wish to be

confused with the facts, and fear of how the 'new' black
man would react on his return to the States was an
overriding concern at the end of the war. Again, Graham
heard the popular white view that because the black
soldier was a 'favourite of the white girls in France, it is
thought that his eye roves more readily to the pure
womanhood of the South'.[22] James K. Vardaman, former
Governor and neo-populist senator from Mississippi, expressed the same thought in his paper *Vardaman's Weekly*.
The Senator had always believed that to 'squander money'
on education for blacks was to 'spoil a good field hand and
make an insolent cook'. At the end of the war his bigger
worry was the return of the 'French-women-ruined negro
soldiers'.[23]

The general fear amongst whites about 'how you were
going to keep the blacks down on the farm, now that they'd
seen Paree', resulted in President Wilson sending Dr
Robert R. Moton to France. The Virginia-born son of
former slaves, Moton had succeeded Booker T. Washington
as principal of the Tuskegee Institute in Alabama in 1915
after the latter's death. When the USA entered the war
Moton had been instrumental in pressing black claims on
Secretary Baker, but possessing the same skills as his
famous predecessor in soliciting funds from whites made
him look too accommodationist for more radical blacks.
Moton's task in France was to talk to the black troops
about their return to the USA and he reportedly told them
that, 'I hope no one will do anything in peace to spoil the
magnificent record you have made in the war'.[24] A less
welcome visitor for the authorities was Du Bois of the
NAACP, who went to France in December 1918 partly to
collect material for a history of the black man in the war.
He was regarded as a dangerous radical, and he did
criticize Moton's mission as being inadequate. William
Colson in the *Messenger* was critical of both: 'Moton
attempted to palliate the unrest among the soldiers and to
prepare them for their homecoming, but his methods were
poor and his statements often misrepresentations. That
Moton did more harm than good is to put it mildly. Du Bois
worked in a narrow, intellectual circle only'.[25]

For black soldiers there were foretastes of what was to
come even before they left French shores. They were not
permitted to march in the Allied victory parade in Paris,
and there were petty restrictions imposed on their pay,
rations and freedom of movement in the post-Armistice
period before their embarkation for home. Nevertheless
blacks continued to hope for change in the USA after the
war, with Du Bois to the fore with his rallying call in *The
Crisis* of May 1919:

> We return
> We return
> We return from fighting

> Make way for Democracy! We saved it in France and by the
> Great Jehovah, we will save it in the United States of America
> or know the reason why.[26]

Dean Pickens of Morgan College, Baltimore, an NAACP
field secretary, echoed these sentiments: 'Our boys here
have been to France and bled and suffered for white
civilization and white justice. We didn't want to go. We
didn't know anything about it. But it's been good for us.
We've made the cause of universal justice our cause. We
have taken a share in world-sufferings and world-politics.
It's going to help raise us out of our obscurity'.[27] Stephen
Graham raised the question being asked by many blacks at
this time as they returned to normality in America: 'What
more absurd . . . than to take a man who is being illegally
disfranchised by the community, and make him fight for
that community?'[28]

In truth, despite the fears of whites that black soldiers
would return from France after the Great War full of big
ideas, post-war America did not herald a new dawn for
them. Lynchings continued: of the 454 who died in the
USA in this way between 1918 and 1927, 416 (including
three pregnant women) were black. In addition the
anti-Semitic, anti-black Ku-Klux-Klan grew apace and
jim-crow legislation remained. Indeed, any dreams that
black veterans returning home from their service in the
jim-crow army had of a better deal were rudely shattered.
Blacks were ill-treated and much of America remained the

same. There were those soldiers who realized this would be the case, as this self-effacing black story showed:

> Two black soldiers sitting on the dock at Brest at the end of the First World War spoke of what they would do when they were shipped home. One said that he would take a lesson from the French, who had no race feelings and drew no color line. On arriving in their home town he would buy a white suit, white tie, white straw hat, and white shoes. 'An I goin' put 'em on an' den I's goin' invite some w'ite gal to jine me an' wid her on my arm I'z gwine walk slow down de street bound fur de ice-cream parlor. Whut does you aim to do w'en you gits back?' His companion replied, 'I 'spects to act diffe'ent frum you, an' yet, in a way, similar. I'm goin' git me a black suit, black from haid to foot, and black shoes, an I'm gwine walk slow down de street, jes' behin' you – bound fur de cemetery!'[29]

When the Americans sent their forces overseas in segregated units in both world wars, they exported their racial problems abroad. The inevitable effect of this was to hand a propaganda gift to the enemy. In both wars the German use of the black-soldier issue was ambivalent – both the effect of segregation and the fear of blacks were exploited. German propaganda aimed at black soldiers asked whether they enjoyed the 'same rights as the white people do in America, the land of freedom and democracy, or are you not rather treated over there as second-class citizens? Can you go into a restaurant where white people dine? Can you get a seat in the theatre where the white people sit? . . . is lynching . . . a lawful proceeding in a democratic country? Now all this is entirely different in Germany, where they do like coloured people'.[30]

Most black Americans spent their overseas war in France. Those who came to England were usually in transit. They would arrive at Liverpool, make their way to Southampton and from there to Le Havre in northern France. Some black pioneer regiments and labour battalions were held back for service in England though only as an experiment 'owing to the objections of [British] Labor Unions'.[31] There were, however, some hints as to the kind of public and private attitudes which would be more fully exhibited in World War II when blacks came to Britian in greater numbers and for longer periods. The attitude of the British military command was revealed in May 1918 when the 92nd all-black division, formed in November 1917, was due to arrive in France. According to General Pershing they were to be given temporary service and training with the British armies, but the British Military Attaché at Washington, acting under instructions from his Government, protested against it. Pershing wrote to Field Marshal Haig and Lord Milner, the British Secretary for War, on 5 May 1918, to clarify the matter. He probably had an inkling of what the British response would be for he noted in his diary on 10 May 1918 that the 'British object to taking coloured troops for training'. Milner's reply to Pershing came on 13 May and was elegantly disingenuous: '. . . I am rather hoping that this difficult question may not after all be going to trouble us, for I see, from a telegram received from General Wagstaff, that the Divisions so far arrived for training with the British do not include the 92nd. I hope this is so, for as a matter of fact, a good deal of administrative trouble would, I think, necessarily arise if the British Army had to undertake the training of a coloured Division'.[32] The US War Department evidently bowed to these wishes and the 92nd Division was not included among those assigned to Britain.

Though there were few American blacks in Britain for any length of time in World War I, there were indigenous blacks and blacks from the British Empire. When these met the white American, particularly when women were involved, there were ugly rehearsals of what was to become a major problem in Britain in World War II. *The Times* reported race rioting at Cardiff in 1919 which had involved British blacks and indicated the white fear that was still paramount over twenty years later: 'The Negro is almost pathetically loyal to the British Empire and he is always proud to acclaim himself a Briton. His chief failing is his fondness for white women, and American naval officers stationed at the American naval base at Cardiff have often expressed their disgust at the laxity of the British law in this connection'.[33]

Nevertheless, William Colson seemed happy about English attitudes in the Great War, and compared the English and the French: 'While in France, the Negro soldiers got their bearings. They discovered that the only white men that treated them as men, were native Europeans, and especially the French with their wider social experience and finer social sense. The Frenchman was unable to comprehend color prejudice. The Englishman was much more democratic than the American'.[34] It may well be, however, that it was because the black soldier was kept in line in Britain in World War I, rather than the fact that he was accepted, that persuaded the US military authorities into thinking it would be safe to send him there in World War II. Major General Strong of the Intelligence Division gave his advice about Britain to the US Army Operations Division on 17 June 1942: '*Great Britain and Ireland.* There are no basic factors tending to prevent our sending negro troops to the British Isles (North Ireland included). A very strict color line is maintained everywhere. The people have been accustomed to the presence of their own native troops, among them negroes. The American negro troops stationed in England during the World War created no unsolvable problems and they were generally well treated'.[35]

Black troops were thus sent to Britain in large numbers from the spring of 1942. The NAACP's *Crisis* however soon found that the situation paralleled that of France in the earlier war: 'Messages and letters – some of the latter in guarded language – are beginning to come home from our boys overseas indicating that white American troops from Dixie are trying to give them the same treatment given black troops in France in 1918. . . . The trouble is with white Southern American troops who do not want the English to treat our men as men and fighters of democracy. There should be no repetition of the shameful treatment of Negro troops in France in the first world war by their own countrymen'.[36] But this is to jump the gun; even before the American entry into the war at the end of 1941 the British Government had exchanged views on racial issues with the NAACP, and with its own black citizens. These exchanges were to give a clear indication of the problems to come in the years of the Second World War.

2
The Early War Years: First Encounters

The years between the end of World War I and the American entry into World War II in December 1941 were important for the development of the United States Army. In particular, for blacks the years between 1939 and Pearl Harbor witnessed vital debates about their participation in the armed forces, though the outcome was a restatement of the policy of segregation. There were those blacks at this time who wished to help the British war effort before their own government became officially involved. By examining the British Government's reaction to these offers we can get some inkling of the racial attitudes which were to be more fully developed from 1942. It is also equally important to gather some idea of the perceptions of ordinary British citizens on matters concerning race and colour before these attitudes were put to the test by Operation Bolero, the build-up of American forces in Britain in the spring of 1942.

After World War I the peacetime Army of the United States was decreased in size; the four black regular units were retained, but there was considerable discussion about their future function. Reports of the black performance in the First World War, together with pseudo-scientific studies of black intelligence, contributed to a strongly supported belief that there should be no combat role for the black soldier. Some observers realized that, as in the Great War, the overwhelming majority of casualties in future wars would be white Americans. If blacks were not allowed to fight (and die) for their country serious political repercussions would take place. A 1922 study for the Army Chief of Staff on manpower utilization concluded that there should be black officers, and for social and economic reasons blacks should serve in service and combat units. The Depression years hit America's blacks particularly hard and Federal measures to alleviate distress were either laced with opportunities to discriminate or made matters worse, especially in the South. Joining up was no escape route either: because of the limitations on black troop strength black Americans were only allowed into the Army to fill vacancies. Moreover the role of the regular units was confined to ceremonial and housekeeping duties while the Air Corps (of the Army) rejected blacks altogether.

Changes in Army policy came with a War Department Personnel Plan in 1937, which received a mixed reception from blacks. They were to form about 9–10% of the Army, their approximate proportion in the American population. This quota was not reached in fact until the end of World War II and was not reached at all in combat units during the war. The disappointment for many blacks was that they were to continue to serve in segregated units. Their roles in other branches of the armed forces were not defined. Perhaps the biggest blow involved the number of black officers. By 1939 there were only five regular officers; three of these were chaplains and the other two were Colonel Benjamin O. Davis (who was to play an important part in race relations in England in the war) and his son Lieutenant Benjamin O. Davis, jun., (later of the Air Corps).[1]

On the eve of the great mobilization of 1940 blacks began to step up their demands for greater participation in the defence forces. Not all organizations were uncompromising on the issue of segregation, but it was a main cause of controversy, as was the whole issue of blacks in labour battalions. The black press, World War I veterans, and the

NAACP all began to exert pressure now, rousing public
opinion and approaching President Roosevelt directly
rather than through the War Department. The Selective
Training and Service Act of September 1940 called for the
induction of 800,000 draftees and whilst it was stated that
'there shall be no discrimination against any person on
account of race or color' the implication was that the basic
pattern of segregation was to remain.

In order to clarify several aspects of the defence policy
and the use of blacks, including a request that units be
formed without regard to race, several prominent black
leaders met the President at the White House on 27
September 1940. At the conference, which had been
arranged with the help of the President's wife, Eleanor,
were Frank Knox, Secretary of the Navy, and Robert T.
Patterson, Assistant Secretary of War. Knox was a veteran
newspaper magnate who had been brought into office in
July partly because his Republican sympathies gave
Roosevelt's cabinet a bipartisan look. Patterson, a Harvard
law graduate, had been recruited by the President specifically in this case as a counterweight to the ageing
Secretary of War, Henry Stimson, who was 72. Presenting
the black programme were Walter White, Secretary of the
NAACP since 1929, T. Arnold Hill, adviser on black affairs
to the National Youth Administration, one of FDR's New
Deal agencies, and Asa Philip Randolph, a doughty
civil-rights worker of the 1920s and 30s who had formed
the Brotherhood of Sleeping Car Porters in 1937. Originally wanting to be an actor he quickly learned from his
preacher father that skill at addressing crowds was a
powerful weapon. In Randolph and White, Roosevelt faced
a formidable team.

It is not clear whether the black leaders expected
anything fundamental to come out of the White House
meeting; it would have been difficult to effect any great
change in Roosevelt's views. He was essentially a racial
gradualist always having to keep a political eye on
southern Democrats in the Congress who viewed concessions to blacks with grave suspicion. James MacGregor
Burns, one of his biographers, has argued that Roosevelt

'was more sympathetic to black aspirations than either his War or his Navy Secretary, but his tendency in wartime to look on race relations more as a problem of efficient industrial mobilization than as a fundamental moral problem left policy largely in their hands'.[2] Stimson, with his puritanical and strictly Calvinist background, was even more conservative. He regarded the black problem in the United States as 'insoluble'; he thought that 'foolish leaders of the colored race' were at bottom seeking social equality, which was impossible because it would mean intermarriage.[3]

Eleanor Roosevelt, however, was an invaluable ally for the black leaders. Using her close personal friendship with Walter White, she kept his activities firmly in front of the President during the war years as her interest in civil rights grew, even though the President himself on occasion would declare that he didn't 'think too much of this organisation' – the NAACP.[4]

The black delegation at the September meeting with the President seemed to think it had gone pretty well. White later remembered that 'one of the steps most emphatically urged upon the President was the immediate and total abolition in the armed services of segregation based on race or color. The President listened attentively and apparently sympathetically, and assured us that he would look into possible methods of lessening, if not destroying, discrimination and segregation against Negroes'.[5] Roosevelt promised to contact the black leaders, but his eventual response was to disappoint them. On 8 October Patterson submitted to the President a statement of policy, already approved by Stimson and General George C. Marshall, the Chief of Staff, to which Roosevelt gave his assent. This document was given to the press the next day with the implication that it had the approval of the black leaders. Henceforth it was treated as the official policy on the use of blacks in the defence forces.

The content as well as the delivery of the statement aroused black anger. The policy stated that blacks would serve in numbers proportionate to their numbers in the population, in combatant and noncombatant roles, and there would be black officers and participation in the Air Corps. The sting lay in the final point: 'The policy of the War Department is not to intermingle colored and white enlisted personnel in the same regimental organizations. This policy has been proven satisfactory over a long period of years, and to make changes now would produce situations destructive to morale and detrimental to the preparation for national defense'.[6] White commented bitterly that 'far from diminishing jim crowism, the new plan actually extended it!'

The resentment aroused by the White House policy statements coupled with the forthcoming 1940 Presidential election helped to explain the subsequent moves of the Roosevelt Administration. Within weeks new black combat and aviation units were announced, and B. O. Davis was promoted to Brigadier General on 25 October 1940. In addition to these measures, and following the precedent of Baker, the Secretary of War in 1917, who had a special assistant for black affairs in World War I, William Hastie was appointed Civilian Aide to the Secretary of War. Hastie, from Knoxville, Tennessee, was an NAACP board member and Dean of the Howard University law school, a black college in Washington, DC.

Despite the apparent finality of Roosevelt's announcement that American troops would serve in segregated units, this was not the end of attempts by blacks to change the policy. Randolph initiated the March on Washington movement. Borrowing the nonviolent tactics of Gandhi in India he urged thousands of blacks (and only blacks) to march on the nation's capital on 1 July 1941 to lobby for equal opportunities in employment and racial integration in the armed forces. With some vehemence he later explained one of the purposes of the movement. Black Americans, he argued, wanted to see 'the stuffing knocked out of white supremacy and of empire over subject peoples'. But, he continued, 'What have Negroes to fight for? Why has a man got to be Jim-Crowed to die for democracy?'[7] As the proposed date for the march approached Roosevelt grew increasingly apprehensive, aware that such an open exhibition of black protest would be a threat to the image of national unity. A week before the planned demonstration the President issued an executive order concerning discrimination in the defence industries which established the Committee on Fair Employment Practices. No changes were made in the organization of the armed forces but Roosevelt had contrived to take the wind out of the movement's sails and the march was cancelled. Randolph pressed on with his engagements despite this setback and continued to draw large crowds in New York, Chicago and St Louis.

William Hastie, once installed in the Administration, continued to attack the problem of racial segregation in the Army and, after ten months' observation, he presented a report to Stimson on 22 September 1941 suggesting certain improvements. He criticized the Army's adoption of the 'traditional mores of the South . . . as the basis of policy and practice affecting the Negro soldier', and urged the employment of soldiers without racial separation.[8] The report was submitted to Patterson at the War Department, who passed it on to General Marshall. It was this recommendation about desegregation which overshadowed the others, and a reply was delayed for several months probably on account of this. The formal reply from the Chief of Staff to the Secretary of War came on 1 December 1941.

George Marshall became Chief of Staff in September 1939, when he was in his late 50s, after a long career in the Army. Of Virginia stock, his military education took place there after he saw service in the Philippines and in France, where he was an aide to Pershing after the First World War. One of his most important posts was at Fort Benning in Georgia from 1927 to 1933, when he was in charge of instruction, a position giving him influence over both army doctrine and those who were to be commanders in World War II. Marshall, like Roosevelt, could be termed a gradualist in racial matters. Forrest C. Pogue, his biographer, has said that 'Among the serious soldier problems Marshall had to deal with was the question of the place the Negro should occupy in the armed forces, an issue that was not settled then, despite his efforts to gain equal treatment for all men in the Army. One must not claim too much for him'.[9] Henry Stimson revealed that Marshall could be quite derogatory about black troops, noting in his diary his agreement with the Chief of Staff's assessment of the performance of the 92nd Division in the First World War: 'As Marshall remarked, the only place they could be counted on to stand would be in Iceland in summertime where there was daylight for twenty-four hours'.[10]

In his reply to Hastie's suggestions on the use of black troops, Marshall spelt out the dilemma of raising an integrated army in a country where to a large extent segregation was the order of the day. Hastie's ideas, he said, would be

> Tantamount to solving a social problem which has perplexed the American people throughout the history of this nation. The Army cannot accomplish such a solution, and should not be charged with the undertaking. The settlement of vexing social problems cannot be permitted to complicate the tremendous task of the War Department and thereby jeopardize discipline and morale. . . . The War Department cannot ignore the social relationships between negroes and whites which has [sic] been established by the American people through custom and habit.[11]

The debate on integration in the military was virtually ended by John J. McCloy, the Assistant Secretary of War, another Harvard-educated lawyer called to government early in Roosevelt's third Administration. In July 1942, ironically just before his appointment as Chairman of the Advisory Committee on Negro Troop Policies – a watchdog committee on the whole question of black troops in the Army – McCloy laconically wrote to Hastie: 'Frankly I do not think that the basic issues of this war are involved in the question of whether Colored troops serve in segregated units or in mixed units and I doubt whether you can convince the people of the United States that the basic issues of freedom are involved in such a question'.[12]

Whether black troops were to serve in segregated or integrated units was of significance to their deployment overseas, however, and contributed to the image presented by the United States to its wartime allies. There was much discussion in American military circles in 1941 about the prevailing belief that segregation was part of the social mores of the United States, and as a result the Army argued that it was unable to change its own policy on racial matters. However, there was no discussion about what was to happen when an American army segregated by race was quartered in a country where such segregation was *not* part of the host nation's way of life. The picture of American democracy thus presented overseas was a contradictory one. Here was a country fighting for its freedom (and in part against racism) and yet when that country's army reached Britain it was exposed as rigidly divided, with white Americans openly proclaiming hostility to blacks. To cap it all, the jim-crow army was a propaganda gift to both Germany and Japan and was exploited by both.

Britain's first involvement with America's jim-crow Army came even before US troops crossed the Atlantic – indeed before the USA even entered the war. With the Lend-Lease Agreement of 1940 Roosevelt agreed to ease Britain's desperate military position in the war by making available fifty mothballed American destroyers (as well as other ships) in return for 99-year leases to military bases in the Caribbean. As with many British colonial areas the bases had mainly black populations governed by white administrators and civil servants. The significance now was that black and white Americans, both military and civil personnel, would soon be working in some of the leased territories.

Speculation about the attitude of white Americans to the indigenous blacks in these areas quickly emerged, including concern about whether they would bring their racial prejudices with them as they had done in Panama forty years earlier. Some of these fears were confirmed. Clashes did occur though there was no real racial tension or widespread trouble. Relations were worst in Trinidad which had the largest number of white Americans, concentrated near urban centres, though even Jamaica, where there were fewer US troops, was not trouble-free.

The *New Statesman*'s correspondent suggested that

> An unfortunate choice was made in the type of American
> sent out to Jamaica. Quite a large proportion of the soldiers
> and airmen came from the Southern States. Their immedi-
> ate reaction to Jamaica was to attempt to put into practice
> the social behaviour of Georgia. . . . American soldiers would
> go into a bar demanding to be served before all these
> 'niggers'. On refusal they would try to wreck the bar. In
> response Jamaican youths organized themselves into bands
> and whenever Americans attempted to create incidents they
> were frustrated by sheer weight of numbers.[13]

On the positive side was the experience for the white
American soldier of meeting middle-class blacks on the
islands.

American racial attitudes were not something the
British could directly control, though these attitudes were
being observed very closely by West Indians who were
being encouraged at this time to come to Britain to help in
the war effort. Certainly one aspect of race relations that
had a parallel later in England became clear – Jamaicans
were not readily going to succumb to American racial
prejudice.

Another problem which arose out of the leasing of the
Caribbean bases involved the British Government in
allegations of racial discrimination and attracted the
attention of the NAACP. The charge, put bluntly, was that
the British did not want American blacks to work or serve
in the West Indian bases, and hence requested the
American Government not to send any. Walter White
wrote to Prime Minister Churchill on 26 September 1941:
'Does the British Government bar these American Negroes
lest the example of qualified Negroes filling executive and
other official positions arouse too great an ambition to do
likewise on the part of under privileged Negro British
subjects in these islands?' White asked waspishly, after
listing his complaints. The reply to White's letter, when it
finally came seven weeks later, channelled via the Foreign
Office, denied that black Americans were being refused
permission to work in the West Indies. This 'must have
referred', the letter continued, 'to persons wishing to enter

the island as immigrants'.[14]

Britain's bland denial is belied by the American evidence. Brigadier General Dwight D. Eisenhower as Chief of the War Plans Division was charged with liaising with the State Department on the use of black troops overseas. In March 1942 he wrote to Chief of Staff George C. Marshall that 'local British authorities are strongly opposed to the assignment of colored units to Trinidad' and it was recommended that 'white units be sent in lieu thereof'.[15] Apart from the customary worries about miscegenation some British Governors in the West Indies were concerned lest the arrival of well-paid and well-dressed black GIs upset the local blacks. In another memorandum in June 1942 the Intelligence Division of the War Department espoused a view of British colonial rule: 'The local authorities try to keep the native populations contented with a low standard of living. Obviously, a situation will be created which will result in an unfavourable comparison which is bound to cause local disturbances. Before the arrival of colored troops at some bases, the [British] white and native populations were getting along well. Trouble arose as soon as our colored troops disembarked.'[16]

The issue of American blacks serving in the British West Indies certainly caused some ill-feeling between the NAACP and the Churchill Government, and the organization was quick to find other charges against it of deliberate racial discrimination. These other complaints (four in all) reached the Prime Minister late in September 1941.[17] They were acutely embarrassing for some British officials and the responses to them did little to lessen black American suspicions. The first charge was that despite the Royal Air Force's desperate appeal for pilots to ferry bombing planes from Montreal to England, the offer of help from a Charles M. Ashe, a qualified pilot, was rejected because he was black. Ashe was told by a Captain of the British Air Commission in Washington, DC, that blacks would not be accepted. In addition he received a written copy of the requirements from the RAF in Montreal which said 'all applicants must be of the white race'. The second charge was very similar in that a qualified black American physician, Walter W. King, had volunteered his services to England after urgent appeals. He was told in May 1941 that the American Red Cross had instructions (presumably from London) that only white people were eligible for this project. The third issue related to the controversial question of blood banks. Having heard that the British did not want 'black' blood, White asked whether it meant 'that English men, women and children would prefer dying to living, if the balance in favor of life is non-Aryan blood?'[18] The NAACP's fifth and final grievance (the bases was the fourth) was its belief that the British Purchase Commission in Washington refused to employ blacks.

The Foreign Office, which was given the task of preparing a reply, was troubled by some of the questions, and the NAACP would have been distressed at some of the comments made during the drafting of the British response. With regard to the ferry pilot request, the answer was that the requirement to be white would be dropped. The blood donor issue was fielded; various agencies in Britain, the Foreign Office argued, 'do not discriminate against Negro blood donors'.[19] Issues two and five, concerning Dr King and the employment of black Americans caused the most foot-shuffling. The first draft response on the doctor issue came from Nevile Butler at the Foreign Office on 12 February 1942: 'The Government have . . . felt obliged to take into account the possible susceptibilities of the patients and to provide a service similar to that to which they are accustomed (there are few, if any, negro doctors practicing [sic] in the United Kingdom)'.[20] Two weeks later an official of the Health Ministry said that there *were* black doctors in Britain so that had better be left out! It was suggested that the reply now read: 'The government have therefore felt obliged to take into account the possible preference on the part of the patients to be treated by doctors of their own race and to provide a service similar to that to which they are accustomed.[21] The Prime Minister's office regarded this answer as unsuitable because the NAACP might use it to advance a claim for black doctors for black people in England! With the help of the Colonial Office it was therefore changed again. This time the argument was that there were few black people in England and 'some people might even never have seen those of a different colour. In an emergency, children, in particular, who do not know of the traditional kindness shown by coloured people to children might be uneasy through unfamiliarity; and emergencies are no time for such complications.'[22] Britain, like the American Army, was not going to play host to a sociological experiment.

In response to the charge of discrimination against blacks in employment, it was pointed out that there were 110 black people employed in British missions in the USA but then a message from Lord Halifax, the British Ambassador, said that in Washington, DC, itself there were five messengers and ten charwomen. A Foreign Office spokesman cautioned against sending this to the NAACP arguing that to 'specify the posts in which coloured people are employed (i.e., the lower menial posts) would only further inflame the sensitive race-consciousness of the NAACP'.[23]

The black press in the United States also had strong views on Britain and it was the image of the country as a colonial power, holding sway over millions of black people in many parts of the world, that gave rise to most comment. This view was often held by those who questioned whether black Americans should fight in a 'white man's war' at all, and later, after Pearl Harbor, whether blacks should take arms against a coloured race. The association of these various themes led to bitter condemnation by some journalists.

George Schuyler in the *Pittsburgh Courier* in June 1939 said that the British Empire was the keystone of race prejudice and discrimination in the modern world, and a few months later thought that there was little to choose between the rule of the British in Africa and the Germans in Austria. Philip Randolph could also be somewhat vitriolic; he was reported as saying to the National Negro Congress in April 1940 that the 'fingers of England and France [are] dripping with the blood of black, yellow and brown colonials'. He did modify this a little later, and conceded that Britain did at least treat blacks as human in contrast to Hitler who looked upon them as half-apes. The *Courier* seemed to adopt an anti-British line, and in March the next year Horace Cayton argued that most blacks in America despised Great Britain as much as Germany.[24]

By the time America entered the war these views had moderated somewhat and, not long after the arrival of the first black GIs in the spring of 1942, they were modified again. Black newspapers despatched their own journalists to the European Theatre and when writers such as Ollie Stewart and Roi Ottley saw how the British responded favourably to black soldiers they contrasted this with the attempts of the American Army command to impose segregation.

If black American perceptions of Britain were often one-sided, British views on black Americans or blacks in general were equally formed in ignorance or from over-drawn pictures presented in the media. Both sides had much to learn therefore about one another.

It is difficult to say with any precision how many black people were living and working in Britain before the outbreak of World War II, but the permanent black population numbered in all probability between 10,000 and 15,000. Most of these were situated in or around dock areas such as Liverpool, Cardiff, Swansea, Hull and London, and it is safe to say that the vast majority of the population had never seen a black person.

Though there were comparatively few black people in the country this is not to say that there were no views on racial issues. The League of Coloured Peoples (LCP) was founded in England in 1931 by Harold Moody, a black physician originally from the West Indies. He could assert during the war years that 'the Colour Bar does exist in Britain', while Kenneth Little, an academic who was also a leading member of the League, argued that 'even up to the time of the present war, economic as well as social discrimination against the coloured man has been far from negligible'. Little believed that blacks in Britain were discriminated against when they were seeking jobs, and when interracial marriages took place. He was also able to show that a considerable number of guest-house keepers would not accept black people as lodgers.[25]

There were British people who sympathized with the racist American view when black troops arrived in 1942, and undoubtedly there were some Britons who expected black Americans to be like the movie image of them. The cinema was, of course, a vital medium at this time and its popularity meant that many people did 'see' black men. However, Peter Noble, a respected British film critic, described the parts that they generally portrayed as 'ignorant servants, lazy janitors, superstitious toilet attendants, nit-wit maids, valets, shoe-shine boys, faithful retainers, tramps and no-accounts, and Uncle Tom roles of every description.'[26]

Once the United States was in the war the British propaganda machinery turned towards America, and the public was bombarded with information about its new ally. Inevitably some of this attention was focused on America's racial problems, and as a result of several polls taken early in 1942 we have some indication of British feeling on this issue at that time. With the help of its twelve Regional Intelligence Officers, each with 150–200 correspondents, the Ministry of Information carried out a survey between January 1942 and March 1943 entitled, 'British Public Feeling about America'.[27] Some of the questions asked were about the racial situation in the United States and the answers suggest that there was little interest in, or knowledge of, this aspect of American life before the arrival of American soldiers. In answer to a question of January 1942 about what was least liked about the USA, only 2 per cent answered 'treatment of negroes', or 'attitude to race problems'. In addition only 1 per cent wanted to know more about racial matters. In response to a similar question over a year later in March 1943, only 1 per cent mentioned colour prejudice this time. This is perhaps not surprising as by the end of 1942 there were still only 7,315 black soldiers in England, and many people had not yet been exposed to white American prejudice.

Another survey, 'America', carried out by the British

Broadcasting Corporation's Listener Research Department
led the BBC anxiously to insist that its findings not be
passed on to the Americans because they contained some
derogatory remarks. As with some members of Churchill's
Government there was a strong feeling in the BBC that
American participation in the war was so essential that
adverse comment should be stifled. Even though the USA
was so vulnerable on the race issue a feeling of 'let's not be
beastly to the Americans' prevailed. The BBC report
confirmed the earlier findings of the Ministry of Information that British views on the race question in early 1942
were undeveloped. This document was produced in the
middle of February 1944, and since the Corporation had
carried out a similar survey in 1942 some interesting
comparisons could be made. Nine hundred local correspondents had contributed to the later report which briefly
mentioned the race problem. It argued that the British
judged American democracy in part by the treatment given
to American blacks: 'It should be remembered that it is
only within the last two years that many people have
actually seen the colour bar in operation, and this has
made a profound impression in some quarters. . . . It is not
unfair to say that two years ago British opinion about the
USA was a little naive'.[28]

Perhaps the most ambitious attempts to monitor British
public attitudes to the American race issue were carried
out by an organization called Mass Observation. Founded
in 1937 and using some ideas from the American pollster,
Dr Gallup, this private institution sought to supply
accurate observations on Britain's everyday life and public
moods. Its two main methods of gathering information
were man-in-the-street surveys, and reports from a large
panel of voluntary observers and diarists. During the war
one of the clients for its work (especially concerning
morale, air-raids and the effectiveness of propaganda) was
the Ministry of Information. Throughout the war Mass
Observation questioned British people on their attitudes to
the foreigners in their midst, particularly the Americans,
and these early surveys give us some important information about the changing interest in, and attitude to, racial

issues.

One early poll was taken in London in January/
February 1942 when people were asked for their views of
Americans. Then, people in seven cities – London, Bolton,
Bristol, Cheltenham, Portsmouth, Salisbury, and York –
were invited to comment on the American forces in their
midst. The overall conclusion of the report was that the
American race problem was now a matter of public debate:
'On the Colour Question as a whole majority view is that
the treatment of negroes in America is not satisfactory'.[29]

From the available evidence it is safe to say that large
numbers of British people in January 1942 had no views
on, or knowledge of, the American racial pattern. This
naivety was to change within a couple of years. In 1942,
however, it was a source of fear to some commentators and
a golden opportunity to others. Captain Harry Butcher was
the naval aide to General Eisenhower between 1942 and
1945 and he was present during some of Ike's press
conferences in the middle of 1942. For him the lack of a
colour line in Britain was a difficulty. 'England,' he wrote,
'is devoid of racial consciousness. . . . [the English] know
nothing at all about the conventions and habits of polite
society that have developed in the US in order to preserve a
segregation in social activity without making the matter
one of official or public notice'.[30]

For Kenneth Little of the LCP, who had carried out some
research into racial attitudes before the war, the imminence of black Americans was a time for theories to be put
to a practical test. He observed that the presence of blacks
in Britain provided 'almost a unique opportunity for the
breaking down of certain strongly ingrained attitudes in
this respect which we ourselves possess. There is little
doubt that these attitudes are based largely on certain
"stereotypes," or conventional ideas of the coloured person,
for taking the population as a whole, it is doubtful if as
many as 5 per cent of us have ever had any personal
contact with a coloured man or woman'.[31] Little's colleague
in the LCP, Dr Harold Moody, was perhaps the most
optimistic in thinking that the war offered a chance to
solve the problem of race relations throughout the world.

He saw the importation of the American racial pattern as a challenge to the British Government. Writing to the *New Statesman* he felt that 'our Government must somehow, and that quite soon, assert that this country will not stand for any "Jim Crow" attitude in relationship to Coloured Americans'.[32]

All three commentators would have been interested in the results of their musings. Butcher was certainly correct in his assumption that the British people in general would not readily accept the American way in race relations, and this conflict was at the root of many of the wartime Anglo-American problems. As Little correctly forecast the presence of black Americans in Britain in large numbers *did* test racial attitudes, and the results and implications of these tests are examined later. As for Moody, his hopes would have been instantly shattered. For most of the decisions which had to be made by the British Government in connection with the black Americans had indeed already been taken by the time his letter to the *New Statesman* was published in September 1942. He was not to know of the feverish, high-level diplomatic activity in both Washington and London surrounding the destination and destiny of the black troops. Far from opposing segregation in the American Army, the British Government tried (and failed) to exclude blacks from the country altogether, or limit their numbers. It was certainly not prepared to risk the wrath of its vital ally by coming out against jim crow.

3

Attitudes and Anxieties: Jim Crow and the British Government

In the autumn of 1941 Prime Minister Winston Churchill asked President Roosevelt, more in hope than anticipation, for the help of American forces. Labour leader, Clement Attlee, the Deputy Premier, delivered a letter of 20 October 1941 to Roosevelt in which the Prime Minister outlined his request. Churchill wanted American troops and armoured divisions and all possible air force help to come to Northern Ireland even though the United States was still officially a neutral country. His belief was that 'the arrival of American troops in Northern Ireland would exercise a powerful effect upon the whole of Eire [which was neutral], with favourable consequences that cannot be measured. It would also be a deterrent upon German invasion schemes. I hope this may find a favourable place in your thoughts'.[1]

Churchill did not receive a formal reply to his request and on his own admission did not really expect one. Once the Japanese attacked the American fleet at Pearl Harbor, however, the United States moved with alacrity. The President delivered a message to Congress on 6 January 1942, promising that American forces would be stationed in the British Isles, and soon after the middle of January the first troops arrived in Northern Ireland as part of Operation Bolero – the build-up of United States' forces in the United Kingdom prior to a joint invasion of Europe. The first troops however were white; the deployment of black soldiers overseas was surrounded by some complications, and they did not arrive in Britain until May 1942.

When America entered the war General Marshall, Chief of Staff of the United States Army, called Brigadier General Dwight D. Eisenhower to Washington. The 52-year-old Eisenhower had graduated from West Point Military Academy in the remarkable class of 1915 which produced fifty-nine generals. Eisenhower was not a brilliant student himself, finishing 61st in academic standing, and 125th in conduct out of 164 classmates. When he went to Washington it was to work in the War Plans Division, a desk job not entirely to his liking. In view of his lack of combat duty it was a surprise to many when shortly afterwards he was appointed as Commanding General of the European Theatre of Operations. In late June 1942 Ike arrived in London to begin the task he had been given in preference to 366 other officers, soon to become a lieutenant general.

Not the least of Eisenhower's preoccupations while he endured his brief stay in the nation's capital was the issue of black troops and their deployment overseas. Officially there was of course no policy prohibiting their use outside the USA. Despite this various countries expressed their reservations about receiving black GIs, putting forward as reasons their fears of miscegenation, their higher rates of pay than local troops, and the weather. Britain did not voice any official opinion one way or the other though initially it seemed that *no* black troops would be sent to the United Kingdom in any case. White American soldiers had been in the country for several months when the War Department in Washington received a cable signed by Marshall in London on 17 April 1942, saying unequivocally that black units should not be sent to the British Isles. Eisenhower quickly corrected this administrative blunder a week later. He claimed that the cable had been sent without the Chief of Staff's authority and the true picture was that black troops could be sent to Britain, including Nothern Ireland, in reasonable numbers in any type of service unit.

Thus the American policy in the early stages was that
black service troops were to come to England. Inevitably
there were those who wanted black soldiers to be sent to
Europe for other than military or political reasons. A Mrs
Fry from Philadelphia wrote to Grace Tully in President
Roosevelt's office early in June 1942: 'For some time, the
negroes in Philadelphia and its suburbs have become
increasingly insolent. It makes one feel that an outbreak
from them is near. Would it be possible to send some troops
of negroes to Europe? The sooner large numbers are gotten
in training and out of the US the better it will be for
American women.'[2]

This advice was somewhat belated for by the middle of
May 1942 there were 811 black soldiers *en route* to the
British Isles out of a projected total at that time of 12,877;
by 20 May some 600 had arrived, quartermaster and
ordnance troops with the Eighth Air Force which at this
time was a part of the Army Air Forces.

There was only a short interval between America's entry
into the war and the arrival of her troops in Britain, and
thus it is hardly surprising that there was a great deal of
ignorance in Britain about the United States and its
people. The British had little acquaintance with *any*
Americans and additional curiosity was aroused by the
blacks. Moreover the American policy of segregation, as
will be seen, was plainly visible and this separation of
whites from blacks was at the very least a source of wonder
to local inhabitants. Some questions of a very practical
nature began to be asked of wartime officials controlling
all aspects of life on the home front by those who came into
contact with the black soldiers and observed their relations
with their white compatriots. In the event of fights
developing between black and white American soldiers,
especially if they happened on British premises, what
should be the attitude of the British? What should be the
reaction if *British* people were involved in any racial
disturbances? One question was certainly at the root of
many anxieties: what advice should be given if British
girls went out with black Americans, and even wanted to

marry them? What about the illegitimate brown babies which would almost inevitably result?

Few in power realized how the black presence in Britain would affect almost every government department, almost every facet of British life and almost every aspect of Anglo-American relations. True, there were many bigger issues to be wrestled with such as the military progress of the war, the relationship of Britain with Russia, the timing of the Second Front and the nature of post-war political organization; but the issue of American race relations and its side-effects on Britain was a constant nagging pain to add to the country's other wartime ailments.

Layer upon layer of British institutions found themselves becoming directly or indirectly caught up in the business of maintaining a segregated American army in Britain. In the early months of 1942 the Colonial and Foreign Offices became embroiled in the question because the racial prejudices imported with the American troops began to affect blacks from the colonies who were already living and working in Britain, and this in turn dragged in the Ministry of Labour which had recruited many of them in the first place. The Ministry of Information was charged with making the Americans welcome and had to tailor its message to two separate armies. In common with the Home Office and the Ministry of Home Security, the Ministry of Information dealt with the delicate questions raised by the various information, intelligence and morale officers scattered throughout the land facing issues they were not trained to handle. The War Office worked closely with the American Army in Britain to sort out all the difficulties that were thrown up, while other services – the hospitals and those who requisitioned accommodation for the troops for example – had to tackle the logistical and supply problems raised in providing for two American armies, one black, one white. Meanwhile countless minor officials and civil servants, from policemen, magistrates and probation officers grappled with the practical difficulties raised by the presence of segregated black troops.

The cast of dignitaries who had some connection with the issue reads like a list of the Anglo-American élite of the period. Churchill and Roosevelt found themselves sucked in from time to time, as, of course, was Eisenhower and, of her own volition, Eleanor Roosevelt. Three future US secretaries of state devoted some of their attention to this area, namely George Marshall, Dean Acheson, and John Foster Dulles, as did future Democratic senator Robert C. Byrd. In Britain several of those who tackled the situation at the Foreign Office became post-war ambassadors, Nevile Butler, Alan Dudley and Francis Evans for example, and for a while future Conservative Prime Minister, Harold Macmillan, was immersed in it. Ecclesiastics wrestled with the racial dilemmas Britain encountered, most notably in the shape of William Temple, the contemporary Archbishop of Canterbury, and Bishop Geoffrey Fisher, one of his successors, while prominent literary figures like Louis MacNeice, and those like George Orwell and Ralph Ellison, whose greater fame was yet to come, were actively involved in it. All this was watched closely by the black press in America and by powerful black pressure groups whose members included Walter White, Roy Wilkins and Thurgood Marshall who would become the first black Justice on the Supreme Court. The drama of jim crow in Britain could not have found a more interesting and varied cast of characters.

The regional reports coming in to their departments expressing some of the concerns surrounding the presence of the black GIs in Britain, meant that several ministers would have been aware of the problems quite early in 1942. These would have included Anthony Eden at the Foreign Office, Herbert Morrison at the Home Office and Brendan Bracken at the Ministry of Information. Despite the level at which the issue was being reviewed, concerted action was lacking. The Government prevaricated, hedged and delayed. When, as will be seen, its attempts to limit the numbers of black troops coming to Britain proved futile, it finally groped its way towards a policy which was formalized in October and November 1942.

In truth the British Government was faced with a dilemma which was not of its own making, and which in reality it did not know how to solve. Thus it seems likely that the Cabinet would have been criticized for taking any kind of action and there were those, such as Oliver Harvey, wartime private secretary to Anthony Eden, and future Ambassador to Paris, who realized this at an early date; he commented in his diary towards the end of July 1942 that to treat black Americans as equals would cause trouble with officers from the South (there had already been a scene in a club in Cheltenham), while to treat them differently would offend their northern counterparts.

The British Government, as it saw matters, had to be careful not to upset its vital ally by actively encouraging the breakdown of the American segregation policy which would, according to some white Americans, make the blacks more 'uppity' and demanding on their return home at the end of the war. On the other hand, to accept the American standpoint would be to give offence to British blacks, to the NAACP, the British colonial territories and armies, not to mention significant elements of the British electorate. All aggravation of these unfamiliar racial problems would, it was believed, impair the war effort. Little wonder then that the efforts of some ministers were, as we shall see, directed towards the apparently simple solution of preventing black American troops from coming to Britain at all. This they failed to do, and the anxieties did not go away.

From the middle of 1942, as black and white Americans came into the British Isles, it was the rigid racial demarcation which seemed most incongruous to the host population, and it was a frequent cause of comment, often by those close to Cabinet thinking. One astute observer was Hugh Dalton, the Labour member for Bishop Auckland and President of the Board of Trade. In early July he visited the north of England with the Ministry of Information officer for the region, and they discussed the kinds of problems which would arise when the Americans arrived in large numbers – their wealth, their relations with girls, their boastfulness and the fact that many of them would be blacks who would inevitably be harried by white Americans in British streets or pubs, perhaps arousing the indignation of British citizens and causing them to take the part of the black soldiers. Dalton was one of several commentators who forecast that the British would find the American system of racial segregation difficult to cope with.

Though black soldiers began to appear in increasing numbers in Britain in the second half of 1942 they tended to be concentrated in certain parts of the country, notably in the south and south-west of England. As they piled into Devon, Gloucestershire, Cornwall and Hampshire in increasing numbers the local inhabitants began to see the fights between them and their white compatriots; they saw how the local girls found the 'tan Yanks' attractive, and above all noticed that they were kept apart from the 'other American Army'.

Many of the early difficulties came to the attention of the regional commissioners for those areas, who were responsible to the Minister of Home Security, Herbert Morrison, the Labour MP for Hackney South in London. Britain was divided into thirteen regions, each headed by a Regional Commissioner for Civil Defence whose primary purpose was to assume full civil power in place of central government if communications between the Government and the regions broke down. The commissioners were a motley group which included colonial governors, civil servants, ex-army officers and other individuals like the noted educationist Sir Will Spens, and lawyer and future Labour Attorney General, Hartley Shawcross. Fortunately they were never needed for their main role but they performed a variety of other tasks which included keeping an eye on relations between black and white GIs and the civilian population. Those regions which were the first to see black soldiers asked anxiously for help with the problems, but several other areas also wanted information about the question of discrimination.

The two commissioners who particularly sought advice were Harry Haig and General Sir Hugh Jamieson Elles. Haig was in charge of the Southern area centred on Reading. Schooled at Winchester he left Oxford with a first-class degree and then joined the Indian Civil Service where at one point he was private secretary to the Viceroy, and in the years immediately before the outbreak of war he was Governor of the United Provinces in India. Elles by contrast was a professional soldier whose background was Clifton and Woolwich. He had been in the Tank Corps in France during the First World War and was Director of Military Training for a spell in the early 1930s. Both men were over 60 when the Americans arrived and paragons of the British establishment. From his base in Bristol as the Southwestern Commissioner, Elles became increasingly frustrated with what he saw as the lack of guidance from central government on the racial issue. He felt that it was extremely difficult to give any advice to anyone anxious about the colour problem while the Government remained silent on the matter, and he returned to this subject repeatedly in his reports. Though he was anxious to know how the British should react when white soldiers operated a colour bar, many of the concerns expressed by him and by Haig were related to the liking local girls openly showed for black GIs.

In the spring of 1942 much of the controversy surrounding the presence of the black GIs in Britain was held in check, with many of the official documents classified as 'Confidential'. The issue entered the public forum on 29 July 1942, however, when the House of Lords debated the Visiting Forces Bill which dealt with the legal procedures relating to American troops committing criminal offences in Britain. Anthony Ashley-Cooper, the ninth Earl of Shaftesbury used this opportunity to bring the racial issue out in the open, noting that it was in no way taken account of in the Bill, and asking the Government, in vague terms, to give it consideration. It was not clear what Shaftesbury wanted, but by this date the Government *had* given some consideration to the question. On this occasion it was the Lord Chancellor, Viscount Simon, who replied sharply to Shaftesbury and his response was carefully noted, and welcomed, in black America: 'I do not suppose that my noble friend suggests for a moment that any distinction should be drawn between white and coloured soldiers. I am certain that neither the British Parliament nor any of us would contemplate that for a single moment'.[3] Although

Simon maintained his liberal approach there were members of the Cabinet who within a very short time were not simply contemplating racial segregation but actively promoting it.

The most public pressure exerted on the Government to 'do something' about the black Americans came with the publication of an article in the popular newspaper the *Sunday Pictorial* on 6 September 1942. The American troops had reached the area of Worle near Weston-super-Mare, and the vicar's wife there had seen fit to address the local ladies about their behaviour towards the blacks. Mrs May's advice to shopkeepers was to serve them but to tell them not to come again, while ladies should move if seated next to them in a cinema. They were to cross the road to avoid meeting blacks, move out of shops and 'of course, must have no social relationship with coloured troops', and on 'no account must coloured troops be invited into the homes of white women'. The *Pictorial*, which reported the incident, also had some advice for Britain's black visitors: 'Any coloured soldier who reads this may rest assured that there is no colour bar in this country and that he is as welcome as any other Allied soldier. He will find that the vast majority of people here have nothing but repugnance for the narrow-minded, uninformed prejudices expressed by the vicar's wife. There is – and will be – no persecution of coloured people in Britain'. Again, these hopes were a little optimistic for as it turned out some of the instructions issued by Mrs May not only coincided with the views of some Cabinet members but were not far removed from the feelings of many churchmen.

Black soldiers came to the notice of the House of Commons in September 1942. During a debate on the pay of British soldiers on 10 September, J. J. Davison, the Labour MP for Glasgow Maryhill, was upset that American forces now in Britain received much more money than their British counterparts. Though the gap narrowed at the higher end of the officer rankings, at the bottom it was quite considerable. A private in the British Army, for example, received 14s per week, while his counterpart in the American forces (be he black or white) was paid $13.85

(equivalent to £3. 8s. 9d.) a week in the middle of 1942. Many people were concerned enough about this gap but that *blacks* should be earning more than their British counterparts seemed galling to Mr Davison.

When Tom Driberg, Independent (later Labour) MP for Maldon, Essex, raised the issue of black soldiers on 29 September, the impact was significant. Was the Prime Minister aware, Driberg asked Churchill directly,

> that an unfortunate result of the presence here of American Forces has been the introduction in some parts of Britain of discrimination against negro troops; and whether he will make friendly representations to the American military authorities asking them to instruct their men that the colour bar is not a custom of this country and that its non-observance by British troops or civilians should be regarded with equanimity.

Churchill may not as yet have read a paper produced by Secretary of War James Grigg on the subject though he was certainly aware of it a few days after Driberg's question. In any case he regarded the question now as 'unfortunate' and added that he was hopeful that 'without any action on my part the points of view of all concerned will be mutually understood and respected'. Driberg argued that because the matter had now been publicly aired it was preferable and wiser to deal with it openly and 'handle this very serious problem firmly and constructively than to pretend it does not exist'.[4] Churchill refused to be drawn and several American newspapers, some of them with their own journalists in Britain watching the reactions to their compatriots with keen eyes, were critical of him because of this. The *Pittsburgh Courier*'s interpretation was that 'Churchill does not wish to act', though in its criticism it differentiated between the Prime Minister, the Government and the British people. *Time* magazine reported that Churchill 'needed all his skill at parliamentary parrying of tricky subjects' in answering this question from 'cocky' Driberg and rightly suggested that the question 'had peeled the blanket of official silence off a complex and dangerous problem'. The cartoonist in the black newspaper, the *Baltimore Afro-American*, chose the occasion to depict Uncle Sam being reprimanded by John Bull for introducing segregation into Britain.[5]

How different would have been the reaction of the *Courier* reporter if he could have witnessed the debate in the War Cabinet a few days later on 13 October, the first occasion on which the black Americans were discussed in any depth at ministerial level. It is clear that some members of the Cabinet had not been impervious to the welter of information coming into their ministries, and though Britain had not been among the countries refusing to accept black soldiers early in 1942 there had been an attempt to reverse this position.

A great deal of energy was spent in July and August, particularly by Foreign Secretary Anthony Eden, in putting forward what seemed an attractive and easy solution to the problem: this was to stop blacks coming to Britain altogether or at the very least to put a strict limit on their numbers. With such a powerful spokesman this idea gained momentum at the expense of any other positive course of action relating to the black soldiers already in Britain.

Although the Government realized that it was going to be difficult to persuade the American authorities not to send any black soldiers to Britain at all, the chance to put the subject back on the Anglo-American agenda came in the middle of July 1942. On the 17th, General Marshall and Admiral King, together with veteran New Dealer Harry Hopkins, who described himself as Roosevelt's 'glorified office boy', arrived in Britain. At that moment relationships between the two countries were a little tetchy. There were disagreements about when any cross-Channel attack should take place and whether there should be a concerted Anglo-American move against the Germans in North Africa. To add to the difficulties the hard-pushed Russians were pressing both Britain and America to open a second front with an invasion of the German-occupied Continent. The visiting party did not begin their trip auspiciously. Ignoring Churchill's invita-

tion to see him in the country first, Marshall and King
went straight into discussions with their British counterparts. When Hopkins went to see Churchill on his own, he
had to listen in embarrassment as the Prime Minister
berated the absent British Chiefs of Staff. Arguing that
they were under his command Churchill angrily tore out
each page of a book of Army regulations as he read it,
throwing the leaves on the floor.

Meanwhile at the meeting of the War Cabinet on the
morning of 21 July, Anthony Eden raised the question of
the proportion of black Americans, thought to be 10 per
cent, which would arrive. He feared that there would be
trouble between the British people and the American
troops 'more particularly, perhaps, through certain sections of our people showing more effusiveness to the
coloured people than the Americans would readily understand'. Eden may well have discussed the racial difficulties
with Oliver Harvey, his private secretary, for Harvey
recorded some strong views in his diary on the same day.
Harvey's arguments were to gain currency later in the
war, with certain officials 'blaming' the American Government for sending black troops to Britain in the first place:
'Both sides,' he wrote,

> were angling for the negro vote in the coming [American]
> autumn elections, hence the decision to send the negroes
> over here just as if they were whites. It is rather a scandal
> that the Americans should thus export their internal
> problem. We don't want to see lynching begin in England. I
> can't bear the typical Southern attitude towards the negroes.
> It is a great ulcer on the American civilisation and makes
> nonsense of half their claims.[6]

One result of the Cabinet meeting of 21 July was the
Prime Minister's decision to raise the matter of the black
troops with the American guests during their visit, and Sir
Edward Bridges, Secretary of the Cabinet since 1938, who
was always certain of the importance of Anglo-American
relations, sent a note to the Prime Minister's office to
remind Churchill to do this.

The Americans did not in fact look at the situation for
another month, but meanwhile Eden, partly through

frustration and partly because of his anxiety to use more than one channel of communication, raised the question of the black soldiers directly with the British Embassy in Washington. In a telegram to the Foreign Office on 12 August, Ronald (Ronnie) Campbell, the bright young British Minister in Washington, outlined some of the difficulties the American Government faced:

> Marshall promises Dill [Field Marshall Sir John Dill, head of the British Joint Staff Mission in Washington] he will look into the problem from the British point of view and let us know the number of coloured troops it is at present proposed to send. The difficulty he says is that 60% of United States army engineers are coloured and provide most of their organised dock labour. Politically the army must accept coloured men on equality with white and the former are quite unsuitable for combatant duties. Engineers, fighting units of which have to be included in field formations are in serious danger of being over-darkened. Marshall has received strong representations from Australia through McArthur [sic] and from every country to which United States troops have been sent including Liberia.

Campbell said that he had already spoken to Hopkins who was going to 'see what can be done'. The British Minister in Washington realized that the whole question of limiting the numbers of black troops coming into Britain was a 'hot potato', adding that Hopkins thought that it would be 'a bad thing if this matter were to be treated formally between United States Government and His Majesty's Government'. Campbell went on somewhat cryptically:

> Very confidential. Winant had mentioned the matter to him [Hopkins] and thought it had started by United States officers from the south who had spoken to British Officers and so on up. He thought therefore that there might have been some introduction in the presentation of the question to you. However, he realises that you and the Prime Minister are genuinely concerned. I emphasised that the problem presented was a genuinely serious and difficult one and by no means a mere matter of sympathy with possible Southern preferences.[7]

Pressed, no doubt, by Campbell, Hopkins reminded

Marshall now they were both back in the USA of their
promise to Churchill to look into the black-soldier issue.
'You will recall,' he wrote in the middle of August, 'that
when we were in England the British brought up several
times the question of colored troops in England. They are
under the impression that we are planing to send about
100,000 over there. I wonder if I could get a confidential
memorandum on our policy relative to colored troops in
England.' Marshall replied a couple of days later, presenting the facts to Hopkins who immediately passed them on
to Ronald Campbell. Marshall said that the present policy
was

> to send colored units to England in such numbers that the
> number of colored men will not exceed 10.6 per cent of the
> total United States Army strength. This is the ratio
> established by the Selective Service System for induction,
> and which we practically have been forced to adopt for all
> theatres. The figure of 100,000 would be contingent upon
> sending about a million to the British Isles. Present colored
> strength in the United Kingdom is 5,683.[8]

These figures were subsequently sent to London and
were raised at a further Cabinet meeting on the last day of
August 1942. Again the War Cabinet expressed its
unhappiness at the number of black Americans coming
over, and Eden introduced a new element into the
argument – the British climate. The Foreign Secretary
believed that the detrimental effect of the English climate
on the health of black troops would justify a reduction in
the number coming to Britain. This view was endorsed by
the War Cabinet.

It was also shared by James P. Warburg, a Harvard-
educated banker who, in July 1942, together with Archibald MacLeish, came to London to set up the main overseas
operational base of the Office of War Information. The
Office had been created the previous month by presidential
order, and grew out of the office of Facts and Figures which
had been headed by MacLeish, the Librarian of Congress
and 'poet laureate' of the New Deal. The London base of the
OWI, which would employ 1,600 people by mid-1944, was
one of forty such overseas operations whose function was to

gather information about local attitudes to the United States and her role in the war, and distribute propaganda material about America. Warburg became the deputy director of propaganda policy at the OWI's Overseas Branch. Certainly he foresaw problems with the black Americans in Britain. 'I think it is a mistake to send colored troops here', he reported to Elmer Davis, the head of the OWI in Washington, in September 1942,

and transplant into this country a problem which we have been unable to solve at home. I recognize the political necessity for using colored troops but I should think that the climate would provide sufficient reason not to send them to these islands and to use them primarily for the Middle East, Brazil, or other hot, tropical parts of the world. Actually it remains to be seen whether the colored troops can take an English winter; I doubt it.[9]

There were British citizens who shared Warburg's doubts about the wisdom of bringing black troops to England though their reservations were of a different kind. One comment made to a Mass Observation enquiry was that 'It was a pity to bring coloured US troops over and let the world see how backward white Americans are'.

Eden apparently explored yet another avenue in his attempt to stop black troops from coming to Britain. It is probable that he communicated with John G. Winant, the US Ambassador to Britain since the departure of Joseph Kennedy in 1941, for Winant, a personal friend of the President's, expressed some reservations about the black Americans in a telegram to Roosevelt on 22 August:

If it is necessary to send a considerable number of colored troops over here I wish you would ask Lloyd Garrison [a member of the NAACP National Legal Committee] if he could come on [over] for a period of time to help work out a wholesome and friendly contact with the civil population. It would take all of a good man's time for some time but I am certain it is worth the effort from every point of view.[10]

Eden mysteriously met Winant shortly after this, discussed the issue of the black troops with him and then passed on a message to Campbell in Washington. The Foreign

Office file on this is closed until 1993 and leads one to speculate that either Churchill and Roosevelt had further conversations about the American blacks in Britain, or members of the British royal family became involved in the issue. Whatever the answer it was felt sensitive enough to be the subject of a fifty year closure ban.[11]

Any hope that Eden might still have nurtured about limiting black troop numbers was quashed by Roosevelt's response to Winant's telegram on 10 September. Not surprisingly, for Marshall had prepared the draft, the President reiterated official Army policy – black troops *had* to be sent to Britain. He realized that there were 'many complications' surrounding their utilization but 'of necessity' a reasonable proportion of them were to be sent overseas.[12] A Foreign Office representative, J. C. Donnelly, reflecting on the black troop issue towards the end of 1943, felt that the Americans had used Britain:

> I suppose there may be military reasons for the presence of coloured troops in this country, but one important motive for sending them was certainly political. We need not begrudge the Administration much needed negro votes, but we cannot reasonably at the same time be expected to save the US Army authorities here from all the resultant difficulties.[13]

The feeling that black troops were sent overseas for political reasons lingered on. In one sense, of course, they were, for the black organizations in America would have raised a storm of protest at the slightest suspicion that blacks, within the limits already drawn for them, were not being allowed to play a full part in the war. As it was, the NAACP was very dubious about Britain's part in limiting the numbers of black troops and its enquiries into this caused considerable embarrassment to the British Government, and at the same time revealed how haphazard and uncoordinated was the official reaction to the black Americans. On 13 November 1942 the NAACP sent a telegram to the Prime Minister. It read:

> We are informed that British Government has requested US Government to send no more Negro soldiers to England because of complications created by prejudice of certain

American troops from Southern States. Will you advise if such request has been made. We trust it has not been as capitulation to race prejudice by Great Britain or US can only injure morale of colored peoples throughout the world.

The answer of course was that the British Government most certainly had made such representations, but it was not about to admit this to the NAACP. Neither was it clear who should reply to the telegram. The Colonial Secretary said that no reply should be sent at all whereas the Foreign Office advised issuing a categorical denial. The Prime Minister's office thought that the Colonial, Foreign and War Offices should reply jointly, but also hinted that the matter be left to Lord Halifax, the British Ambassador in Washington. The War Office was not anxious to get involved. Consequently over a month went by and no reply was sent. One Foreign Office spokesman thought there was a 'possibility that the PM might have said something of the sort to Mr Hopkins' therefore it was not wise for Halifax to deny it. But, he continued,

If the PM is now asked, and authorizes a categorical denial, Mr White [of the NAACP] will rightly conclude that if it took us six weeks to answer his simple question there is more in it than meets the eye. He would not have asked his question at all if he had not got wind of our approaches to General Marshall and Mr Hopkins, and to a sensitive negro the difference is slight between asking for 'no more' and asking for 'as few more as possible'.[14]

His advice was to bury the issue, not pass the buck to Halifax in America. The Prime Minister's office concurred with this and no reply was given to White, an action which once more cannot have endeared the British Government to the NAACP.

The most significant aspect of the British attempt to limit black troop numbers was that it was exceedingly time-consuming and diverted the attention of the War Cabinet from doing anything about the problems surrounding those black Americans who were already in Britain or on the way here. From many sources the Government was being made aware that the presence of the black Americans in Britain, and their relationships with their white compatriots, was giving rise to concern. Despite this the War Cabinet declined to provide any guidelines or policy statements on the issue. It preferred to direct its energies into stopping black soldiers from entering Britain rather than attempting to find solutions for a problem which had already arrived.

It was ultimately the activities of one man which prodded the Government into action. That person was a Major General A. A. B. Dowler who presented his views in a paper of 7 August 1942. These 'Notes', as he called them, became not only the basis of all Cabinet discussions from that point onwards but were in part incorporated into the definitive Government statements about the black Americans.

By 1942 Arthur Arnold Bullick Dowler had been a professional soldier for nearly 30 of his 47 years. Educated at Tonbridge School and Sandhurst he was commissioned into the East Surrey Regiment in 1914. During the First World War he saw service in France and Belgium and was both wounded and decorated. In the interwar years he was engaged in various activities at the War Office and in the mid-1930s he became a general staff officer in India. After the outbreak of the war he served with several branches of the Army, including the Welsh Division, until he was made the acting Major General in charge of Administration in the British Southern Command in April 1942. Based in Salisbury in Wiltshire, his main function was to liaise with the American troops in the area.

Dowler's interest in the black American GIs is on record at least as early as July 1942 when he arranged for one of his men, a Major G. Wills, to visit black troops in the Somerset area. Wills, accompanied on the inspection by Major Wilber M. Gaige, jun., an American liaison officer, was to gather 'informally' information on the relations of the black troops with the community and to note the solutions of any problems that had arisen. It is not clear whether Dowler accompanied them but it is clear that a policy document was in the process of being framed.

In Yeovil, a large country town some forty miles from Salisbury, the party saw how segregation had affected an engineering regiment. Cinemas in the locality had set aside reserved seats for the black GIs and up to a quarter of them were allowed 5.00 p.m. to midnight passes at any one time. Some seventeen miles or so further away the 92nd Engineering Regiment used Chard for their social life because Taunton, which was nearer, was out of bounds to them. In Chard there were also to be separate sections in cinemas and a suggestion of segregated dances. In addition segregation had hit the pubs, some displaying notices reading 'Off limits to 92nd Engineering' and refusing to serve black troops. The black regimental chaplain had become very upset about this, as had some Czech troops who fraternized with them. Major Gaige, who reported on the situation, proposed to re-educate the civilian population who, along with British troops stationed nearby, persisted in their friendliness towards the black soldiers.

In the absence of any statement from the civil powers it was the military authorities who had to work out some relationship with the American Army in Britain, and they made the running over the black troop issue. A meeting about racial matters was convened at the War Office on 5 August 1942, addressed by an American officer. The Colonial Office was represented by John Keith, who was particularly interested in the welfare of black Britons. The meeting was 'off the record' but there were hints of what was to come. Keith was especially worried by the chairman's assertion at this meeting, echoing Gaige, that British civilians needed to be educated out of their hospitableness towards black Americans.

James Grigg, Secretary of State for War, later described the meeting as being in 'furtherance of the policy of working in this matter in close relation with the American authorities' and the American officer giving the talk offered 'guidance' as to the course to be adopted. The most significant aspect of the meeting was its secrecy. Grigg commented that 'Owing to the delicate nature of the subject it was suggested that it would be better to issue no written instructions on the matter, but that the policy should be made known to the troops and ATS by lectures from their officers.[15] Clearly the whole operation was fraught with political danger.

It was in the context of this secrecy that Major General Dowler's Notes proved to be such a bombshell. They were issued to his district commanders in writing, a clear breach of the decision made at the War Office meeting, and without reference to his political or military superiors. In the preamble Dowler explained his motives. He believed that soldiers, plus those in the Home Guard and the ATS, needed 'educating' about relations with blacks. The Notes however were not to be distributed in writing as official policy because for 'political and other reasons, the declared policy of US Commanders must be that no distinction must be made between white and coloured American troops'. In addition Dowler noted that he had sent copies of the Notes to Regional Commissioners Haig and Elles who were 'taking steps through civilian channels to educate the civilian population as far as possible on the same lines'. Dowler also suggested the use of the Army Bureau of Current Affairs to get the message over to the soldiers.[16]

Why were the Notes so important? The answer is that they were the first official British pronouncement of any attitude to be taken towards the black soldiers; they would inevitably reach a wider audience, military and civil, and they would not have been out of place coming from a nineteenth-century southern slaveholder. As a monumental example of racist arrogance the paper is worth examining in some detail.

The Notes fall into several distinct parts: they give a brief summary of the problem facing the British; this is followed by a historical 'analysis' of the black man in America and they conclude with a list of do's and don'ts for British people. The most important piece of advice was that the British attitude should conform to that of the white American citizen so that 'amicable relations' with the US Army would not be disturbed. Highly paternalistic and offensive was Dowler's summary of the 'negro character':

> While there are many coloured men of high mentality and cultural distinction, the generality are of a simple mental outlook. They work hard when they have no money and when they have money prefer to do nothing until it is gone.

In short they have not the white man's ability to think and act to a plan. Their spiritual outlook is well known and their songs give the clue to their nature. They respond to sympathetic treatment. They are natural psychologists in that they can size up a white man's character and can take advantage of a weakness. Too much freedom, too wide associations with white men tend to make them lose their heads and have on occasions led to civil strife. This occurred after the last war due to [too] free treatment and associations which they had experienced in France.

Dowler proceeded to argue that certain practical points necessarily followed from these 'facts' and he offered five pieces of advice. The first was to be 'sympathetic in your mind towards the coloured man, basing your sympathy on a knowledge of his problem, of his good qualities and his weaker ones'. The second point perhaps lay at the root of everything: 'White women should not associate with coloured men. It follows then, they should not walk out, dance, or drink with them. Do not think such action hard or unsociable. They do not expect your companionship and such relations would in the end only result in strife'. The third piece of advice was aimed directly at British troops: 'Soldiers should not make intimate friends with them, taking them to cinemas or bars. Your wish to be friendly if it becomes too intimate may be an unkind act in the end. Try and find out from American troops how they treat them and avoid such action as would tend to antagonize the white American soldier'. Finally Dowler urged the British soldier to avoid political extremists who wanted to stir up racial trouble, and never to pass on stories which would antagonize relations between the British and black troops. Such stories, he argued, would be a propaganda gift to the enemy, though no consideration seems to have been given to the effect which the distribution of Dowler's *own* Notes might have on black and white relationships, or indeed the document's own propaganda value to the enemy.

Dowler's plea for his advice to be kept confidential was naive in the extreme. The Notes had also been given to the civil authorities in two regions and would eventually and inevitably filter down to the humblest fire-watcher or defence volunteer. In addition there would be those soldiers who would resent the advice in any case and would choose to publicize it, as was quickly shown. On 22 August 1942, just a couple of weeks after the Notes were issued, the *New Statesman* reported that a British soldier had contacted its London Diary column. The soldier had written to complain that in an English port part of a well-known restaurant was barred to black troops. He had reported that the employees of the restaurant disliked discriminating against blacks, and that local British soldiers also resented colour prejudice. But, according to the *New Statesman*, his unit had been called together and instructed to be 'polite to coloured troops, answer their queries and drift away'. They were not to eat or drink with coloured soldiers. Dowler's Notes, it seemed, were already in use.

The Colonial Office got wind of Dowler's Notes from Sir Hubert Young on 26 August 1942. Young, an ex-Indian Army major, had served in the 1930s as a governor in Africa, first in Nyasaland and then in Northern Rhodesia. In 1938 he became Governor of Trinidad and Tobago, a post he relinquished in 1942 after a heart attack, though in the post-war period before his death in 1950 he was a Liberal MP for a while. Young had attended a Southern Command conference of Home Guard battalion commanders at Wilton in Wiltshire and the Notes were distributed to those present, as Dowler said would happen, with oral instructions to read them to their company commanders. Young was absolutely indignant:

> I am reluctant to believe that the passages I have underlined [the document has not been traced] correctly represent the policy of His Majesty's Government and as I am still drawing salary as Governor of Trinidad (where no such instructions were issued for the guidance of British subjects) I should be glad of your advice on what action I should now take. The matter is urgent, as great harm may be done if these instructions are obeyed.[17]

Sir George H. Gater, Permanent Under-Secretary at the Colonial Office, took the issue further by giving a copy of the Notes to Sir Ronald Adam, Adjutant General to the forces since 1941. Clearly Dowler's idea of 'education' was not to Adam's liking though for the time being he restrained himself, saying only that the Major General's wording was 'injudicious'. He did agree with Gater that this was a matter calling for comment from higher authority and it was suggested that Viscount Cranborne, the Colonial Secretary, and Grigg should meet prior to raising it in the Cabinet.

The two ministers did make contact and one of the consequences was the position paper produced by Grigg in early September (see p. 65), modified by a second paper of 3 October 1942. In both documents Grigg was faced with the repercussions of Dowler's Notes. The Notes had been the cause of considerable anxiety, but had received some support, and, what was probably more important, had already been issued. Any retraction of them now would inevitably lead to more publicity, though given the will Grigg could have withdrawn the Notes with little damage to his own position. The Secretary for War chose not to do this. In the first of his two papers Grigg argued that Dowler, despite the War Office prohibition on written instructions, decided to issue his Notes 'in view of the difficulties which were already occurring'. Now Grigg leapt to the General's defence claiming that the instructions were issued in 'close consultation' with local American commanders, and were generally 'welcomed as affording guidance to a uniform policy'. Moreover, he added, relations between British and American troops had improved, even though putting instructions in writing had caused them to become known to a 'wider circle than was originally intended'; but that was his only guarded criticism.

In his second paper of 3 October 1942 Grigg defended the Notes more aggressively, placing increased emphasis now on his department's role and the sexual aspect of the problem: 'the War Office has held that it is desirable for British troops, especially British ATS [Auxiliary Territorial Service – part of the Women's Auxiliary Services] to understand the American background on this matter and so regulate their conduct as not to give cause for offence either to the white or coloured troops'. Though the War Office had wanted no written instructions, Grigg thought it 'desirable' that some factual statement 'should be made available to the Army generally'. In that sense Dowler and Grigg were the victors in this policy issue, for the impending Cabinet meetings centred on Grigg's papers, which in turn owed much to Dowler's Notes.

Although Dowler had acted in defiance of War Office instructions, his career prospered – he was knighted in 1946 and in the same year he assumed the important role of Chief of Staff, British Army of the Rhine, and later became the General Officer Commanding in the East Africa Command between 1948 and 1951.

As Grigg feared, and as would have been obvious to most observers, Dowler's Notes received wider publicity than was intended. In addition there were occasions when they appear to have been quite crudely interpreted and as a result the more sensational was the publicity. The *New Statesman* reported in September 1942 that the policy in one place was to move to another area any ATS girl seen associating with a black soldier, and to give a bogus reason for her transfer. When Tom Driberg questioned Prime Minister Churchill in the House about discrimination, Communist MP Willie Gallacher used the occasion to ask the Premier whether he was aware 'that I have received a letter, a copy of which I have sent to him, from a number of serving men informing me that an officer has given them a lecture advising them on the necessity for discrimination in connection with negroes who are in London?'[18] Churchill had no comment to make.

Perhaps the most unfortunate aspect of the Southern Notes was that they emanated from the top. There was no surge of requests from the 'ordinary' soldier for rules about how to behave towards the black Americans. On the contrary, some British tommies resented the advice offered by Dowler's Notes, as Denis Argent, an ex-journalist serving in the Signal Corps, pointed out to Mass Observation in 1943:

During the Summer of 1942 there was that Army order about keeping aloof from coloured troops to avoid the risk of rows with white US troops. That, I'm glad to say, was very unfavourably received by the troops – both non-combatants and Royal Engineers of the bomb-disposal company in which I was at the time. It savoured of Hitlerism. 'Just like Hitler and the Jews' was one typical RE reaction to the order, I remember.[19]

Ironically the general belief was that any rules about discrimination against black soldiers must have had their origin in the US Army – it was barely conceivable to many that the British would act in this way. Thus the *Daily Herald* carried a story about black Americans being banned from entering a dance at Eye in Suffolk at the request of the American military authorities, while the British Army command had not objected to black Americans and British soldiers mixing. The Americans, it appears, had also been refused entry to the town's reading-room with its recreational facilities. The incident received wide publicity and was the subject of a detailed investigation by the US authorities. Colonel Plank, the American officer in charge of the Eastern Base Section, not only discovered that some of the discriminatory acts had been instigated by the Eye town council but also that the commanding general of the 54th Division of the British Home Forces had warned the members of his command not to associate with the black Americans. Though this area was not part of Dowler's command the spirit of his Notes seems to have drifted outside his region.

Some of the regional commissioners were amongst those who thought Dowler's advice was admirable and consequently there were demands that advice be given to others besides military personnel. A Home Intelligence report towards the end of October showed there was some concern at the association of white girls with black Americans, and suggested that female civilians as well as service women should be advised on their behaviour in this respect. This kind of reaction encouraged Grigg to continue to press for a comprehensive official policy towards the black Amer-

icans, and the discussions which took place between the
War Office and the Colonial Office meant that such a
policy would be framed at the very highest level of
government. Further support for Grigg came from the
suggestions put forward at another meeting held a few
days after the publication of Dowler's Notes. This was the
Bolero Combined Committee (London) of 12 August 1942,
which was devoted exclusively to a discussion of the
'problem of American Coloured Troops' and was apparently
called at the initiative of the War Office.[20]

The Bolero Combined Committee (London) met at
Norfolk House in St James's Square and was the most
important body dealing with the reception, accommodation
and maintenance of the US forces in Great Britain. This,
and the various committees associated with it, dealt with
the transport and movement of troops, shipping and the
medical services. One of the problems underpinning all the
arrangements was that the segregation of black GIs from
white had to be considered at every step. The fact that this
committee, whose members included some of the most
important civil servants of the day, devoted at least one
special meeting and parts of many others to racial issues
showed how pervasive the matter was and how it affected
many areas of the Government's work.

Excluding the secretariat the meeting of 12 August was
attended by a small, select group of nine people. In the
chair was Sir Samuel Findlater Stewart, a Scot who had
been a teenage academic prodigy at Edinburgh University,
and who was now in his early 60s. Stewart was yet another
of those with experience of Indian affairs as Permanent
Under-Secretary of State for the subcontinent between
1930 and 1940. As the principal officer of the Bolero
Committee he was highly regarded by the Americans who
gave him the US Medal of Freedom with gold palm after
the war. From the War Office came Major General
H.Willans, General Sir Walter K. Venning, Quartermaster
General to the Forces since February 1939, Colonel Brian
Rowe, on special duty as an Anglo-American liaison
officer, and Sir Frederick Bovenschen. Bovenschen had
wide experience at the War Office and had been Perma-

nent Under-Secretary of State for six months. The Ministry of Information, totally involved with the reception of American soldiers, was represented by E. St J. Bamford, the Deputy Director (later Sir Eric Bamford), and R. H. Parker, Director of the Home Publicity Division, and known as 'Judge' Parker because of his judicial career in India. Completing the group were F. E. Evans of the Foreign Office, and Thomas Herbert Sheepshanks of the Ministry of Home Security. Francis Edward Evans, an Ulsterman in his mid-40s, had already had extensive consular experience in New York, Boston and Los Angeles, and was to be a post-war ambassador to Israel and Argentina. Sheepshanks was the youngest of twelve children of a former Bishop of Norwich and again was a civil servant of long standing. He was an intelligent, strong character, a trait important in his main role of dealing with the assorted bunch of regional commissioners. Conspicuously absent from the meeting was any representative from the Colonial Office even though that department was very involved with black people and their perceptions of Britain. Oliver Harvey, in his diary, implied that the Office had little political clout, even though it was one of the most important government departments.

Colonel Rowe told the meeting that currently there were about 11,000 or 12,000 black GIs in Britain and it was planned that there would be about 100,000. There was general agreement that as yet no great problems had occurred though this might change as some of them, the truck drivers for example, moved about the country. The 'problem' as yet was undefined though the meeting did concern itself largely with the black and white sexual issue (which is more fully explored later). Rowe considered one of the main difficulties to be the need to avoid the mixing of races in entertainment offered by the British. Parker endorsed this, adding that the churches in Britain would need to be aware of this precaution. In one of the few notes of dissent the Foreign Office spokesman commented that 'progressive elements in America were now strongly opposed to any form of discrimination' and he felt that nothing should be done on the British side 'to offend these

elements'. General Venning voiced a concern that was
already becoming evident from the Intelligence reports:
'the effect on British opinion of what might be regarded as
the undemocratic American attitude to the colour
problem'.

It was left to General Willans to make explicit the
implicit: 'The only difficult problem that remained was the
question of the association of coloured American soldiers
with British women', a sentiment with which Venning was
'in complete agreement'. Willans therefore offered the
solutions: first he recommended that the British public
should learn of the historical background to the white
American attitude to the blacks, and because this was
based on years of experience the implication was that the
British attitude should be the same. Willans particularly
wanted female service personnel in the ATS to have
guidance on the issue of black American men.

The meeting concluded that any practicable segregation
of the races was an American not a British concern, but an
Army Bureau of Current Affairs statement would be
drafted with consideration given to its publication for the
civil defence forces also. In the meantime British canteens
were to serve American troops, white and black, without
discrimination.

The Secretary for War must have been encouraged that
this important committee, directly responsible to the
Cabinet, expressed views that coincided quite closely with
Dowler's. Thus heartened, Grigg pressed his views more
forcefully on his ministerial colleagues.

The Bolero Committee discussion was not, however,
without its critics. In a significant Home Office directive of
4 September 1942, sent out to Chief Constables and
marked 'Confidential', Frank Newsam seemed to dissociate his department from the Bolero Committee's deliberations. Newsam was another of those with long civil service
experience, mainly in the Home Office. Born in Barbados
he had served with the Punjabis in India during the First
World War. Though admitting that 'difficulties' might be
caused by the presence of black troops and their relationships with other troops and British women, his paper

was otherwise strongly worded. The British, it clearly stated, should have nothing to do with segregation:

> It is not the policy of His Majesty's Government that any discrimination as regards the treatment of coloured troops should be made by the British authorities. The Secretary of State, therefore, would be glad if you would be good enough to take steps to ensure that the police do not make any approach to the proprietors of public houses, restaurants, cinemas or other places of entertainment with a view to discriminating against coloured troops. If the American service authorities decide to put certain places out of bounds for their coloured troops, such prohibition can be effected only by means of an Order issued by the appropriate American Army and Naval authorities. The police should not make themselves in any way responsible for the enforcement of such orders.[21]

It was not this Home Office paper, however, but Grigg's first document on black GIs issued a few days later which had the greater influence on the definition of Government policy. Grigg began by stating that black soldiers would be coming to Britain in increasing numbers. They were, he continues, 'not considered to be well fitted for combatant duties' but as they constituted about 60 per cent of army engineers there could be no question of them not coming to Britain, and hence, 'various difficulties' would arise. Grigg gave a brief outline of what had happened up to then – the 5 August meeting at the War Office, the publication of the Southern Notes, and the Bolero meeting of 12 August. All this had put some pressure on the Secretary for War to explain his position as every action had, on the face of it, been a War Office initiative. Now he added there were other pressures which were likely to cause the matter to be 'opened in the political field' and therefore it was desirable that it should be brought to Cabinet. These further influences were the wider distribution of the Notes than had been intended, the September article in the *Sunday Pictorial*, the concern of Viscount Cranborne for West Indian and British Empire opinion, and the enquiries of left-wing MP Denis Pritt (who had been expelled from the Labour Party in 1940 for defending the Russian invasion of

Finland) about 'whether any instructions on this subject, which have a definite basis of racial discrimination', had been issued and his request for a copy.

Grigg, with perhaps more candour than most of his previous deliberations had shown, began to describe the problems as he saw them. They all stemmed, he argued in the same vein as some others, from the fact that the British, 'with little experience of a colour problem at home, are naturally inclined to make no distinction between their treatment of white and coloured troops and are apt to regard such distinctions as undemocratic'. He then spelled out the three consequences of this British feeling. In the first place the average white American would lose his respect for Britain if he saw the country's inhabitants 'drawing no distinction between white and coloured'; secondly came the 'uppity nigger' argument – 'the coloured troops themselves probably expect to be treated in this country as in the United States, and a markedly different treatment might well cause political difficulties in America at the end of the war'. Last came Grigg's fear that *British* troop morale would suffer at home and abroad if there was any 'unnecessary association' between black Americans and British women.

Grigg proposed the answers to these problems. He realized that there could be no official discrimination but he considered it 'desirable that the British troops, especially British ATS, should understand the American background of this matter, in order that they may so regulate their conduct as not to give cause for offence either to the white or to the coloured troops'. While making token gestures to *all* political shades of opinion in the USA it is clear that Grigg was mainly concerned with white views for in another part of his paper he talked about not arousing 'resentment' in America. It must have been obvious to him, however, that the publication of his *own* paper would give great offence to black organizations like the NAACP, and would go against those 'natural' British instincts he himself had outlined. Grigg did have some political sense; realizing that the War Office's views on the American racial problem had up to that point been heavily influenced by the American Army, he urged some caution: 'It has to be recognized . . . that the view of the American Government is not quite the same as the view of the [American] Army; it has been questioned whether they would commit themselves formally to any measure of social segregation, and there is a risk that they might object if we committed ourselves to it in any authorized document.' Despite this caveat Grigg's three practical suggestions remained:

(a) To follow the general lead given by the USA Army authorities, adapting where necessary to local conditions.

(b) To give the [British] Army through ABCA a knowledge of the facts and history of the coloured question in the USA and the USA Army.

(c) To educate, without the issue of overt or written *instructions*, [emphasis in original] the personnel of the Army including the ATS, in the attitude which should be adopted towards the USA coloured troops.

This paper was circulated to a few select government departments in September 1942, but in the meantime the Home Office had issued its memorandum to chief constables and, on 20 September, an article entitled 'Colour bar must go', by Brendan Bracken, the Minister for Information, had appeared in the *Sunday Express*. One of the main criticisms of the Government's action during 1942 is that it sometimes equivocated on this issue, and sometimes contradicted itself, and in short was sometimes full of cant and hypocrisy. In this context Bracken's article has significance. It was not only inconsistent with his Cabinet colleague Grigg's advice, but diametrically opposed to it. As it was one of the few public ministerial statements on race, and as the minister concerned, a close confidant of Prime Minister Churchill, was intimately involved with the US troops, Bracken's position is worth looking at closely.

Brendan Bracken was in many ways a strange, mysterious figure, in part because we know less about him than others on the public stage since he ordered his papers to be destroyed after his death. Born in Ireland he spent some of

his teenage years on a sheep station in Australia. As a
young man he became a protégé of Winston Churchill's and
he entered the House of Commons in 1929 as Conservative
member for North Paddington. His friendship and loyalty
to the 'Boss' was rewarded when Bracken became Minister
of Information, following Duff Cooper, in July 1941. In his
Sunday Express article Bracken's sentiments were admir-
ably liberal:

> It is in fact true that there is still some colour prejudice in
> this country and still social barriers against coloured people
> . . . the British Government is in favour of putting an end to
> this prejudice as quickly as possible. It should die a natural
> death as many prejudices have done in the past, and it
> should be helped to die quickly . . . we in Britain do not
> intend to stand fast upon theories of political equality and
> economic freedom without seeing to it that the negro peoples
> actually enjoy them in our country. . . . Removing the
> misconceptions and prejudice which arise is largely a
> question of education. Only continued contact between our
> two races and a great deal of effort on both sides will do it . . .
> Those in this country who still have a prejudice against
> colour will also be taught in time to overcome it. Certainly
> it is the desire of the British Government that this
> prejudice should go. . . . The barriers still standing in the
> way of the social equality of coloured peoples must be with-
> drawn. The prejudiced must be taught by precept and
> example to overcome their prejudices. This is a process
> which will take time, but responsible people in Britain are
> determined that it shall be carried through, and the sooner
> the better.

As will be seen, theory and practice were to be as far
apart as ever. In many respects, particularly when it came
to organizing receptions for GIs, Bracken's own ministry
did its best to ensure that the barriers between the races
that he mentioned in the *Sunday Express* did not tumble.
Similarly there were people in the Cabinet, and others,
like Haig and Elles in the regions, and some in the Church,
who were determined to see that the Second World War,
particularly where black Americans were involved, should
not increase interracial contact.

Grigg's paper of September 1942, together with Dowler's

earlier Notes, were the first steps which led towards a crucial Cabinet discussion on the black Americans on 13 October 1942, and this in turn produced important government statements. In the early stages, therefore, Grigg was anxious to solicit the comments of the Colonial and Foreign Offices, the two ministries most likely to be concerned with the subject of his paper.

Within the Colonial Office it produced, not surprisingly, a fairly hostile reaction. Once again it was J. L. Keith who held the strongest view, partly because of his anxieties about the welfare of black citizens of the Colonial Empire at that time resident in Britain. After studying at Lausanne and Oxford, John Lucien Keith went to Africa as a young man of 23 in 1916, eventually entering the Colonial Service in Northern Rhodesia, primarily dealing with African education. On his return to Britain he went to the Colonial Office in 1939. From 1941 his official role was as head of the student department and it was in this capacity that he became involved with the issues affecting black GIs and West Indians.

Believing in racial equality as an ideal for the Empire, Keith rejected suggestions that Britain should follow the American lead: 'such action,' he remarked, 'would attempt to induce the British public to discriminate against American negroes. It is the first step which counts in this sort of thing'. Keith's deeply-held convictions show that there were officials in important positions arguing against the racist practices being proposed by some American and British authorities:

> Our relations as human beings one to another are conditioned by religious and social ideas . . . the relations between one man and another are personal matters. We should let the British people in uniform and out find their own level in their relations with American Negroes, and we should not allow anything to be done to encourage racial prejudice.

Keith went on to suggest that someone like Sir Reginald Coupland, Professor of Colonial History at Oxford since 1920, should be asked to write an attractive history of American blacks but, he pleaded, 'We should not allow any nonsense about rape, VD etc., to deter us from sticking to our main principles and resisting the so-called Southern American attitude towards Negroes'. Finally Keith came to the pragmatic crux of the matter as he saw it: '[Grigg's memorandum] fails to appreciate how vital it is for the Colonial Empire that race relations in this country should be on a sensible and what one might call a Christian basis'.[22]

Harold Macmillan, with sixteen years as an MP already behind him, had been Parliamentary Under-Secretary for the Colonies since February 1942 and, in September, he also expressed some concern. He felt that the people should be given impartial instruction on the issue and then allowed to exercise their common sense in dealing with it; and he was at a loss to see how such education could be given to large numbers without the use of written instructions.

When Grigg's suggestions came to the attention of Colonial Secretary Viscount Cranborne the response was more aloof and less committed than that of his subordinates. Educated at Eton and Christ Church, Robert Arthur James Gascoyne-Cecil, known as 'Bobbety' to his friends, was heir to and scion of one of the country's most prominent aristocratic families. Cranborne was not at all enthusiastic about Grigg's paper. He viewed the issue of race as an American and not a British concern; and in any event the matter of relationships with black troops should simply be viewed as a matter of good manners.

In response to reactions from the Colonial Office Grigg said at the end of September that he would redraft his paper as the original was too long, and that since the modifications were not significant he would circulate the revised version to the War Cabinet. When Colonial Office officials saw Grigg's new paper they decided that there had indeed been little significant change to it and they set to work to produce a separate paper under their minister's name.

At the Foreign Office Grigg's revised paper was received at the end of September 1942 by Nevile Butler, the son of a clergyman and former headmaster of Harrow School.

Butler was a career diplomat who valued precision. His first reaction to what he read was to enquire what exactly the American Army's policy on black troops was, bearing in mind Eisenhower's continued public emphasis on non-discrimination. Grigg's suggestion that the British Army adopt the American attitude to race did not find favour. Anthony Eden himself, the Foreign Secretary, became involved in the search for suitable words to replace Grigg's advice two days after the paper was received in the Foreign Office. Eden was critical of Grigg's language and thought the advice in Butler's revised version was 'certainly better'. This was for the British 'to adapt their attitude towards US coloured troops to that of the US Army authorities so far as may be possible without practising obvious or offensive discrimination'. Butler argued that it was a less slavish acceptance of American attitudes, and, perhaps of greater importance, was easier to defend in Parliament. Butler went further than the War Office on the question of whether there should be written instructions. His own personal inclination seemed to be towards a written policy and he conceded that Dowler's Notes were 'pretty good' but went 'too far as regards our civilians'.

Richard (Dick) Law at the Foreign Office saw the issues in wider terms. The son of former Prime Minister Bonar Law, he had worked and travelled widely in the USA as a newspaperman in the late 1920s, marrying an American girl from New York State. Back in England he entered Parliament as a Conservative MP in 1931, and became Parliamentary Under-Secretary at the Foreign Office ten years later. With his experience of America his observations on the presence of black troops in Britain were perceptive. By and large he accepted the War Office paper and said that the amendment suggested by the Foreign Office was as far as it should go. He had other comments too:

> From the point of view of Anglo-American relations I don't see that Mrs Roosevelt can have any valid grouse if we base ourselves on the US Army. And more broadly, the really important thing is that we sh[oul]d not have considerable friction between the two armies, and that American troops

sh[oul]d not go back to their homes with the view that we are
a decadent and unspeakable race.

With a pragmatic ear cocked to the American scene, Law's
comments display a sense of Foreign Office expediency
which recognized that continued American support for
Britain's war effort and post-war role in the world would
depend on walking a tightrope, without alienating either
the right or liberal wings of the American political
spectrum. Eden reluctantly added a 'very well' on 5
October 1942.[23]

A Cabinet meeting was arranged for twelve noon on
Tuesday 13 October 1942 at the House of Commons to
discuss the issue of the American black troops. As a
consequence of the circulation of Grigg's paper and the
impending Cabinet meeting, several more ministers, not
all of them Cabinet rank, prepared memoranda as contributions to the debate. Lord Cranborne, as his department had promised, produced a paper on 2 October 1942,
followed by the Lord Chancellor Sir John Simon (9
October); Home Secretary Herbert Morrison (10 October);
Minister of Information Brendan Bracken (12 October);
and Lord Privy Seal Sir Stafford Cripps (12 October).[24]

Surprisingly there were some Cabinet ministers who
submitted nothing at all prior to the meeting on the black
Americans. Attlee, Oliver Lyttelton and Stafford Cripps
attended all the Cabinet meetings in July, August and
October of 1942 which discussed this issue but of these
three only Cripps produced a paper of his own. Attlee's
Labour Party colleague, Ernest Bevin, in an attempt to
alleviate the manpower shortage, had brought black West
Indians to Britain, but he likewise produced no document
though one might have expected the socialists to have held
strong views on racial equality.

As John Keith had a hand in writing it the Colonial
Office's contribution to the material produced for the
Cabinet meeting was severely critical of Grigg's proposals.
Cranborne's ministry had special concerns about the
welfare of those black people from the Empire resident in
Britain but the main thrust of its views was that no official
instruction about how British troops should behave to-

wards the black GIs should be issued at all. Butler in the
Foreign Office took a different tack believing that the
British had to look to the US Army for help because
producing regulations 'of our own' would obviously be 'a
very tricky business'.

The Lord Chancellor, Sir John Simon, whose second
wife, Kathryn, was an active member of the League of
Coloured Peoples, was not happy with Grigg's proposals,
though he did admit the presence of black GIs had given
rise to a 'ticklish' problem. In his own paper Simon
concentrated on both the practical and ethical effects of
toeing the American line. He argued that the segregation
practiced in the southern states of America would be both
difficult to effect and unacceptable in Britain as Service
clubs, the YMCA, the Church Army, and the Salvation
Army all had facilities for soldiers and would all refuse to
ban black Americans, as would publicans. His advice was
not to yield to American sentiments but to make the
American authorities aware of British feeling on the
issues. This was that there was 'a profound British
conviction underneath the surface in most of us that if a
coloured man behaves himself he is entitled to the same
treatment as a white man'.

Herbert Morrison's overriding concern was with the
sexual issue and the rumours that British wives and
daughters were being 'debauched by American coloured
troops', though he did admit that the black GIs had on the
whole 'behaved well'. In addition to this Morrison was
amongst the first to express some anxiety about the
'procreation of half-caste children', which would, he correctly forecasted, create a 'difficult social problem'. Morrison's ministry had by this time already been in discussions
with the US Army authorities and it was reported that
Eisenhower was in 'complete accord' with the Home Office
circular put out by Under-Secretary of State Frank
Newsam in early September 1942. Consequently the
minister was optimistic that American commanders would
not want segregation in Britain, which a 'large body of
opinion in this country' would 'strongly resent' anyway. On
the other hand Morrison admitted he could see a case for

giving 'some warning' on the subject of black troops to the women's services.

Brendan Bracken's contribution to the debate was surprisingly brief and insignificant given the thundering tone of his *Sunday Express* piece the previous month. It consisted largely of a letter that he had written to Grigg in the middle of September. Contrary to the theme of his article Bracken now did not favour any general discussions on the problem because these 'tend more to diagnosis than cure', and no solution was going to be found in Britain at this time anyway. The Minister of Information's advice can best be described as *laissez-faire* – he was sure that the American policy of segregation was the best practical contribution to the avoidance of trouble, so suggested that it be seconded 'in every way'. This was advice contrasting sharply with his publicly stated position. He did believe that those who would be meeting the black Americans should be made aware of the problem and be encouraged to 'use all their tact to avoid offending or insulting the White American in their relations with the black', but written documents for either service personnel or civilians were to be avoided.

The final and most significant contribution to the pre-Cabinet debate on the black American troops came from the austere, legalistic Lord Privy Seal, Sir Stafford Cripps. Up to that point his political career had been somewhat chequered. Son of a Tory MP Cripps himself had joined the Labour Party at the relatively late age of 40, only to be expelled in 1939 before the outbreak of war for advocating a popular front against Fascism. Perceived by many as a member of what today would be called the 'lunatic left', he injected money into *Tribune*, the radical weekly, when it was founded in 1937. Some of his contemporaries were not sure what to make of him; Oliver Harvey thought Cripps a brilliant but unstable man, kind but unpredictable.

As the war continued Cripps's ambition grew though few seemed to know where his talents should best be directed. Returning to Britain early in 1942 after almost two years as Ambassador in Moscow, he became Lord Privy Seal and

Leader of the House. Through the first few months and into the spring of 1942 Cripps remained second only to Eden in public standing, and was considered the one most likely to succeed Churchill as Prime Minister. This strength seems to have been reflected in the confidence with which he approached the question of the black GIs in Britain.

In his memorandum of 12 October 1942 Cripps took a different approach to that taken by the other ministers. In the main the other papers had all concentrated on Grigg's notes, criticizing them or offering amendments. Cripps concerned himself with the Notes produced by Dowler, and he produced a revised version of these for Cabinet consideration.

Cripps made some changes to the Notes. He added an extra point that British soldiers should recognize the background to the US situation and the difficulties when black and white people live together, and should be aware of the differing attitudes towards blacks exhibited in America. Like Dowler, he proceeded to outline the historical background, noting that in the South, 'Like children, coloured people commonly inspire affection and admiration; but they are not considered "equal" to white men and women.' Caution was his watchword: the British, Cripps advised, should not 'embarrass' the Americans who were 'making a great experiment in working out a democratic way of life in a mixed community, even if we have different views on how race relationships should be treated in our own country and in the Empire'. The British soldier therefore was to 'understand' and 'respect' the white American point of view.

Cripps ended by offering several pieces of advice, not so far removed from Dowler's conclusions but phrased a little more circumspectly. The first point was: 'Be friendly and sympathetic towards coloured American Troops – but avoid intimate relationships'. Secondly: 'If you find yourselves in the company of white and coloured troops . . . make it your business to avoid unpleasantness. It is much the best, however, to avoid such situations'. The third point raised the old taboo: 'It is undesirable that a white woman should go about *alone* in the company of a coloured

American. This is bound to lead to controversy and
ill-feeling. This does not mean that friendly hospitality in
the home or in social gatherings need to be ruled out'. The
fourth piece of advice was to listen to white Americans
without necessarily agreeing with them. It was suggested
that the listener could avoid disputes by admitting that if
he happened to live in Alabama he would probably 'think
the way they do'. The last of Cripp's suggestions was again
almost identical to Dowler's – this was to avoid listening to
those who stirred up trouble, and to be careful not to hand
the enemy a propaganda weapon.

So the stage was set for the War Cabinet debate of 13
October 1942. Present at the meeting were regular Cabinet
members Churchill, Sir John Anderson, Attlee, Cripps,
Bevin and Lyttelton, but a notable absentee was Anthony
Eden. In addition those ministers who had submitted
papers but were not normally of Cabinet rank were also
there – Cranborne, Grigg, Bracken, Morrison (soon to be a
regular member) and Simon. According to Sir Alexander
Cadogan, Permanent Under-Secretary at the Foreign
Office, the debate was a disappointment: 'Everyone spoke
at once while PM read papers (a formality he had omitted).
Discussion was on a low level'. The only contribution made
by Churchill appears to have been in answer to Cranborne
who pointed out that one of his black Colonial Office staff
was being excluded from a certain restaurant because of
white Americans. The Prime Minister's response was:
'That's all right: if he takes his banjo with him they'll think
he's one of the band'.[25]

'Low level' as the discussion might have been, the
meeting did produce some conclusions.[26] It was generally
agreed that in determining the British attitude to black
Americans some regard had to be paid to the US Army's
views on the question. This led the War Cabinet to
conclude that 'it was desirable that the people of this
country should avoid becoming too friendly with coloured
American troops'. Cranborne was the only one courageous
enough to record his uneasiness at this recommendation.
He was considered a skilful parliamentarian, but clearly
on this occasion he had neither the personal authority nor

that of his office to effect much change. The Cabinet also felt that Grigg's suggestion that the British Army should be educated to adopt the US attitude went 'too far' and the Secretary for War agreed with this. A nice piece of semantic history was recorded when it was agreed that the term 'American negroes' was now more desirable than 'United States coloured troops'.

It was Sir Stafford Cripps's paper which dominated the Cabinet's conclusions for it was 'generally agreed' that his memorandum 'corresponded very nearly to the general view of the War Cabinet and should be taken as the basis for further consideration of this question'. In the light of the discussions of the previous few weeks this conclusion appears at the least to be an odd one. The fact that Cripps's notes so closely resembled those produced by Dowler made them a rather unexpected basis for further action as the earlier advice had been the subject of considerable criticism.

There are several explanations as to why the Cabinet took the turn it did. An important factor in 1942 was the political rivalry between Cripps and Eden. This was a period when Cripps was growing in confidence and stature. His evangelical stance on the left of the political spectrum might have been expected to temper his views on race, but in fact he pursued his position like a lawyer clinically dissecting a case. He was the only regular member of the Cabinet to submit a paper and while others had been content merely to criticize Grigg, Cripps was also the only one to put forward positive proposals, albeit that these were a rehash of some old ones. With Eden absent the Lord Privy Seal was the most dominant figure in the Cabinet.

Another important factor in the acceptance of Cripps's viewpoint was that it was still deferential to the US Army position and there was a strong body of opinion that this was crucial at this time for despite the elaborate committee structure underpinning the Anglo-American war effort, the machinery on both sides of the Atlantic was not running as smoothly as it should. At the same time Wendell Willkie, the defeated Republican presidential candidate of 1940, had embarked on a major tour of China and Russia and had talked to Archibald Clark-Kerr, the British Ambassador in Russia. According to the Foreign Office the main point made by Willkie seems to have been the dislike Americans had for Britain. Clearly the Anglo-American boat had to be placed on an even keel.

As for the Labour members of the Cabinet, Attlee may well have remained his silent self for as Nye Bevan once remarked he always brought to the 'fierce struggle of politics', such as may have occurred in this particular debate, 'the tepid enthusiasm of a lazy summer afternoon at a cricket match'. His colleague Ernest Bevin may well have been subject to subtle pressure from John Winant, the US Ambassador. Winant had become familiar with most of the British union leaders while working for the International Labour Organisation in Geneva in the 1930s. Indeed Bevin was one of those who suggested to Roosevelt that Winant should come to the Court of St James's after Kennedy's departure, optimistic that Labour links with the US would need to be close in the post-war period. There is evidence that Bevin and Winant exchanged information in 1942 and 1943 and doubtless there was some discussion of the racial situation and the need to avoid embarrassing the US by overtly criticizing the American pattern of segregation in Britain.

After its deliberations the Cabinet reached two major conclusions. Cripps was to consult with Grigg and Morrison to prepare a revised version of the Lord Privy Seal's memorandum, which would then be issued confidentially to Army officers of the rank of colonel and above. These officers would then use the notes orally to give guidance to the troops under their command. This revised paper was to be circulated to the War Cabinet for its approval. Secondly the same trio of ministers was to consider the draft of the long-awaited ABCA article. Again the absence of the Colonial Secretary from these arrangements was a notable one.

The ministers did not waste time. The revised notes were ready by 16 October, and printed the next day.[27] This new version of the Lord Privy Seal's paper showed remarkably little change from the original, which is one reason why it took just a few days to redraft. The background notes, apart from the odd word or two, were practically identical and the few alterations which were made were related to the recommendations at the end which were now a little less stark. The suggestion that the British should avoid 'intimate relations' with 'coloured American troops' now became: 'remember that they are not accustomed in their own country to close and intimate relationships with white people'. The fears about sex were similarly amended, the instruction now being that 'for a white woman to go about in the company of a Negro American is likely to lead to controversy and ill-feeling'.

The Cabinet meeting of 20 October 1942 quickly approved the new document and the ABCA article. Thus the culmination of several months' hectic activity came when the notes were circulated by the War Office on 25 November 1942, while the article, 'The colour problem as the American sees it', was published in the Army's journal *Current Affairs* on 5 December 1942.

As the war progressed the feeling grew that the ordinary soldier did not know enough about the issues for which it was being fought. Consequently the Army Bureau of Current Affairs was established in the autumn of 1941. The Director of the Bureau was William Emrys Williams who had been Secretary of the British Institute of Adult Education from 1934 to 1940, and was also associated closely with Penguin Books. Williams, who was knighted after the war, partly for his services to the Arts Council, had worked as a liaison officer in the Northern Command before moving to ABCA in 1941. The Bureau published two journals, *War* and *Current Affairs*, both of which provided the background notes for officers to discuss current affairs with the men and women under their command. *Current Affairs* dealt generally with the events in the news and it was this journal which was chosen to carry the feature on black Americans.

The article was more moderate in tone than the notes issued by the Cabinet because it was obvious that it would have a wider circulation. In general though the watchword was the same – caution. The objective was to 'understand the feelings' the colour problem aroused in the average American. As in the Government's note, the strongest words were reserved for the 'dangers' of white women meeting the soldiers. It was argued that the situation was so 'new and unexpected' for the black GIs that they might not understand it. After expressing the hope that the British would not break down the American forms of social regulations, the article concluded somewhat piously that the war might possibly have a deeper meaning for black people because its 'primary object' was to preserve 'freedom in its broadest sense'. The essence of the advice however was that Britain was not to make too many contributions to such ends.

As the contents of the document approved on 20 October 1942 seeped out and as the Government's gentle public relations efforts took hold, it was inevitable that the Cabinet would be accused of speaking with two voices. The *New Statesman* saw this inconsistency in the Government's position and, even under conditions of wartime censorship, expressed its criticism in its issue of 17 June 1944:

> Some confusion has resulted among the British from the contradictory regulations issued by the Home Office and War Office. According to the Home Office every effort should be made to treat Negroes as equals. The War Office regulation, on the other hand, has laid down that British soldiers must be polite to coloured troops, but not fraternise with them, or offer them drinks.

The *Daily Herald* was amongst those newspapers which saw to it that the instructions on race were given continued exposure. On 17 May 1944 the paper reported that the Admiralty instructed new recruits on the colour bar and it quoted verbatim the words of an officer on board a British warship:

> Although the black soldiers are a very useful addition to our war effort, their presence certainly raises a problem. So that there can be no friction in the manner of dealing with them, I want your standards to conform as near as possible to those of our American Allies. In the States Negroes are separated

from white men. The American regards a Negro as a child and not the equal of the white races. Please conform to that idea.

The papers and documents produced in 1942 were the main contributions to the debate about the presence of black Americans in Britain, but the issue would not go away and official publications continued to comment on it as the war progressed.

One of the boldest references to the American racial problem in such an official publication came in 1943. This was in a Ministry of Information pamphlet published perhaps predictably late when American soldiers had been here for some time. It was obvious soon after the American arrival that the soldiers, both black and white, would be enormously popular with children, if for nothing else than the seemingly endless supplies of chewing gum and Hershey chocolate bars, and a brief guide was produced for teachers. *Meet the US Army* (published for the Board of Education) was written by left-wing poet and intellectual Louis MacNeice, who had spent some time in the USA prior to the outbreak of the war before returning to join the BBC Features Department. MacNeice referred to the black Americans and though his words were still a little circumspect he reached an unequivocal conclusion:

> The American negroes require a special comment. There are many Negro soldiers now in this country, and those Britons who have met them have been very favourably impressed by their pleasant manners and their readiness to be pleased. These Negro troops are not, on principle, separately brigaded, the US War Department having rightly declined to differentiate them from other American citizens. It must be remembered, however, that while the Negroes form a very large section (one in twelve) of the American nation, they are in the unique position of being descended from slaves; this memory of slavery being still fresh, retains a psychological hold both on the Negroes themselves and on many of their white fellow-citizens (especially those in the old slave States, i.e. 'The South'); from this they will only gradually break free. Any American negro who comes to Britain must be treated by us on a basis of absolute equality. And remember *never* call a negro a 'nigger'.

It is easy, with hindsight, to be critical of the British Government's *laissez-faire* attitude to the racial issue in 1942. In its defence it can be argued that the war was at a crucial stage and few politicians wanted to upset the Americans. In the light of the problems raised during the rest of the American stay in Britain, however, it is entirely possible that the Cabinet would have done far better to have taken the people into its confidence. Several ministers forecast correctly that in the event of trouble many British people would side with the blacks and therefore some frank discussion of the dilemmas the Government faced would have been helpful. Articles in newspapers, publication of the US Army's views on discrimination, the Home Office directive and other materials would have both informed the British public that the Government was not simply sitting on the problem, and would have been instructive for black and white Americans alike. In addition it might well have impressed Colonial governments and at the same time reduced the value of race as an enemy propaganda weapon. At the very least a more open debate about the legal difficulties of mixed marriages in the USA could have saved some heartaches. The Cabinet chose not to do this and as a result myth, rumour and exaggeration abounded. It may well be that the Government was fearful of being exposed as hypocritical. Some of its actions subsequent to the 1942 debate were proof that it did not entirely live up to its declared policy.

During the debates of 1942 the Cabinet had been very specific about segregation: whilst it would not interfere with American arrangements it would not aid or abet them. The Home Office circular of 4 September 1942 had stated categorically that it was 'not the policy of His Majesty's Government that any discrimination as regards the treatment of coloured troops should be made by the British authorities'. This was reinforced at the Cabinet meeting of 13 October. The Americans, it was minuted, 'must not expect our authorities, civil or military, to assist them in enforcing a policy of segregation'. There were, however, occasions when, without American provocation, ministers obtrusively and actively supported the jim-crow policy of the United States Army in Britain.

One major British concern was the logistical problem of accommodating the American troops when they arrived. Providing for a racially segregated army was both expensive, as nearly all the facilities had to be duplicated, and time-consuming as these extra facilities had to be built. The American insistence on having small camps to keep the blacks and whites apart slowed down the construction programme and strained the country's already creaking resources. Nevertheless, the British authorities, through the 4th Key Bolero Plan in November 1943, showed an almost excessive zeal in bowing to American requirements by themselves insisting that no building in Britain occupied in any part by white civilians was to be used to quarter black troops. Thus the short-term housing problem for black GIs could only be solved by putting them (rather than whites) under canvas, which in the English climate was not always a pleasant experience. When the British were made aware of the niceties of jim crow they responded quickly to American customs. At the end of July 1942 the American forces in Britain did not yet have their own hospitals, and on 24 July a medical subcommittee of the Bolero Combined Committee asked its parent body how it should look after the American soldiers. It was told a few days later that it should discuss with the Ministry of Health the provision of separate lavatories, if not separate wards, for black GIs being treated in British hospitals!

In other circumstances where the British Government did have control it went further along the American road to segregation than it needed to. In Liverpool the premises of the British Council, which were used by American troops, were segregated and specific rooms reserved for whites. On British troopships under the control of the British War Office, prior notification had to be given of black people travelling. On one occasion an army captain and a civilian technician, both black Americans returning home on a British ship, were served their meals in the dining saloon behind a partition next to the kitchen.

The most blatant and unapologetic segregation practiced by the British Government came with its provision of recreational clubs for the American soldiers. The facilities were offered entirely on racial lines and the policy was stated categorically and quite openly. An example of this occurred with Lady Reading's Women's Voluntary Service organization.

Lady Stella Reading was one of those leisured philanthropists many of whom found fresh challenges during the war. She had worked with the British Red Cross in the First World War and in the mid-1920s was a member of the Viceroy's staff in India. As the war clouds gathered in 1938 she founded the WVS when she was in her mid-40s to promote the recruitment of women into civil defence. When the war broke out the WVS became involved in the problems of evacuation, rationing, air raids and hospitality. At the beginning of 1944 the suggestion was put forward somewhat belatedly to establish 'Welcome Clubs' for American servicemen to stimulate offers of hospitality in British homes, though membership was not to be extended to 'the wrong type'. Two hundred and sixty clubs were established, each receiving a grant of £30, and many of them were organized by the WVS. The problem was the black troops. The worried WVS representatives visited the Ministry of Information which had been charged with coordinating civilian hospitality to the American troops in Britain. They explained to the ministry that the 'primary purpose of the Welcome Club was to promote contact between the American soldiers and British men and women. The kind of contact which the MOI sought to foster through the Welcome Club schemes was 'not altogether applicable in the case of coloured soldiers'. What lay behind this concern, of course, was the usual question of sex for, according to Home Intelligence reports, the WVS was concerned that 'on no account should American coloured troops be entertained in private houses owing to the prevalence among them of veneral disease'.

Hence the WVS proposed 'Silver Birch Clubs' for black soldiers, which like those for their white compatriots were to be established with MOI grants. Clubs were founded at Bala in North Wales, Penarth in South Wales, and Birmingham, though the one there for American Army women postal workers was undercut by the many offers of private hospitality. Further clubs were proposed but not ultimately established for Weobley and Keresley in the Midlands and Nailsea in the West Country.

The British Government, unable to cope with the problems of American discrimination, would have preferred to will the problems away. Its indecision and lack of direction inevitably resulted in a form of British discrimination by default from 1942 onwards. When it could not bring itself to tell the American authorities that it expected white GIs to treat black Britons with respect the results were predictable. Black Britons became subject to jim-crow treatment while civil servants from the Foreign and Colonial Offices and the Ministry of Labour exchanged increasingly rancorous notes without agreeing on where to place any blame or what action to take. In addition black citizens who were temporarily resident in Britain returned to their own countries with a legacy of bitterness which had important repercussions in the post-war era.

It is difficult to estimate the number of indigenous black people in Britain before the war but their numbers were swelled in the first few years of the conflict. About 10,000 West Indians were recruited into the RAF, 1,000 British Hondurans came over as forestry workers and about a further 1,000 West Indians were brought to work as electricians and technicians in factories in the north-west, mainly around Bolton and Liverpool.

It soon became evident that racially prejudiced Americans were not going to shed this part of their cultural baggage even though they were in a foreign country. In March 1942 two white US Marines assaulted a West Indian near a Lyons tea house in London, one of them threatening him with a knife. After protests, with the Colonial, Foreign and Home Offices all becoming involved, the US *chargé d'affaires* was called to account.

As more and more West Indians became the victims of American racial discrimination, the Colonial Office turned its attention to practical ways of preventing the assaults. One novel, if naive, solution was that black Britons should wear a badge to distinguish them from black Americans.

Harold Macmillan thought it a splendid idea and suggested that black people all wear a little Union Jack in their buttonholes. Though the suggestion was endorsed by Cranborne himself it was not adopted.

Autumn 1942 drew on and James Grigg provided some unequivocal thoughts in a departmental paper:

> We should get the United States Army authorities to explain to their own troops our attitude towards coloured persons and to impress upon them the importance of avoiding the treatment of any British coloured persons whether in or out of uniform in a way which would antagonize opinion in this country . . . I am seeing that the matter is taken up with the USA Army authorities.[28]

Cranborne not unnaturally agreed with Grigg and he in turn was supported by Simon. Even Nevile Butler at the Foreign Office was in favour of telling the Americans that the British and the American attitudes towards black citizens were different. When it came to action, however, again the British dithered. Grigg, contrary to his earlier strong words, did nothing, and Cripps, too, was wary lest the British embarrass the Americans. The Cabinet meeting of 13 October did state that the Americans 'should recognise that we had a different problem as regards our coloured people',[29] but no recommendation was proposed and no approaches to the US Army command were made. Discretion proved the better part of valour.

The problem of course would not go away. Particularly around Merseyside West Indians were harassed and attacked by white GIs, and were barred from places of entertainment because of American pressure. The burdens fell upon people like Learie Constantine, the 39-year-old Trinidadian cricketer who had been living and working in the north of England for some time. He was appointed early in 1942 as a welfare officer for the Ministry of Labour with the task of looking after the men who had been recruited to work in Liverpool. The League of Coloured Peoples witnessed the problems there that began to grind Constantine down. Within a year of his appointment, he reported attacks on himself and other West Indians to his superiors:

> I cannot lay sufficient emphasis on the bitterness being
> created amongst the Technicians by these attacks on
> coloured British subjects by white Americans . . . I am . . .
> loth to believe that coloured subjects of the Empire who are
> here on vital work could be attacked at random and at the
> will and pleasure of these white American soldiers without
> the means of redress . . . I have lived in this Country for a
> long time and claim many friends among the white popula-
> tion, and I shiver to think that I am liable to attack by these
> men if I am seen in the company of my friends. I suggest
> something should be done about the position, and done
> urgently, as I can foresee a crisis approaching.[30]

Nothing was done; the difficulties remained as did the exchange of memoranda between the civil servants. Sir George Gater from the Colonial Office, who had been so vocal in his expression of British principles on the race issue, and Bracken simply did not want to approach the Americans.

In the event, deciding not to say anything to the US authorities and therefore acquiescing in their treatment of British blacks, was a wasted opportunity. There is every evidence that the Americans were sympathetic to the British viewpoint and wanted to eliminate the problem. Colonel Pleas B. Rogers of the London Base Command, US Forces, admitted that in London the 'negro British nation-als are rightly incensed. They undoubtedly have been cursed, made to get off the sidewalk, leave eating places and are separated from their white wives in public by American soldiers'.[31] With the help of the League of Coloured Peoples some individual cases of discrimination against Africans and West Indians, such as those men-tioned by Rogers, were brought to the attention of the American Army and offenders were punished.

The Americans, far from being upset in the way that made British officials so nervous, were as cooperative as they could be as was evidenced by a film called *Welcome to Britain*.[32] The film was commissioned by the Ministry of

Information, produced by Strand films and directed by
Anthony Asquith. 'Puffin' Asquith, the son of former Prime
Minister Herbert Asquith, was a film director with a
growing reputation and two box-office successes behind
him in the immediate pre-war years – *Pygmalion* and
French Without Tears. Released in December 1943, *Welcome to Britain* featured American actor Burgess Meredith
and was an hour-long guide to British ways and behaviour,
intended for newly-arrived American servicemen. It included a quite remarkable sequence on race, asking the
American soldiers to respect the different attitudes they
would find in Britain. In effect the film granted the request
that Keith at the Colonial Office, amongst others, had
wanted all along – the right to inform the Americans of the
British view on this matter. In the film Burgess Meredith
plays a white soldier who is the narrator. In the sequence
about race, Meredith, an English woman and a black
soldier are in the same compartment of a railway carriage
and during their conversation the woman and the black GI
discover that they both come from towns called Birmingham. On leaving, the woman invites both soldiers to tea if
they are ever in her Birmingham. This is the point at
which Meredith turns to the camera:

> Now look men, you heard that conversation; that's not
> unusual here, it's the sort of thing that happens quite a lot.
> Now let's be frank about it. There are coloured soldiers as
> well as *white* here and there are less social restrictions in
> this country . . . You heard an Englishwoman asking a
> coloured boy to tea. She was polite about it and he was polite
> about it. Now . . . look; that might not happen at home but
> the . . . point is, we're not at home, and the point is too, if we
> bring a lot of prejudices here what are we gonna do about
> 'em?

Probably no one was more surprised than the black GI at
the invitation to tea, and the script implied that there
would still be little social change in America after the war;
nevertheless these were at this point frank words on race
relations coming indirectly as they did from a ministry
which had been a party to previous government statements
of a very different nature.

The sequence continued with an appearance by the respected American General, J. C. Lee, who made a stirring statement about democracy and the war: 'When the Army needs Americans to fight for the country it takes Negroes along with whites. Everyone's treated the same when it comes to dying'.

The film was well received by those British critics who managed to see it, and General Lee's statement, encouraging US soldiers to take a fresh look at their racist attitudes, was especially commended. There was also extreme irony in the situation. Here was a British Government department (the Ministry of Information) which had in 1942 contributed to a policy encouraging the British to respect segregation because that was the American way, making a film the following year, with American actors and senior American staff officers, encouraging the Americans to respect racial integration in Britain because that was the British way!

For the British civilian population all these discussions on the presence of the black GIs in Britain were academic. Despite the demands of regional commissioners that some guidance should be given to nonmilitary personnel none was offered even though some very practical questions were now being asked such as the legality of marriage to the black GI. Given the dearth of information it was natural that apart from the published books about American life, information was sought from members of the clergy.

Harold Moody of the League of Coloured Peoples got wind that some instructions might have been issued by the Government in November 1942. Having being assured that there were none, he felt that the presence of the black GIs offered a unique opportunity to Christians and Churches to help improve race relations. The Established Church seemed to be in tune with this sentiment too; the Lichfield Diocesan magazine of October 1942 was one of several publications to carry this optimistic message: 'The whole British nation will desire to welcome the large numbers of American troops who have come from overseas, and the Archbishops have expressed their strong desire that the Churches will take their full share in such a welcome'. The reality was that various religious organizations, far from seizing the opportunity outlined by Moody, saw the presence of the black Americans as a problem and sought a more terrestrial solution for it. The story of their acceptance of the Government's position is a revealing and shabby episode.

The Ministry of Information, acting in its capacity as coordinator of voluntary bodies, had warned churches in the middle of 1942 to consult American Army chaplains before inviting GIs to their functions so that race mixing could be avoided. As black troops crowded into various parts of the country individual churchmen took local initiatives. In Bristol the Lord Bishop had called a conference to discuss what he considered to be bad conduct by black troops. The Lord Bishop of Bristol since 1933 had been the Reverend Clifford Salisbury Woodward, former Chaplain to the King, who went on to become the Bishop of Gloucester until his retirement in 1953 at the age of 75. The gist of the concerns was, as usual, the prospect of interracial sexual relations, and sometimes this was made very clear. The Bishop of Salisbury insisted that the sharp distinction drawn between black and white across the Atlantic was justified by experience, and stressed that white women should not associate with black soldiers. The bishop here was the Right Reverend E. Neville Lovett, a septuagenarian who had also been Chaplain to the King. Like many others of the ruling élite of the day, such as Harry Haig, Sir Ronald Adam and Sir Frederick Bovenschen, Lovett was a member of the Athenaeum club. One can imagine the postprandial conversations about the colour bar that took place there.

Towards the end of 1942 the black American issue attracted the attention of the British Council of Churches, a powerful body with the authority to influence many more church officials and churchgoers. The Council, which was founded in 1942, is the official instrument of the Anglican, Presbyterian and Free Churches in the British Isles for furthering, amongst other things, the cause of Christian unity and for facilitating common action on social, educational and international questions. In the middle of November the Secretary of the Council's Department of International Friendship reported that a small group had been established to discuss the question of the black GIs. After a great deal of handwringing the full executive committee of the BCC met in the middle of January 1943. Among its important members were Geoffrey Fisher the Bishop of London (and soon to become Archibishop of Canterbury), and the Bishops of Bristol and Lichfield who had already been involved in the black GI question. The Executive had (if the metaphor is not inappropriate) seized upon the Government's Notes of November 1942 as if they were manna from heaven. For this, of course, it could hardly be criticized – if the matter had been discussed and concluded at the highest possible level of government who were the members of this committee to question it? What is interesting is the letter which the BCC distributed with the notes. It commended the Government's statement dealing 'exhaustively' with the black American issue, but was a little shamefaced about it all: *'For obvious reasons* it is important that this statement must not be printed in Church magazines and elsewhere, nor quoted at public meetings, nor generally distributed'. It apparently was too conservative a statement for some of the committee however. The letter continued: 'We feel . . . that we have cause for thankfulness for the words in the official document; *and though it may be some might privately have desired that it should go still further* we think, in the circumstances, it can be regarded as satisfactory. [Author's emphasis]'[33]

The BCC's statement was somewhat ironic in view of the fact that during the war one of the most popular activities associated with the black Americans was the singing of Negro spirituals in British churches.

Just as the Government spoke with a public and private voice on the black GI issue, the Church too issued statements that were at variance with the BCC pronouncement. Thus in complete contrast to the thinking behind the

Government's Notes and by extension the BCC attitude, was an address by Dr Temple, the Archbishop of Canterbury, to the Convocation of Canterbury in May 1944, which was reprinted in the MOI's religious journal. William Temple, who was educated at Rugby and Balliol College, Oxford, had a lengthy sojourn as Archbishop of York before coming to Canterbury in 1942. Socially aware, Temple was regarded by many as extremely left wing and he was indeed a member of the Labour Party for a number of years after the First World War. Now Dr Temple urged 'special care for the coloured folk, who, because of the treatment they have sometimes received here or elsewhere, often suppose that they are not welcome, for example, in our churches . . . It is one main function of the Church to bind together those whom the natural ordering of life tends to set apart from one another'.[34]

Again, of course, all these deliberations did not slake the thirst of civilians for information about Americans, black and white. Initially there was, as American broadcaster Ed Murrow discovered, little available; Americans were making no effort to explain their way of life to their allies. This soon changed as the American troops piled into Britain. The Ministry of Information was amongst several Government departments which employed writers throughout the war to maintain the flow of information about Britain's allies, her enemies, the progress of the war and sundry other issues. In the sense that all material was liable to be censored it could be said that *everything* published in the war years carried the seal of approval, but particular attention needs to be paid to the involvement of some prominent writers; their publications at the very least could be regarded as semi-official. Several of them were sent to the United States in various capacities. Those that had comments to make on the racial situation said little that would have upset southern racist attitudes, though some did point out the realities of racial discrimination in the USA. Most adopted the Ministry of Information 'it's none of our business' approach, while some went even further, displaying racist or patronizing attitudes.

One of the better known of those writers who turned their attention towards America was Phyllis Bentley who had toured the United States three times before the outbreak of war. With an already established reputation as a novelist of the West Riding of Yorkshire, she joined the American Division of the Ministry of Information in 1942, and worked there for two years. her booklet, *Here is America*, which was published in 1942, can certainly be seen as reflecting official views. She had adopted some southern attitudes, referring to 'coloured piccaninnies', and planters 'who were usually genuinely attached to their negroes'. She did comment on the huge expense of duplicating everything because of segregation, and the 'desperate sense of the negro being a millstone round the South's neck', but she did not greatly advance the pre-war movie image of the 'grinning negro'. Blacks were, she wrote, 'childlike and affectionate . . . people who show such a beautiful desire to make other people happy'.[35]

The following year saw two important books about America. John Langdon-Davis was an honorary wartime Army officer who had conducted several lecture tours in the United States. Langdon-Davis pointed out in *American Close-up: Portrait of an Ally*, that there was an obsession in the South about the danger to white supremacy, which often led to blacks being prevented, by various unscrupulous means, from voting. He rightly pointed out that discrimination in the USA was providing a propaganda gift to the Nazis. The other book of 1943, by Maurice Colbourne, was entitled *America and Britain* and went further than Phyllis Bentley's in its attitude. Colbourne had also travelled in the United States as an official representative of the British Information Service, and again it is probable that some official sanction was given to his writing. Like Bentley, Colbourne outlined some of the disadvantages the black man suffered in the southern states – the ban on interracial unions, the segregation and the separate schools in particular. He then addressed himself to the particular question of Britain and the black GIs: now they were in the country people were taking a 'perplexed and apprehensive' interest in the question of race. 'How, Britons asked themselves, should they treat this amiable curiosity equipped with a broad pearly smile, the accoutrements of war, and, by British standards, pocketfuls of money?' Colbourne's answer to this was to leave the issue alone, for the colour bar was 'an American domestic problem for Americans themselves to solve'. Ultimately, he argued, you could silence any discussion of the problem by coming back to the 'problem' of marriage:

> Britons with no colour problem, and imagining themselves free from colour prejudice, easily slip into violent denunciations of the American colour bar as a disgrace to and denial of democracy. Whenever I encounter a Briton waxing eloquent along that line I ask him, preferably in front of others: 'Would you like your sister to marry a Negro?'[36]

Hilary St George Saunders, who described himself as a pamphleteer, wrote several official books on the work of the Combined Operations Command. As a result of one of these becoming a Book of the Month in America, he was invited to speak there as a guest of the Office of War Information, and he travelled 12,000 miles in two months. Saunders, who was to become librarian at the House of Commons after the war, published his reflections on America in *Pioneers! O Pioneers!* and like the other writers he expressed views on the racial problem. He realized that it was a difficult and abiding social problem, but here was a country 'where discrimination against free-born, equal citizens, because they are coloured, have woolly hair, and are the descendents of slaves, is a social phenomenon which confronts the foreigner wherever he goes'. Then the barriers were raised again for just when Saunders seemed to be about to give some guidance on the black American guests to an eager British public, he grew cautious:

> The [negro] problem is essentially domestic, and visitors would do well to bear this in mind. It is not for us to make suggestions regarding its solution unless we are ready to risk receiving the kind of rebuff administered to Mrs Jones when she tells Mrs Smith over the backyard wall how to bring up her children.[37]

Certainly the most controversial matter of all involving the black Americans as the war progressed was that of marriage and sexual relations, and writers like James Lansdale Hodson returned to the theme frequently. Hodson was a radical and perceptive journalist who contributed much to the record of the war, not least by his work on official films such as *Desert Victory* and *Russian Victory* between 1943 and 1945. Hodson travelled the country, subsequently writing about his meetings with people and the tempo of wartime life in Britain. The obsession with sex that he and writers like him displayed undoubtedly contributed to the formation of public attitudes: 'In theory all men are equal whatever their race,' wrote Hodson, 'but if I am asked whether I should be pleased to see my daughter marrying a negro, the answer is in the negative.'[38]

During the winter and spring of 1943 Hodson travelled in the USA as a uniformed Air Officer in the employ of the British Information Service. He produced a book about this in 1945, and while it was not specifically about race he did have some comments to make. While talking with a professor at Harvard he repeated his assertion that he would not agree to his daughter marrying a black, and later used the expression 'a touch of the tar-brush'. Returning to Britain by ship he remembered sympathizing with a white American colonel who could not understand how some English girls were going out with the black Americans and even having children by them. Hodson's opinion was that 'every country had a certain number of women of that sort'.[39] By late 1943 the early welcome given to the blacks in England was fading. The continual emphasis on the sexual issue was without a doubt one of the reasons for this trend.

Whatever the amount of propaganda issued, many British citizens only looked to those magazines, or listened to those stories, which reinforced their image of the black American. Certainly it would appear that there was still an enormous amount of ignorance about the black soldiers considering the frequency of rumours about them barking like dogs or having tails. Such stories as these were disseminated by some white Americans and believed by some British citizens in 1942 and 1943. Less malevolent but equally significant were those stories which harkened back to the pre-war days, carried by popular publications like the illustrated weekly, *Picture Post*. On 31 October 1942 it welcomed the first black American Red Cross girls, who had the 'typical liveliness and humour of the negro'. A year later, on 16 October 1943, the same journal reviewed a concert by Roland Hayes and a black American choir, talking of the traditional talent of the black and the 'gift of singing. Music – simple rhythmic music – seems inborn in the negro race'. On 18 December 1943 the *Picture Post* investigated the new black dance, the Lindy Hop: 'Dancing is to the coloured people what sport is to the British, or warfare to the Germans – their truest form of self expression. It is a racial heritage, tracing back to the dark ritual of the tom-tom'.

Whether stereotyped views were modified as a result of contacts between the British population and the black Americans from 1942 onwards remains to be seen. Certainly there was some initial astonishment when blacks landed in Northern Ireland; one recollection is that 'the appearance in Lurgan of black GIs with such names as "O'Mahoney" and "Concannon" came as a surprise, until the locals discovered they were common in black communities in Tennessee or Kentucky'.[40] Not all subsequent surprises about the American soldiers and race relations were as superficial. As 1942 progressed the ugly reality of the American jim-crow Army became evident across half of Great Britain, in isolated rural communities and towns alike.

4

Jim Crow in Britain: The US Army and Racial Segregation

Wortley is a small village of less than 1,000 inhabitants nestling in what used to be the West Riding of Yorkshire. Situated on the edge of the picturesque Peak District National Park it is not a place you would easily come across by accident. It has nearly always been dwarfed by its industrial and coalmining neighbours, Sheffield and Barnsley, and life has flowed along as quietly as the nearby River Don.

In the summer of 1942 the village had more excitement than it could probably cope with. In the middle of July, 177 men of the all-black 65th Ordnance Company arrived from Fort Dix, New Jersey, and they were joined a month or so later by a further 98 black GIs and 45 of their white compatriots, forming two separate quartermaster companies. All the troops had come to service an aerial bomb depot which was located in the vicinity. Such was the curiosity, interest and comment aroused in this sleepy English village by the arrival of over 300 Americans, the vast majority black, that at the beginning of October two US captains of the Inspector General's office spent three days probing into the situation in detail. Their report was fascinating and full of the stuff of drama: the complexities and ramifications of the black American presence in Britain were all encapsulated in the Wortley experience,

an experience which few in their wildest imaginations
could have dreamt of just one year earlier.[1]

The investigation was occasioned by allegations against
the black troops which emanated from a variety of sources.
There were British military reports of a fight between an
English sergeant and a black GI and further charges of
rape, and the case of one soldier wanting to 'loan' a
civilian's daughter. In addition the Chief Constable of
Sheffield some eight miles away detailed attacks by blacks
on the villagers, an assault by blacks on a Canadian
soldier, and a fight in a local restaurant. An RAF officer
stationed nearby described an attack on the captain of the
black quartermaster company by one of his own men,
adding in his view that the American troops were poorly
disciplined. The last straw was that the local squire, Lord
Wharncliffe, viewed the 'fraternization' between blacks
and local white girls as 'serious'. Almost all the accusations
related to events in September and of course had to be
looked into.

The estate and grounds of Lord Wharncliffe had been
requisitioned by the Air Ministry for RAF use and in turn
had been handed over to the American Army Air Forces.
The white troops occupied part of Wortley Hall, the manor
house, while the blacks were quartered in tents in the
grounds. Morale and discipline among the black ordnance
troops and the quartermaster company were not all they
should have been. Part of the explanation was that the
white ordnance captain had only two years' active duty,
was short of officer personnel and was only 22 years old
himself.

In their off-duty activities the black GIs were having a
good time. They had 'considerable relationships' with local
girls and those from Sheffield. Prostitutes and factory girls
came from there in taxis to be paid for their favours in
money or rations. All 'actively solicited' black soldiers, and
some lived on or near the military area for up to ten days.
Some, including one girl of 16, set up tents with their GIs,
undiscovered because proper bed checks of the men were
not made. It was while he was disturbing a black GI in the
sexual act that the captain of the black quartermaster

company was punched.

The English 'bobbies' tried to break up these activities by arresting some of the women but did not appear unduly exercised by it. On the contrary Wortley and Sheffield police thought the black Yanks were 'better behaved' than the British or Canadian troops, and the Inspector from nearby Penistone stated that 'the people in this community had no prejudice against coloured soldiers because they were coloured'. The only worry that the Sheffield police had was that some of the black GIs carried long knives.

More concerned about the sexual angle was Lord Wharncliffe, who, the American investigators' report noted, 'occupies a powerful position in the area'. If today you travel to Wortley from Sheffield the name is everywhere – Wharncliffe Crags and Wharncliffe Wood run alongside the River Don and the village of Wharncliffe Side is close by. Lord Wharncliffe – Archibald Ralph Montagu-Stuart-Wortley-Mackenzie, had succeeded to the title in 1926 when he was in his early 30s. Educated at Eton he had been in the Guards and at one time was an aide to the Governor General of South Africa. Invalided back to England, Wharncliffe returned home to Wortley where he now lived with his wife, the daughter of Earl Fitzwilliam. By the time the US investigating team arrived on the scene a new black engineering unit had moved into the area, replacing the white troops in residence at Wortley Hall. Evidently there was no barrier between their quarters and the private part of the house and this was now the principal cause of complaint. On one occasion Wharncliffe was having breakfast and looked up to see 'a big black face grinning at him through the windows'. His wife similarly had found black soldiers peering through the family picture album in her library. The village police constable meanwhile, without elaborating, viewed Lord Wharncliffe as 'a source of continual trouble to the inhabitants of the Wortley community'!

Locally the black GIs were well liked. In Sheffield they used low-grade pubs and were preyed on by women because of their high pay, though in these places they were treated as equals. Wortley inhabitants resented the influx of 'tarts' and the blatant sexual behaviour of blacks ('far beyond the normal standard of the community') but they had sung and preached in church and had been to people's homes for tea. The only exception to the 'very satisfactory' relationships the blacks had with British civilians, soldiers and police was the taunting of them by 'hoodlums' in a local restaurant serving cheap food late at night. The local lads resented the fact that the GIs had collared many of the lower-class women and had more money, and they began to call them 'black bastards'.

The Wortley situation had all the ingredients that were to prove so volatile the longer the black GIs stayed in Britain. These were British class attitudes, the difficulties in pubs, the sexual and financial attraction blacks had for 'camp followers', the difficulties with young girls, the low black morale and above all the stark racial segregation.

Segregation for GIs of course did not begin in Britain, but started as soon as young black men volunteered for the services back home, or were drafted. It was in the camps scattered throughout the United States where blacks did their basic training that the realities of jim crow in the Army became apparent. If camps housed blacks and whites, the blacks were often in the worst part with no access to cinemas, recreational or post exchange facilities. Some camps were isolated from towns with transport nonexistent or operated on a whites first, blacks last basis. What irked many soldiers was that despite their training and education, opportunities for them were very limited and they ended up again as labourers in uniform. At Pampa Air Field, Texas, for example, basic training was even limited. A gun was something a black enlisted man training to go to war was unlikely to see 'except a 45 on the MP's side, ready to blow your brains out if you resent[ed] being treated like a dog or being called a nigger or a Black son of a b....'.[2]

Segregation continued while the troops were *en route* to Britain. Some prestigious ocean-going liners were brought into service as troop carriers during the war, the *Queen Elizabeth*, *Queen Mary* and *Aquitania* among them. The crossing could take as little as four or five days, or up to seventeen if the ships were travelling in convoy, and it was a totally jim-crow experience. On board blacks had their quarters and whites had theirs. The two groups would often not be permitted to associate with one another, even using different mess halls.

While the troops were on board ship they were given a handbook produced by the War and Navy departments, *A Short Guide to Great Britain*. The handbook was a useful little publication for the GI with advice on how to behave in the host country – don't brag, don't make fun of English accents or criticize the King and Queen. Soldiers were told not to 'sound off' about the food or the lukewarm beer, though many later ignored that advice and suggested it should be poured back in the horse. Clutching the handbook as they disembarked at Glasgow or Liverpool, black troops in particular must have been very anxious about the reception they would receive as their trains sped them to all parts of Britain, especially since the *Guide* contained no mention of race, nor any reference to the notion that the British might treat blacks differently.

It was obvious from their experience in the US that the segregation of the troops appeared to the blacks to be accompanied by an equal measure of discrimination against them. Damaging though this problem was at home, the Army authorities were not so insensitive that they failed to see that the difficulties would be multiplied a hundredfold when the troops were overseas, particularly in the cramped British Isles. Before the arrival of black soldiers in the country attempts were made to defuse the situation. In the middle of February 1942 the Adjutant General's office in Washington issued some instructions to its commanding generals on how to treat black soldiers.[3] They were to avoid insulting racial epithets, 'tyrannical or capricious conduct' and abusive language. Everything was to be done to assure the black GI that the Army made no 'differentiation between him and any other soldier'. Most importantly, as the Army expanded, newer officers were to have 'a full realization' of these factors.

The first indication of a racial policy specifically for Britain came in July 1942. Eisenhower had been in Britain

by then for a couple of months and he held a press
conference on the 14th. According to Harry Butcher, Ike's
aide, several of the reporters present were curious about
the black troops. Butcher later wrote that Eisenhower told
the press as background that 'his policy for handling
coloured troops would be absolute equality of treatment
but there would be segregation where facilities afforded.
The coloured troops are to have everything as good as the
white'.[4] Further detail was added a couple of days later
when Eisenhower sent a policy document on black soldiers
to General Lee of the Services of Supply, in which most
blacks served. The statement contained suggestions for
implementing the 'separate but equal' policy which was to
operate in Great Britain. Problems would be raised which
would require the 'constant and close supervision of
Commanding Officers', but it was the desire of Headquarters that 'discrimination against the Negro troops be
sedulously avoided'. Eisenhower realized that it would be
impossible to segregate black and white soldiers on leave
in London and other big cities, but he did make some
tentative proposals for meeting the situation elsewhere:

> A more difficult problem will exist in the vicinity of camps
> where both White and Negro soldiers are stationed, particu-
> larly with reference to dances and other social activities.
> This Headquarters will not attempt to issue any detailed
> instructions. Local Commanding Officers will be expected to
> use their own best judgement in avoiding discrimination due
> to race, but at the same time, minimizing causes of friction
> between White and Colored Troops. Rotation of pass pri-
> vileges and similar methods suggest themselves for use;
> always with the guiding principle that any restriction
> imposed by Commanding Officers applies with equal force to
> both races.[5]

By this time Great Britain had been divided for ease of
administration into various commands by the American
authorities. The areas were: Northern Ireland, Eastern,
Western, Southern and London Base (later called Central
Base Section). General Lee passed on Ike's letter to all the
base section commanders in the first week of August
adding a little note of his own that the 'resourceful'

commander could employ various methods to minimize racial friction. In addition to the rotation of pass privileges he suggested that dances could be 'equitably regulated' on an organizational base.[6] What he meant was that instead of a function being advertised for black or white troops it would be for the 89th Quartermaster Company or whatever. As troop units were either black or white, and to the initiated the name indicated this, it was simply a more discreet way of maintaining jim crow.

Eisenhower left England towards the end of 1942 and did not return for about fourteen months. Lee was designated Deputy Theatre Commander as well as being Commander of the Services of Supply, and his suggestions about black troops were obviously taken seriously.

John Clifford Hodges Lee was a controversial figure during the war. Born in Kansas in 1887 he was named after his maternal grandfather who had been a captain in the Confederate Army. Lee graduated from West Point and then became a young engineer officer working in many parts of the world. His dealings with blacks began early in his army career in France and continued between the wars when he was involved in flood control on the Mississippi. Throughout his career he maintained a southern paternalistic attitude to blacks. Just before coming to Europe he was in charge of the Second Infantry Division in Texas where he tried without success to get permission to enlist blacks as mess personnel because he remembered 'as a child how good cooks negroes were'. As commander of the SOS he was demanding and stern and his religious views earned him the nickname of 'Jesus Christ' Lee. Though he was not averse to attending services where blacks preached he doubted whether blacks and whites were 'equal in God's sight'. He agreed with Eisenhower that in wartime Britain the black soldier had to have equal rights but 'we recognized,' he said, 'this should be modified when it concerned women and liquor'. Lee was not a popular figure but he worked hard at his job as he ostentatiously toured Britain in a special train on his inspection trips.[7]

General Lee was clearly aware that his methods of controlling racial friction were somewhat hypocritical, and late in September 1942, after reports of disturbances in East Anglia, he was a little embarrassed about how they should be presented. Writing to Colonel Plank, the commanding officer of the Eastern Base Section, he said that 'the Organization Commander should be reminded that in accordance with my policy, mixed parties should be avoided. While color lines are not to be announced, or even mentioned, entertainments, such as dances should be done "by organization". The reason, if any given for such an arrangement should be "limitation of space and personnel".'[8]

Since Eisenhower's preference had been to leave much of the minutiae of segregation to subordinates, they now began to suggest all kinds of ways in which jim crow could best be effected in Britain. In August 1942 Chaplain Edwin R. Carter, jun., usually a sensitive commentator on black affairs, prepared a memorandum on the racial problem in Britain.[9] As he saw it the only real solution was absolute segregation of the races though he realized that this was 'impossible'. The measures he advocated came pretty close to it however. He suggested separate, and distant camps for each race, leave passes for designated areas and duplication of facilities where both races used the same area. Carter was not alone.

Colonel Montgomery of the personnel section of Lee's own command had a particularly simple approach: if you kept the black guys 'happy in their own camps' fewer would want passes to go out and hence no racial problem. He suggested that travelling libraries should visit the camps every two weeks, and there should be lectures by the British, and other educational classes. In addition the men were to be encouraged to form glee clubs and drama groups, and to take part in athletics. Motion pictures would keep the men 'at home', Montgomery argued, though at that moment there were plenty of films but no projectors! If all else failed the men were to be induced to invest in war bonds which would give them less spending money and again reduce the demand for passes.[10]

From a description of life in one black camp near Penistone in Yorkshire it is clear that vast improvements would have been needed to divert the men there from their main goal – the 'wine, women and song' of Huddersfield. In camp they had little apart from gambling, ping-pong tables and draughts. Forums were abandoned because they were never well attended, and when they had the films and a projector there was no operator. Even when all the accoutrements for an evening of film-watching were at hand the spools would come unwound only to be shown in the wrong order, and the projector would break down on numerous occasions to be 'mended' by beefy hands carrying crowbars and blow torches.[11] Not surprisingly Montgomery's suggestions were never officially adopted; if they had been the number of black soldiers guilty of being absent without leave would have kept the military courts busy long after the end of the war!

It was in the late summer of 1942 that the American authorities were jolted by Frank Newsam's letter from the Home Office saying that the British police had been told not to assist with the arrangements for segregation. There now arose the very odd situation of both countries bending over backwards trying not to upset each other on the race issue. The Americans announced that Eisenhower was in 'complete accord' with the Home Office instructions and the US Army policy was one of nondiscrimination. They added a statement which was, however, already blatantly untrue in the areas of Britain where black troops and white troops were stationed in close proximity:

> With reference to the question of placing certain places out of bounds, we do not make any restrictions of that kind on the basis of color. The policy followed by United States Army authorities is that places out of bounds for United States soldiers are out of bounds to all United States personnel.[12]

Eisenhower himself seems to have had a real understanding of the delicacy of the American position and a willingness to be bold. He showed his concern by sending Lee a copy of Newsam's Home Office note. The various reports of disturbances now reaching him prompted Eisenhower to state the problem in blunt terms. 'There is,' he wrote, practically no colored population in the British Isles. Undoubtedly a considerable association of colored troops with British white population, both men and women, will take place on a basis mutually acceptable to the individuals concerned. Any attempt to curtail such association by official orders or restrictions is unjustified and must not be attempted.[13]

In private Ike was not quite so sanguine about the sexual angle. He told Merle Oberon, the Hollywood movie star who came to Britain in August 1942, that he was worried about the black troops because they were running off with English girls.[14]

The most comprehensive instruction about how to operate jim crow in Britain came on 25 October 1943, and it was really a confirmation of what had been happening for some time. This statement came from the office of Lieutenant General Jacob L. Devers, who had taken over the command of the European Theatre in May 1943 when the old flying buff, General Frank Andrews, was killed in a plane crash in Iceland. Devers' instructions emphasized that discrimination was still not permitted though much was again left to local commanders. The Army's stand on segregation, reflecting the reality of the situation, was that it was not to happen in localities where it was 'contrary to custom and accepted practice'. This of course meant everywhere in Britain but now two exceptions were made: firstly, 'in the interest of military discipline and avoidance of possible disorder', and secondly, to 'ameliorate over-crowding of facilities'.[15]

In practice the policy of segregating black GIs from the whites was very carefully worked out though in such a restricted space as Britain there were obvious difficulties. Where there were large numbers of soldiers of both races stationed in small towns or villages in the same general area, such as parts of the West Country or East Anglia, access to any town could be limited to one race by the use of passes. If one large town in these areas was the magnet for all troops because of its facilities (Bristol and Ipswich were such towns), pass control could again effectively restrict the use of certain pubs or dance halls in those towns to one race. If, as often happened in remote parts of Britain, troops were based in places where opportunities for recreation were few, then rotation of pass days would allow those scarce facilities to be shared. In other words it was 'blacks Tuesday, whites Wednesday'.

Much of the detail of segregation in Britain comes from the reports of the Inspector General's Department. The officers assigned to this section were dispatched when there were rumours of interracial trouble or complaints from the civilian population. One of the most energetic and even-handed of these men was Colonel, later Brigadier General, Oliver Haines, who arrived in Europe in September 1943, soon to travel miles all over Britain on inspection tours. Haines, a graduate of the University of California, was 52 years old when he was sent overseas. Like many of his contemporaries he had served in France in the First World War and on his return to the States spent much of his early army career with the cavalry in Texas and Kansas. After this he attended the Command and General Staff School in Kansas and the War College in Washington, DC. He joined the Inspector General's Department in the middle of 1939, serving in Texas again, Louisiana and Kentucky, doubtless gaining experience with black troops before his European assignment.

At the end of 1943 Haines discovered that there were some 5,000 black troops in and around Liverpool at Maghull, Aintree and Huyton, and others in Manchester. There were about 2,500 whites in the same area and another 3,500 at the large air depot at Burtonwood near Warrington. Both races used Liverpool and Manchester and relations there were said to be satisfactory, in part because both cities had separate Red Cross Clubs for blacks and whites. In smaller towns other arrangements were made. Two black truck battalions in Bamber Bridge used nearby Preston, while white Americans a dozen miles away at Warton were sent for their off-duty recreation in the opposite direction either south across the River Ribble to genteel Southport, or north to the popular resort of Blackpool. The result, it was reported, was that there were few contacts between blacks and whites, and few incidents,

none of them serious. Further south at Marbury Hall near
Northwich in Cheshire there were complications because
black and white troops were in close proximity there, and
another 600 whites were about six miles down the road at
Delamere. The local commanding officers of these troops
therefore agreed that the issue of passes would determine
that Northwich was the black town while Chester about
fifteen miles away was the white town.[16]

Jim crow was even more pronounced and carefully
regulated in East Anglia which Haines had visited just
prior to going to the north-west. Here there were important
air bases with whites involved in combat duties and blacks
performing essential backup tasks as engineers, truck
drivers and ordnance workers. Blacks were stationed at
Eye, at Debach near Ipswich, and in Haughley Park near
Stowmarket where they were particularly popular with
the locals because of their swing bands and dances. The
white troops were in different towns – Martlesham,
Wattisham and Horham. For both races the night life was
in Ipswich with its 150 public houses! There being more
white than black troops, their commanders decided that
the whites should have access to the majority of places of
entertainment, and so just eight pubs, a Co-op dance hall
and a Red Cross club were 'reserved' for blacks alone. In
the larger area local officers determined that the ironically
named River Dove, a tributary of the Waveney which
flowed through East Anglia, was to be the border line. Eye
and Diss were 'black' towns but all the villages east of the
Dove were 'out of bounds' for the blacks. Locals in Eye
must have shaken their heads in amazement at the
American Army's arrangements. Eye being just on the
river was a 'black' town, while Horham, four miles away,
was 'white'. Evidence that segregation was strictly
adhered to was provided by the frequent arrests of blacks
found in areas out of bounds to them.[17]

It was these arrangements, particularly as they applied
to Ipswich, which were so appalling to Truman K. Gibson,
jun., who became the black civilian aide to the US
Secretary of War at the end of January 1943. He wrote an
angry letter to Assistant Secretary of War John J. McCloy

condemning the exportation of jim crow overseas. The European Theatre of Operations had, he claimed, imposed

A rigid pattern of racial segregation in Great Britain, community patterns in that country to the contrary notwithstanding . . . it is exceedingly interesting to note that the practices in Great Britain conform with those that exist in many parts of this country. Here, segregation of Negroes goes much beyond their separation in military units. . . . It is common in the South also to have portions of towns declared 'off limits' to Negro personnel. It would therefore appear, superficially at least, that the Army has taken to England practices that exist widely in this country and that are regarded by many persons as constituting *the* solution to the racial problem.[18]

Despite protests from Gibson and others segregation remained virtually absolute in Britain during the war years; it lasted until the end and, as was shown with Joe Louis, black heavyweight boxing champion of the world, it was no respecter of persons. Louis joined the American Army and served largely in a morale-boosting role – appearing on recruitment posters, fund-raising tours and entertaining troops overseas. One such tour brought him to Britain early in 1944, where in Salisbury, Wiltshire, he encountered the heavy hand of Jim Crow. Entering a cinema, he later recollected, the

ticket taker told us we'd have to sit in a special section. Shit! This wasn't America, this was England . . . the theatre manager . . . knew who I was and apologized all over the place. Said he had instructions from the Army. So I called my friend Lieutenant General John Lee and told them they had no business messing up another country's customs with American Jim Crow. He was real sorry; after that there was no more Jim Crow in the English theater.[19]

Joe Louis's assertion however was not true – his stand had little permanent effect on long-term army policy. When a WAC postal battalion of over 700 black women arrived in Birmingham in February 1945, it was warmly welcomed by local people; civic receptions were laid on and there were invitations to people's homes. The US Army command however decided that one of the local swimming baths should be placed out of bounds to the battalion. In the local council Labour members voiced their dissatisfaction, but an anti-colour bar resolution in the general purposes committee was defeated by 49 votes to 31.[20]

Recurring features of the reports written by Haines and his colleagues in the Inspector General's Department were the need for proper military policemen (preferably from both races) in areas where blacks and whites mixed, and the need to fill the authorized 25 per cent increase in officers in black troop commands. Generally where there had been race friction it was almost always attributed to the lack of proper 'indoctrination' (that was the word used) in the US military's racial directives. As the inspections continued it became clear that the amount of indoctrination units received varied considerably though it was generally agreed that efforts had been concentrated on black troops. It was also revealed that particular branches of the Army had their own statements on the black and white issue, implying that the overall policy was not sufficient. For example, the VIII Air Force Service Command unit newly-arrived in Stone, Staffordshire, had its own detailed programme. First the troops were advised that now they were in Britain it was wise to avoid conversations about politics, religion and the Duke of Windsor. Then a further thirteen minutes were devoted to race. Black soldiers, the audience heard, were Americans too. The advice continued:

> The English do not have a negro situation like we have in the States, and some of the English do not draw the color line as we do. To the English they are American soldiers who came across the ocean to win this war. So if you should see an American negro soldier walking down the street with a white English woman, you will simply look the other way and don't start an argument. We are telling you this so you will know how to act if you should be stationed near our negro troops.[21]

Clearly, despite all the memoranda that were issued by the US military, despite all attempts at indoctrination, however well-meaning and sensitive these attempts might have been, in the final analysis the implementation of directives on the issue of race rested with individual local commanders and officers. No amount of paperwork whatever its form could get round this reality. President Roosevelt had by February 1944 conceded this point too. In that month he held a special press conference for representatives of the Negro Newspaper Publishers Association. After listening to a tirade about civil rights and discrimination in jobs and the Army, Roosevelt admitted resignedly:

> It is perfectly true, there is definite discrimination in the actual treatment of the colored engineer troops, and others. And you are up against it, as you know perfectly well. I have talked about it – I had the Secretary of War and the Assistant – everybody in on it. The trouble lies fundamentally in the attitude of certain white people – officers down the line who haven't got much more education, many of them, than the colored troops and the Seabees and the engineers for example. And well, you know the kind of person it is. We all do. We don't have to do more than think of a great many people that we know. And it has become not a question of orders – they are repeated fairly often, I think, in all the camps of colored troops – it's a question of the personality of the individual. And we are up against it, absolutely up against it.[22]

What explains the attitude of the average American officer to the black troops under his command? Put at its simplest of course it was that officers, like the white GIs, reflected the attitudes of American society and hence many held racist views. More specifically many white officers believed it to be a punishment to command black soldiers, as well as a dead end in terms of further promotion. Stories were circulated that the only way to avoid this unpleasant duty was to feign illness to ensure that you were in the sickbay when black units embarked from the USA for Europe. Then there were the officers who believed that black soldiers meant harder work. One captain of an engineering unit felt that the majority of black troops were 'more of a detriment than an asset. They are for the most part unreliable and require constant supervision. Slave-driver tactics is the only way to get work out of them. The officers must continually push from morning to night. It's . . . tough work and in the end one is liable to crack under the strain'.[23] Perhaps most fundamental and most common was the opinion held by some officers that black troops were simply inferior. No wonder, therefore, that they could not get too exercised about central directives advocating an equality for blacks which they could not support. Thus Air Force Major General Henry J. F. Miller believed that 'one of the basic reasons for the current racial problems [in Britain] is the unrealistic manner by which these problems are handled. So long as the natural fact is ignored that all races were not endowed with the same intelligence and therefore the same standards cannot be demanded of them, troubles will multiply'.[24] Similarly Colonel R. S. Edwards, sometime Deputy Chief of Staff of the European Theatre, responding to a request from Operations Divisions for information about black troops, stated that problems in England were the result of the absence of a colour line. In addition there were the 'usual problems emanating from the comparative lack of discipline, low intelligence and laziness of coloured troops'.[25]

Possibly the most extraordinary attempt from the American military to provide guidelines on the issue of commanding black troops came from Colonel Plank on 15 July 1943. At that time he was still officially Deputy Chief of Staff at SOS headquarters in Britain, but he moved to the Eastern Base Section, centred at Watford, the next month and took command of it soon after. Plank was from Missouri with, one assumes, Anglophile parents who named their son Ewart Gladstone after the British Prime Minister. Graduating from West Point with a science degree, his grooming for higher office came when, like Eisenhower and others, he was sent to the Command and General Staff School at Fort Leavenworth, Kansas. Leaving there in 1940 he spent some time in Washington, DC, before his posting to Britain.

Plank's memorandum, headed 'confidential . . . of a personal nature', and unsigned, was for all officers working with black troops. The notes were entitled 'Leadership of colored troops', and the Colonel later explained that they were a summary of the experience and methods used by his commanders 'to make leadership more effective'.[26]

The preparation of Plank's notes bore a remarkable resemblance to the circumstances surrounding Dowler's, which had such an influence on British thinking. The content of both memoranda had much in common: both revealed that local initiatives in the absence of comprehensive central guidance could be dangerous, and in spite of considerable criticism the careers of both officers prospered. Plank was careful to avoid actual discrimination between blacks and whites, but it was his analysis of the 'negro character' which proved to be the most offensive:

> Colored soldiers are akin to well-meaning but irresponsible children . . . Generally they cannot be trusted to tell the truth, to execute complicated orders, or act on their own initiative except in certain individual cases . . . the colored race are [sic] easily led, extremely responsive, and under stress of certain influences such as excitement, fear, religion, dope, liquor . . . they can change form with amazing rapidity from a kind or bashful individual to one of brazen boldness or madness, or become hysterical . . . The colored man does not look for work. He must be assigned a specific task that will keep him busy . . . The colored individual likes to 'doll up,' strut, brag and show off. He likes to be distinctive and stand out from the others. Everything possible should be used to encourage this . . . In the selection of NCOs the real black *bosses* should be picked rather than the lighter 'smart boy'.

Plank gave special attention to the problems which Great Britain was presenting, and in doing so made some judgements which would quite clearly have distressed the female inhabitants of the country. The particular difficulty, as he saw it, was the problem of black solder/white girl relationships. The Colonel saw the situation very simply: for him three types of girls associated with black soldiers, and all could be easily categorized. There were the recognized prostitutes, who could be dealt with by the civil police; then there was the 'semi-respectable older woman of

loose morals' looking as much for drinks as money; finally
there was the problem of the minor, and this again could be
solved by collaboration with the local police.

The limited circulation of Plank's unsigned memorandum succeeded in generating so much protest, from black
and white officers alike, that Lieutenant General Devers,
the Assistant Adjutant General, requested all copies of
Plank's letter to be destroyed. Plank was gently admo-
nished and acknowledged the 'inapt language' of parts of
his directive.[27] Shortly thereafter Plank was promoted to
Brigadier General and within a year of so was further
upgraded to become a two-star (temporary) major general.

Even if the American Army had devised within the rules
of segregation the most liberal and clear-cut regulations,
in turn administered by far-sighted and caring officers,
racial matters would still have gone astray. Segregation,
especially when it is supposed to be accompanied by
equality, is almost impossible to achieve and in the
jim-crow army in Britain the policy discriminated against
whites as well as blacks. Restricting certain towns and
villages to the soldiers of just one race, for example,
curtailed the leave opportunities of *both* races. The net
result was that at certain times troops were denied access
to some of Britain's best-known and most historic towns.
Equally inhibitory of recreational opportunities was of
course the alternate-day system. On occasions when white
troops were in a clear majority in a particular location the
alternate-day system was still employed, and there was
much resentment that this elaborate procedure was just
because of the presence of a handful of blacks. One white
GI who spent some of his days in Somerset was reminded
that it imposed an additional cause for concern. The policy
'was all right until the white soldiers happened to ask their
English girl friends who they went out with on the
coloured nights'.[28]

Eisenhower returned to Britain at the beginning of 1944
and during the next few months tried again to bring home
to the men through his commanders the 'lack of a color-line

in the United Kingdom'.[29] In addition the War Department
in Washington issued in February 1944 its most effective
pamphlet, 'Command of Negro troops'.[30] It was a sound
statement of the issues concerning black troops, their lack
of education and their history of discrimination, disadvantage and stereotyping – but it was two years too late! With
black and white troops crowding into Britain as the
invasion of France approached, attitudes were too entren-
ched. One recruit from New Jersey told black journalist
Roi Ottley that since his arrival in Britain he'd been
'constantly reminded' that he was 'a negro'.[31] As one
soldier has recently reminisced there were those anxious to
tear down the barriers of segregation: 'Blacks were given
the least desirable towns to go to. Often, some of our more
aggressive young men would say, I'm going to the nice
town. I'm not gonna go to that crummy town. They'd have a
conflict. We were fightin' a war before we went to the real
war'.[32]

   In the meantime the British were viewing jim crow at
first hand, and on occasions taking part in the 'practice'
wars between black and white GIs. Their comments on
what was happening are a unique and unrehearsed record
of a country meeting large numbers of black people for the
first time.

5
Novelty to Familiarity: The Home Front

For Americans and British alike wartime Britain presented a new and unique situation. This was true particularly with regard to the racial issue. The country had never before witnessed such a large influx of friendly aliens and certainly had never seen so many of a different race at any one time. Many of the black Americans, as they crowded into Britain straight from Chicago or Chattanooga, Montgomery or Mobile, met a freedom and friendliness they had rarely encountered before in the company of white people. At the same time this caused distress to many white GIs, particularly those from the southern states. The results of this antipathy were the physical confrontations between black and white Americans which many towns and villages witnessed between 1942 and 1945. The bewildered spectator of all this in Bristol and Liverpool, in the quaint market towns of Suffolk and in the remote villages of West Wales, tried to put it in perspective . . . and tried not to be an ungracious and critical host to the allies he was constantly told were vital to his well-being. Fortunately for the historian forty years on, the records relating to the acting-out of this drama remain vital and fresh.

During 1942 the British Government went to great lengths to draw up guidelines for its troops suggesting what their attitude should be towards the black GIs. Nearly all the official propaganda had been aimed at the

servicemen and women and not at civilians, and as a result
Tommy Atkins and his female counterpart were supposed
to understand the racial situation in the American Army,
but lean towards the white viewpoint.

Despite all the effort it is clear that the real situation
was not as simple as that. It may be that the British were
just more questioning in the war, or that the Army Bureau
of Current Affairs was *too* successful in arousing soldier
curiosity. ABCA of course had its critics, many of whom,
like right-wing Tory MP Maurice Petherick (who also had
strong views on the black GIs), felt it was a front
organization. For him the 'education of the forces racket'
was far too left wing, and he feared that unless political
subjects were avoided the 'creatures' would be coming back
'all pansy-pink'.[1]

Whatever the reason the British soldiers did not simply
accept the official viewpoint. One letter-writer from Dorset
was agreeably surprised 'at our coloured friends'. They
were 'real gentlemen, well behaved and well spoken . . . a
credit to their unit. British troops get on well with them,
we can't help it. They don't boast and flash their money
about or make themselves unpopular, we mix quite freely
which does seem to surprise them rather . . . we don't have
a colour distinction'.[2] Given the amount of time that had
been spent on drawing up its racial guidelines the Army
authorities must have been surprised by the continuing
interest in the colour bar. President Roosevelt and the BBC
had made 'Brains Trusts' – panels of acknowledged experts
– respectable and popular, and this example of education
by stealth spread to the Forces. *The Times* reported on 11
May 1943 that over 200 Anglo-American Brains Trusts
had been held in Army and RAF camps in the previous
year, with both British and Americans on the panels. The
secretary was quoted as saying that in 'the first six months
there was virtually no meeting at which the disparity in
American soldiers' pay did not arise. The subject has now
been allowed to drop. The same is true of questions about
the colour bar'.

Transatlantic was a monthly journal devoted to Anglo-
American affairs, first published by Penguin in September

1943. In its second issue, in October, Geoffrey Crowther
expanded on the racial theme. He wrote that four questions
always cropped up at the Brains Trusts. The first three
were isolation, lend-lease and education, and the fourth,
'asked over and over again by the British troops, will
surprise only those who have had their eyes shut'. This
was, 'How is the civil equality of the negro to be reconciled
with the discrimination against him shown, for example,
in the US Army?' Crowther remarked that there was no
use pretending that this was other than 'a very difficult
and delicate question, on which it was fatally easy to
mislead or to give offence'.

Despite the anxieties of some Government officials in the
regions, no guidance on race was given to civilians and it is
not surprising therefore that they were as curious about
the black soldiers and the colour-bar question as were their
compatriots in the armed forces. It was part of the Ministry
of Information's brief to satisfy that curiosity. The regional
Information Officers with their local committees organized
meetings, film shows and campaigns, and reported back to
the Ministry's headquarters in the Senate House of the
University of London on what they thought the public
needed to know.

This curiosity created a mass of evidence on the interest
in, and reactions to, the black GIs in Britain. Much of it
ironically was provided by the Ministry of Information
whose head, Brendan Bracken, was so anxious to under-
play the issue. All this evidence points overwhelmingly to
the conclusion that the blacks were warmly welcomed in
Britain, and the action of the white Americans in furthering a colour bar was roundly condemned. Stories about
black Americans, which probably had their origins in
truth, assumed the status of popular myths. Everywhere, it
was reported, pubs were displaying signs reading, 'For
British people and coloured Americans only'. Similarly bus
conductresses in all parts of the country were said to be
telling the blacks not to give up their seats to whites as
'they were in England' now. Probably the most popular
story came from a West Country farmer. When asked
about the visitors he replied: 'I love the Americans but I

don't like these white ones they've brought with them'.

Although this kind of reaction was widespread two important qualifications must be made. In the first place the initial welcome for the blacks, for various reasons which will be examined later, began to fade somewhat in the second half of 1943. Secondly, even in areas where the reception to the black GIs was at its most cordial, there was an almost universal dislike of the blacks associating with white British women. Even those who made the most liberal and far-sighted observations about the state of race relations in Britain could almost always be relied upon to express grave misgivings about such interracial mixing. A rough analysis of the Home Intelligence weekly reports demonstrates both these trends.

The Home Intelligence Unit was one of the two agencies set up by the Government in 1940 to monitor public reactions, in this case to prepare reports on the morale of the civilian population. These were the responsibility of the regional intelligence officers and from May to September 1940 their reports were produced every day, while from October they came out weekly. From June 1941 the officers were assisted in their tasks by panels of correspondents recruited by them. The panel members were supposed to be people who had contact with the public, such as newsagents, parsons, doctors and publicans. Each officer could have up to 400 contacts, a proportion of whom were asked questions each week. The reports were supposed to be a record of current feelings *not* facts and this caveat prefaced them; because the reports were, and were intended to be, so subjective they have come in for criticism. Historian A. J. P. Taylor, at that time a tutor at Magdalen College, Oxford, was one of those panellists whose brief was to record impressions from meetings and private conversations, but he has since expressed reservations about this method of operating:

I took little notice of these impressions and merely put down what I myself thought at the time or wanted to advocate. I suspect that most contributors to Home Intelligence did much the same. Home Intelligence was in fact propaganda in reverse. We were trying to instil some common sense into the mandarins of Senate House. We did not have much success.[3]

Despite Taylor's cautionary note, the reports coming in during the second half of 1942, when the black Americans were arriving in Britain, were consistent both in attitude and from region to region. The blacks were a success with the broad mass of the British population.

Perhaps the most novel piece of evidence testifying to the popularity of the black GIs was the catchy popular song, published in 1944, 'Choc'late Soldier from the USA'. There were several recorded versions of the tune including one by Lou Praeger, a popular bandleader of the day. It was composed by Elton Box, Sonny Cox and Lewis Ilda, noted Tin Pan Alley tunesmiths, Box and Cox being credited with 'In the Quartermaster's Stores', a song done to death by many a boy scout. The cover of the 'Choc'late Soldier' songsheet featured a grinning black GI driving his jeep through the rolling English countryside. Judged from the perspective of the 1980s the song appears patronizing and offensive but it was no doubt meant as a tribute at the time.

> Choc'late drop, always fast asleep
> Dozin' in his cozy bed,
> Choc'late drop, has got no time for sleep,
> He's riding in a jeep instead;
>
> They used to call him Lazybones in Harlem,
> Lazy good for nothin' all the day;
> But now they're mighty proud of him in Harlem
> CHOC'LATE SOLDIER FROM THE USA.
> They used to call him just a choc'late dreamer
> Until the day he heard the bugle play;
> They made a coloured Doughboy out of dreamer,
> CHOC'LATE SOLDIER FROM THE USA.
>
> Never in the schoolroom always in the poolroom
> For a nickel or a dime he'd croon.
> His idea of Heaven was seven come eleven
> And dancin' ev'ry evening 'neath the yellow Harlem moon,
> He used to get a scolding from his mammy
> But now you'll hear his mammy proudly say,

He's 'somewhere over there for Uncle Sammy'
CHOC'LATE SOLDIER FROM THE USA.[4]

The admiration for the black soldier which inspired this
song discomfited the American authorities. As Hugh
Dalton and other politicians had predicted the British
sided with the blacks when colour difficulties emerged. The
Bureau of Intelligence of the American Office of War
Information came to this unwelcome conclusion after
studying the situation in December 1942: 'The special
problem of American troops stationed in Britain has given
rise to certain difficulties, chiefly in terms of British
attitudes'.[5] Writing for the *Observer,* the *Tribune* and the
BBC, George Orwell also recorded the same impressions.
In January 1943 it was his view that people seemed to
prefer the blacks to the white Americans and it was much
the same in the following December: 'The general consen-
sus of opinion seems to be that the only American soldiers
with decent manners are the Negroes'. As late as April
1944, Orwell was still claiming that 'everyone says they
like the Negroes better'.[6]

Aside from the Ministry of Information's efforts the
other organization most involved in gauging public opinion
during the war was Mass Observation. Included in their
regular surveys of British attitudes to the foreigners in
their midst were people's perceptions of the black Americans. Part of the methodology devised by Tom Harrison
and Charles Madge, Mass Observation's founders, included
'Panel Directives'. These Directives were issued to a
nation-wide group of voluntary 'observers' who reported
upon themselves by answering and commenting on questions relating to specific issues. In addition the observers
were asked to keep diaries during the war and some of
these were still being returned years later.

The charge has been made that the panels were not
representative bodies, were biased towards the middle
classes, were composed of people with above average
intelligence and that the whole venture was leftist and
somehow dilettante. Certainly the people responding to the
Directives discussed here tended to be white-collar –

clerks, teachers, lawyers, civil servants – but this did not
mean they were more liberal on racial issues. Moreover the
anonymity of which the observers and diarists were
assured led them presumably to provide their responses in
complete honesty, so much so that on other issues relating
to the conduct of the war, it was not rare to come upon
defeatist, panicky and even disloyal responses. Still, while
it is wise to evaluate statistics cautiously in the early days
of public opinion surveys, the input that was fed to Mass
Observation presents a useful picture of British attitudes
towards blacks in the early 1940s.

The most detailed comments on racial issues came as a
result of the Panel Directive of June 1943.[7] Among the
questions asked then were: 'What is your personal attitude
towards coloured people, and is there any difference in
your attitude towards members of different coloured races?
Have wartime events or experiences had any effect on your
attitude in this respect?' The survey was not categorically
directed at the *American* racial problem and thus many
replies were exclusively about Africa or India, but interest
in the black GIs was indicated by the fact that 1 person in
15 spontaneously mentioned them.

The individual viewpoints were fascinating, though on
Mass Observation's own admission this was a sample of
middle-class bias and more-than-average broadminded-
ness. One person in 50 showed no interest in, or was vague
about, colour; 1 in 20 had no strong feelings; 1 in 10 had an
anti-colour bias, and 1 in 15 felt 'coloured races' were
inferior. A conclusion which the American Army authorities might have been interested in was that 'once an
acquaintanceship between a white and coloured person
had been established, anti-colour bias tended to decrease or
even disappear'. The presence of black Americans had
made a marked impression for the report noted that
everyone who spoke of the American race problem

> expressed disapproval of the way these people are being
> treated, and many were shocked at the attitude of American
> white to black troops in this country, though some showed
> understanding of the difficulties involved. Few observers
> have come into actual contact with American black troops,

but of those who have, all approved of them as people, many comparing them favourably with other American troops.

Perhaps of even greater impact sociologically, considering the disinterestedness of most of the British in racial issues at the start of the war, was the conclusion that nearly a quarter of the observers had now changed their attitude and had become 'more friendly and more pro-colour'.

Given that the British public had little knowledge of, or interest in, *any* black people before the war, why did they welcome black Americans so warmly and so forcefully condemn racial discrimination? Three reasons suggest themselves. In the first place the black soldier was quickly recognized as an underdog in his army and the British generally clung to the view that they sympathized with underdogs, particularly at this time when the war was being fought in part for the rights of minorities. There was a gut feeling that racial prejudice was inappropriate at this moment in history. Mass Observation recorded two pertinent comments: 'I think it's horrible, especially just now when we shout about Hitler's racial theories', said one commentator, while another thought discrimination 'a nasty business' which played 'right into the hands of Goebbels'.

Secondly, a more prosaic explanation of the welcome given to black soldiers in Britain was an economic one. The white Americans, regarded already as overpaid (though there was no differentiation in black and white pay), complained loudly and bitterly about the lack of the conveniences of modern living in Britain – cars, radios, refrigerators and central heating. Their black compatriots did not share this resentment because in the main they were not used to such luxuries at home. Thus the blacks and the British experienced a similar standard of living and this economic bond increased the friendship between them.

There is no doubt that many white GIs disliked much that they found in England – from the beer to the plumbing. Shopkeepers were old-fashioned and leisurely.

Hotels were uncomfortable, the lavatories were outmoded and there were dirty towels in the barber shops. English food and waitresses were abominable, and the beer was foul-tasting and warm. Many GIs believed that the monetary system was an example of carrying a national joke a bit too far . . . and then there was the weather! So many were the grouses that one popular story towards the end of the war was of a bemedalled Yank grinning from ear to ear. In answer to a dour Englishman enquiring as to the reason for his happiness, his response was: 'we're going home, you have to stay here'.

The final factor in the welcome afforded to the black American soldiers was what can be termed 'the negro as stereotype'. Most British people had received their image of blacks from the cinema screen and when in reality some soldiers *were* unassuming, *were* kind to children and *did* sing and dance, it was reassuring. The publicity given to black choirs locally, and to the huge one which gave concerts all over Britain, reinforced stereotypes. Thus it is not surprising that surveys came up with phrases such as blacks being 'regarded as children and liked for their smiles and their kindness to children'. Individual comments illuminate these generalities: a canteen lady from Hull preferred the 'dusky lads' as you could always find a good singer, a pianist, or some dancers among them and thus 'canteen nights never drag'. Similarly a letter-writer from Bradford, Wiltshire, preferred the black Americans to the whites because they had 'better manners' and were 'better dancers. Some of them took over the band during the evening and we had some real swing and jitter bugging'. Out in East Anglia black companies had several big bands including the '923 Reveilleers' and the 'Rhythm Rockets', offering enormous excitement to locals of all ages.

Oddly enough even bad behaviour could sometimes be tolerated because this was in the 'negro character': 'lawlessness and lack of self restraint among coloured people is to be expected,' said one commentator, 'and does not cause surprise'. For others it was the contrast to the preconception that was welcome. A 45-year-old man interviewed in Bristol thought the black soldiers 'a decent lot. Different from what we've seen of them on the films. They're not all dull and stupid – they're educated some of 'em'. Proof, though, that even the movie image was not a uniform perception came from another observer who liked the American negro soldier 'with his shining smile, seductive southern voice and spontaneous love of enjoyment, (familiar already in the pictures)'.[8]

Kenneth Little, an academic who was a member of the League of Coloured Peoples (founded in England in 1931), took a specific interest in the reasons for the popularity of the blacks. After observing them for several months he realized that many were very apprehensive about living and working in close proximity with white people in Britain, and were on their guard. This attitude seemed to be a welcome contrast to the bombastic manners of many of the white GIs. In the *New Statesman* of 29 August 1942, Little noted that the black soldiers were said to be

'too reserved', 'careful', 'too self controlled and disciplined', and the construction put on these 'observations' is that the coloureds have been 'cowed' by past inter-racial experiences in the States. In short, there is an obvious and fairly definite tendency in many quarters towards championing the cause of the 'Blackies' (note the diminutive) against the white Americans.

The Ministry of Information's report on British attitudes to America, issued in the middle of 1943, reinforced Little's early opinion. It said that the most common attitude to the black GIs was one of

'paternal tolerance', not unmixed with sympathy for 'the underdog'. There is a tendency to regard the negroes as 'childish, happy and naive fellows who mean no harm' and this sympathetic attitude has been increased by the good behaviour, kindliness and humour of the coloured troops themselves.[9]

As director of the black Red Cross Club in Bristol, George Goodman had plenty of experience of observing black Americans at first hand and it was his view that they shared some characteristics with their temporary hosts:

> The graciousness of the Negro plus his inclination to be
> self-effacing had an astounding conformity to the English-
> man's conservativeness. It did not matter that the negro had
> acquired his over long years of bitter experience and that the
> Englishman had absorbed his chiefly from his environment.
> The important fact was that it established a common ground
> for understanding.[10]

To most people it was a simple issue. The blacks were
polite, inoffensive and kindly. As one civil servant remarked, Englishmen 'were deeply impressed with the
extreme modesty of behaviour of the Negroes, their
softness of voice, their gracefulness of movement and their
adaptability to strange custom and surroundings. If any of
them happen to think ill of us or our country, they don't
reveal it'.[11] When longer acquaintance made it clear that
most black GIs were doing the hard, unglamorous work in
the American Army, British sympathies for them were
further heightened.

British resentment at the colour bar had important
repercussions on the perceptions of its ally and was one
factor in the anti-Americanism which lingered on in the
post-war era. Constantly fed since Pearl Harbor with the
view of the USA as the home of democracy, many found
this belief increasingly untenable as the evidence of racial
discrimination in the American forces mounted. A Cambridge civilian in early 1943 wondered why the 'poor
darkies' had been sent overseas. While he conceded that
social mixing and intermarriage might have its difficulties, 'to refuse to eat in the same room! and to get off buses'
was going 'too far, especially in democratic England'. This
was, perhaps, a touch of smugness easy to understand in a
society which was yet to face its own racial tensions. One
British soldier may have hit the nail unerringly on the
head:

> One of the slight awkwardnesses is the colour question and
> that is entirely the fault of the English – you see we are not
> used to having Negroes in the country and many stupid and
> soft-hearted people tend to treat them as if they were a sort
> of 'super-white', they make more fuss of them than they do of

the white men, merely to show in a pompous and shortsight-
ed way that they are not afflicted with any 'colour-baritus'.[12]

And what did the Americans make of the British
response to their race issue as imported by the US
military? *Time* magazine took the view that the British
used the question of race as a peg on which to hang their
anti-Americanism. Its argument went something like this:
there was a view in the country that the United States had
again come late into the war, and was leaving much of the
fighting to the British. Racial discrimination was one
indication that America was less than perfect and this
enabled some British people to 'cock a snook' at their
over-confident ally. The magazine commented that 'Great
Britain . . . had never faced the "race problem" at home.
Ninety per cent of Britain's citizens had never actually
seen or talked to a black-skinned human being before.
America's polite, liquid-voiced, smartly uniformed Negro
soldiers were a surprise, a pleasure, and a happy opportunity for them to thumb the nose of moral self-righteousness
at the US'.[13]

Of course racist prejudices against the black soldiers
were not unheard of among the British, even during the
early stages of the troops' presence in Britain when the
majority of the population regarded them with sympathy
and affection. Not surprisingly in view of the institutionalized racism fostered by some arms of the Government, any
racist tendencies among Britons could be viewed with
toleration. Thus there were occasions when black Americans were refused service in British pubs and restaurants
(ironically at one time in a Chinese restaurant). *The Times*
of 2 October 1942 reported that one commanding officer
felt it necessary to issue his black troops with a note to
show restaurant owners: 'it is necessary that he sometimes
has a meal, which he has, on occasions found difficult to
obtain. I would be grateful if you would look after him'.

Moreover, despite all the Army orders proscribing the
spreading of remarks or epithets designed to stir up racial
hatred, many white American soldiers disseminated derogatory stories about their black colleagues. This persis-

tent peddling of racist ideologies was one factor which led
to an almost imperceptible change in the attitude of some
British people towards the black Americans. Though it is
impossible to date this with any precision there is evidence
that the 'cooling-off' started about the middle of 1943.
Ultimately the question of numbers was bound to weigh
against the blacks. White Americans were in the majority
and many of them did not like their black colleagues being
so warmly received. Hence it was more convenient for
Britons to go along with the white viewpoint. One town
councillor reportedly said that he personally had 'no
feeling of racial prejudice' but he'd been led to believe
relations with American white troops would be better if the
country conformed to what he understood to be 'American
practices of discrimination'.[14]

The gradual shift in British public attitudes is well
documented by the weekly reports from Home Intelligence
as well as the responses from Mass Observation panellists.
Whatever the stated objective reasons for the change may
have been, clearly familiarity did breed some contempt,
especially after the novelty of the black presence had worn
off. Disappointments set in with the discovery that black
men were not much different from others when it came to
human failings.

Before turning to the American perspective on the racial
situation in Britain it is interesting for a moment to see if
class or political affiliation had any bearing on the
formation of people's views.

The Second World War stirred up the whole political and
sexual melting-pot and wrought a total change in the
nature of British society. The black American troops in
this country, and the issue of race, served to throw British
class attitudes into stark relief. So was colour prejudice the
prerogative of any one particular group in society? The
short and blunt answer seems to be that the 'lower' and
working classes were more in favour of the black GIs than
the middle and upper classes. Of course in wartime people
have a tendency to be anti-authoritarian, a feeling cap-

tured so well by David Low's creation, Colonel Blimp, who symbolized right-wing politics and pompous militarism. Certainly there appeared to be this vague feeling that class and other barriers were an irrelevance at this time in Britain's history. Obviously no contemporary surveys were carried out specifically to pinpoint the class dimension of the racial issue among Britons during the war, but from an extensive reading of the British Government reports, the Mass Observation responses and the reports of the American military investigations into incidents, it is hard to avoid the impression that antipathy towards the blacks increased in direct relation to people's status on the social scale.

It would be too tedious to quote all the instances which help to form this judgement, but a few contemporary viewpoints are worth raising. One British journalist, Donald Attwater, published his views in an American weekly stating that in general the attitude of the host population had been 'positively friendly' with exceptions 'to some extent . . . a "class" phenomenon. The upholders of a color-bar are mainly,' he believed, 'in the upper-middle class, and . . . in a less degree, in the professional class, and it takes a mainly social form'. He had heard that the advent of the American blacks had increased colour prejudice amongst all classes, but he had 'little evidence of feeling against coloured people among the working and lower-middle classes'.[15] The following year Eric Dingwall, the co-author of the Government-inspired ABCA article in 1942, agreed with this judgement. He believed that colour prejudice had increased in the last fifty years among all classes, with the middle and lower classes following their 'superiors'. However, this had changed somewhat when the black GIs came: in areas 'of perhaps a more sophisticated kind, especially in urban, inland, provincial areas' white Americans had been successful in introducing some discrimination. His conclusion was that there seemed 'little doubt that a number of the younger women of the middle and upper class' had 'taken over from [white American soldiers] a good deal of their colour prejudice' and this was true of 'many of the less intelligent among middle-class girls', who had 'never thought about the question'.[16]

Lord Wharncliffe's intervention in Wortley (see pp. 97–100) did not typify the attitude of the landed gentry, but the responses of the Wharncliffe family to the situation in which they found themselves was an entirely plausible one. Another incident which came to the attention of the Foreign Office in July 1944 rings equally true.

At that time there were about 1,200 black troops in the small Cotswold village of Westonbirt, near Tetbury. There had been a rape there and as a result a Peter Lloyd, a 'gentleman farmer of some substance', who owned a local hotel and once owned a newspaper, registered a complaint. Through his MP and the Lord Lieutenant of the county, he suggested that a state of 'terror and alarm' existed in the vicinity because of the presence of black GIs, and this necessitated him sitting up all night with a shotgun. The situation was investigated by a British liaison officer who talked both to locals and Americans. His report was short and succinct: the behaviour and discipline of the blacks was no problem and this pleasant area of Gloucestershire still presented a 'calm and peaceful English rural scene'. What the reporting colonel was sure about was that Lloyd had strong 'anti-negro' feelings, regarding black troops as 'little more than animals'.[17]

Similarly, over in Norfolk, Mrs Carr, wife of Brigadier Carr the owner of Ditchingham Hall, sent her complaints about black GIs to Lord Cecil who passed them on to the American authorities. Like Lady Wharncliffe in the north, Mrs Carr didn't like blacks in the Hall. She was upset that the blacks attracted women and, according to her, sent trucks into town to collect them. An American investigation showed that the allegations were unfounded, a view echoed by the caretaker's wife. She said simply that she found the black GIs 'very well behaved . . . no trouble to us'. Her little girl had cried when they left and in her opinion there had been greater numbers of camp-followers around when British troops were based in the area.[18] In the light of these and other incidents it is hardly surprising therefore that the US War Department was told in October 1945 that Britain was one of the European countries where 'the lower classes . . . have accepted the Negro almost without reservation'.[19]

Political generalizations about reactions to the black Americans are more difficult to make. The Cabinet deliberations of 1942 revealed that Herbert Morrison, one Labour minister to make a contribution, appeared to be overly concerned with the sexual issue while the Government's ultimate position was based largely on the very conservative position of Sir Stafford Cripps. The Left it seems could not be relied upon to take a radical stance on discrimination and often were more uncritical of the US Army's position at the highest level than their colleagues like Sir John Simon and Lord Cranborne from the other parties. At the grass roots the Independent Labour Party and on occasions the Common Wealth Party, took a firm line on humanitarian issues, while the Labour backbencher who spoke out on racial topics – people like Reginald Sorensen, John Rhys Davies, Dr Haden-Guest and Arthur Creech-Jones – was often interested in other 'radical' issues such as civil liberties, Colonial freedom, the abolition of the death penalty or pacifism. Some were also active members of the League of Coloured Peoples.

The extremist opinions of Conservative MP Maurice Petherick on the black GIs are examined in detail later, but they do show that there were those on the Tory benches whose views would certainly be deemed racist today. He was perhaps exceptional as was Lady Astor though she – Tory, patrician and an American southerner to boot – best exemplified the patronizing attitude to blacks displayed by some of the 'ruling class'. The Virginia-born daughter of a Confederate civil-war veteran, Nancy Astor came to England in the early 1900s for the social and hunting seasons. Vivacious and wealthy she met and married Waldorf Astor who was elevated to the peerage in 1919. Nancy became the first woman in the House when she won her husband's former seat in Plymouth. Lord Astor was mayor of the town during the war and Nancy kept up people's spirits by performing cartwheels in the shelters.

For some unknown reason Walter White was invited to the Astor country home at Cliveden when he was in Britain in 1944, but the grandeur of the place had less impact on him than Nancy's words. White was a very light-skinned black man with white features who, unlike others of his hue, chose not to cross the colour line. Nancy must have been surprised by this, exclaiming: 'You're an idiot! You *are* an idiot calling yourself a Negro when you're whiter than I am, with blue eyes and blond hair!' Totally justifying her reputation as insensitive and cruel she told White after luncheon: 'We never have any trouble with the good black boys, it's the near-white ones who cause the trouble. They're always talking about and insisting on rights'. The NAACP Secretary kept his thoughts to himself but realized, as he later wrote, that 'no hint of a newer world' in which blacks had some say would come from Cliveden or other bastions of conservatism.[20]

Reactions of the white Americans to the British reception of the blacks depended in part on which section of the United States the soldiers came from. Some disliked the segregation they encountered in the Army in Britain, but others despised the new freedom given to the blacks in the British Isles and found comfort only in the belief that the blacks would find rigidly enforced segregation on their return home. As one US captain wrote in a memorandum in July 1942: 'it is not our task to create a race line for the British when they don't themselves see one. However, this does not mean the same line will not be re-established upon the Negroes [sic] return to the States'.[21]

Others still took a more charitable view of the British, conceding that since their hosts had little experience in such matters they should be helped. 'In fairness', wrote a US Army chaplain, 'we must help guide them where such guidance seems necessary. The problem is one entirely foreign to them and while it is by no means our intention to make them race conscious, thus segregating a small portion of our Army, carefully guided information regarding the problem can and should be given their leaders'.[22]

Despite the edicts from their commanders the ordinary white American soldier *was* concerned about what his black compatriot was getting up to in Britain. Although many white GIs rarely came into contact with blacks – whites were far more numerous – most heard about them from their colleagues or from the British themselves. Early morale reports give an indication of how vitriolic were some opinions about black soldiers. This white sergeant wrote home in September 1942: 'One thing which would make you sick at your stomach tho is the niggers over here tell the English that they are North American Indians . . . so the English girls go with them. Every time so far that we have seen a nigger with a white girl we have run him away. I would like to shoot the whole bunch of them. I guess I will always be a *rebel*.' If the topic of interracial sex was guaranteed to provoke comment, responses from soldiers from below the Mason-Dixon line were almost as predictable. This corporal was in hospital in Britain, with a black soldier in a nearby bed: 'Oh how I'm gonna love the South after this – where a nigger knows his place and the whites feel they are above sleeping and eating with the damned niggers'.

By 1943 these initial reactions were followed by another which was perhaps inevitable. As the British continued what some of the visitors saw as their 'pampering' of the blacks, white American hostility, and sometimes loathing, began to be directed towards their hosts. A corporal writing home from Cheltenham was bitter about the British and 'the niggers – believe it or not – the English seem to actually prefer them to the white boys. Especially the girls – not that I give a hang for them anyhow, but it is disgusting, to say the least. Maybe the south is right – keep 'em in line, one way or another. That is enough to make me inclined to look down on the English in general to start with'.[23] By the spring of 1944 all that Britain was to some white Americans was a 'nigger-loving' country. In May, George Orwell was told by a recently arrived GI that anti-British feeling was general in the US Army. The first question asked by this soldier as he came off the boat was 'How's England?' In reply an American military policeman

had told him: 'The girls here walk out with niggers . . .
They call them American Indians'.[24]

The reactions of the black Americans were more complex:
some were in awe of, or felt ill at ease in, an almost totally
white world, but most were delighted at their reception.
These impressions were backed up by a significant survey
into the attitudes of black soldiers in the European Theatre
of Operations undertaken by the US Army in November
1943, and published in February 1944. Four hundred and
twenty-two black soldiers and an equal number of white
soldiers of the same home, educational and age background
were used as control groups to examine the attitudes to
service in the United Kingdom. The survey is quoted in
more depth later but suffice it here to cite the responses to
the question, 'What sort of opinion do you have of the
English people?': 80 per cent of blacks answered 'favourable', 9 per cent 'unfavourable', while the remaining 11 per
cent had 'no answer'; (white responses were respectively
68, 28 and 4 per cent).
   Though the ETO survey showed that the overwhelming
majority of black soldiers in Britain liked the British, some
of their reactions, as with the white GIs, depended on
which part of America they came from. Some met more
segregation in Britain than in the US. One black north-
erner commented that his outfit was made up of southern
officers 'who voluntarily insist they have no prejudices but
who allow us as few passes as possible and restrict us from
many towns'. A southern black was equally upset: 'I don't
see why we should be robbed of our great opportunity over
here by white yanks. Why we colored soldiers have off
limits to some places an [sic] white soldiers don't. Why
shouldn't we kick. After all we are fighting together. They
are no more important than we are'. Superiors were often
blamed for black woes including attempts by white
American officers to prejudice the British against the black
GIs: 'most of the white officers up to generals have know
[sic] respect for a colored soldier, except trying to poison
the minds of English against us. I call it sabotourering [sic]

their own people'.[25]

Making things more difficult for the black soldier in Britain was the knowledge that he was in a novel environment, people were examining his conduct closely and officers were constantly reminding him to be on his best behaviour: in short he was on show. One aviation sergeant expressed this predicament bluntly: 'I sincerely hope that the boys will learn to handle themselves well here so the world will know we are not apes dressed in clothes'.

Despite all the pressures on blacks in Britain, there is little doubt that the vast majority formed favourable impressions of the British. Many soldiers spent their first few months in Northern Ireland and it was from there that blacks wrote about their early feelings towards their adopted country: 'the Irish treat us as if we were one of them'; 'fine people, never hear of discrimination and stuff like that'; 'I am living the happiest days of my life', they commented on their new surroundings.[26] One wry wartime story showed that the black GIs did realize that prejudice had other than racial forms. In Belfast a Catholic priest was surprised to find himself magnificently saluted in the street by a black soldier. He stopped him and said: 'You must surely be a good child of the Church of Rome'. 'Holy snakes, no,' said the GI, 'it's bad enough being a Negro in Ulster.'

Ralph Ellison probably captured the emotions of many black Americans best in a short story published in 1944, *In a Strange Country*. Ellison tried his hand at many things before settling in New York where he still lives, studying music at Tuskegee and at one time playing jazz trumpet. Today he is best known for his 1952 novel *Invisible Man*, regarded by many as one of the most influential in post-war American literature. Ellison was a merchant seaman for part of the war and his travels took him to Swansea, Cardiff and Barry in South Wales, and this provided the setting for his story. In it a black merchant seaman has docked at night in South Wales anxious the next day to see this strange country with fresh eyes, 'like those with which the Pilgrims had seen the New World'.

Attacked by white Americans he was rescued and taken to a pub by a Welshman. At first those present were included in his rage, but not for long as they were 'genuinely and uncondescendingly polite'. Though his new friend thought the racial violence was 'a disgrace to our country', he was told not to worry – 'it's a sort of family quarrel', the American explained.

Ellison later said that the story was 'an attempt to give fictional form to some of the American racial conflict that was to be observed in the European Theatre of Operations at that time, and to suggest the perspective of irony afforded a young Afro-American by a voyage to Wales'. He had no personal experience of racial difficulties himself, only pleasant memories of 'the warm hospitality of a few private homes', and the ladies working in a black Red Cross Club north of Swansea who prepared 'amazing things with powdered eggs and a delicious salad from the flesh of hares'. Like the subject of his story he enjoyed 'a memorable evening of drinking in a men's club where the communal singing was excellent'.[27]

When the black leaders came over to visit the troops they could hardly believe that the welcome their men and women had received was consistent with the attitude of the British Government whose policy it was to encourage Britons to go along with segregation. Walter White's report in February 1944 to the US War Department reflected this puzzlement. He expressed his appreciation of the letter the Home Office had sent to Chief Constables instructing them not to assist American efforts to enforce segregation. To him the subsequent British Government statement on race could only have originated from, or been inspired by, the Americans. How else to explain the inconsistency?[28]

White was not to know that he was misguided, that the Cabinet's 1942 guidelines were entirely British in origin and not dictated by any American pressure. The gradual realization of the truth certainly harmed the black perception of the British Government. For many blacks Britain was a country where the gap between leaders and led was a mile wide and unbridgeable.

Anyway, by 1944 the British Government's notes were in effect almost irrelevant. By then the tension between black and white GIs in Britain had increased in the run-up to D-Day to such an extent that a whole new set of problems had come into being. This friction had on occasions grown into full-scale violence, and many of the country's citizens wittingly or unwittingly were dragged into the conflicts. For many the days when the second American civil war was transplanted to Britain were to remain their most vivid memories of the period from 1942 to 1945.

6

Dixie Invades Britain: The Racial Violence

In late 1943 the 3,500 inhabitants of Chipping Norton, a normally tranquil town situated near Oxford, anticipated the coming cold weather with less gloom than usual. As talk of a Second Front grew they hoped that this winter, the fifth, would be the last one of the war. For some of the 700 black GIs stationed in the town and at the nearby village of Kingham more immediate matters were pressing.

At 9.30 on Saturday night, 13 November, the rural peace was shattered when some of the black GIs attacked three white Americans, also from Kingham, leaving one badly beaten. Later the same evening another party of white GIs, who had come over by truck from the neighbouring village of Shipton-under-Wychwood for a night out in Chipping Norton, were menaced by blacks. At the same time black GIs also attacked a lone white soldier twelve miles away in Banbury. Many towns in Britain had witnessed similar scenes before though in many cases such violence appeared to be spontaneous and random. In Oxfordshire what was interesting was its apparent coordination. The root of the trouble lay in an incident two weeks earlier; but it also showed that the segregation of American troops could have quite the opposite effect to what the authorities intended.

The American Army not only ensured that its black and

white troops did not work together but did its best also to
ensure they were kept apart when they were off duty. This
it did by the alternate-pass system, supported by the provision of separate Red Cross Clubs wherever troops of both
races were in close proximity. On Saturday 30 October
1943 this policy was evidently breached when some black
GIs from Chipping Norton went to a dance at the Red Cross
Club in Oxford, good enough reason for the white troops
from an air base to take the offensive and cause a fight.
The upshot was that Oxford became out of bounds for black
soldiers who then took Chipping Norton as exclusively
'their' town. Hence their attack on whites from Kingham
and Shipton with cries of 'this is our town and we don't
want you in here'! Segregation, it seemed, had the potential for conflict.[1]

The American Army authorities continued to maintain
during and immediately after the war that incidents of
racial violence such as these were generally few and not
serious. To have admitted otherwise of course would have
been to admit that the jim-crow army was not 100 per cent
successful and logic would therefore have dictated that a
measure of integration should be tried. That did not happen and segregation continued to be the order of the day for
a number of years after the end of the war. There *were*
many incidents between black and white Americans
throughout the country in the wartime years and, despite
the censorship, news of the serious ones quickly spread.
Though some reports were inevitably exaggerated GIs of
both races were killed in anger, and at least one Briton was
caught and killed in the crossfire. By May 1944 morale
reports based on intercepted letters indicated that 90 per
cent of the comments by soldiers on the other race were
unfavourable. As a captain in the ETO historical section
tersely observed: 'The predominant note is that if the invasion doesn't occur soon, trouble will'.[2]

Conflict between black and white GIs in Britain began
almost as soon as there were members of both races in the
country. Towards the end of July 1942, Americans and
British soldiers had almost come to blows on the question
of Britons fraternizing with the blacks.[3] Many blacks spent

their first few months in Northern Ireland and by the end
of August 1942 one began to wonder whether he had been
sent overseas 'to fight against our white soldiers or against
the Nazis'. A white lieutenant felt it had been 'necessary to
lay down the law to the Irish and the coons' while by the
middle of the next month a corporal bleakly claimed that
the 'civil war' had started among the American troops in
Ireland.[4] In October that war claimed its first casualty as a
result of a brawl in the streets of Antrim. Ironically racial
violence temporarily replaced sectarian violence in the
province and left one black GI dead and one white seriously
wounded.

How extensive a problem was the racial violence, and
how serious were the disturbances? On 17 June 1944, after
D-Day, the *New Statesman* reflected on the situation with
an equanimity that those who monitor race relations in the
Britain of the 1980s would find very incongruous, conceding that there had 'of course, been incidents, fights and a
few deaths'! Perhaps death had become commonplace on
the home front or perhaps implicit in this attitude was the
relief that the race problem wouldn't be with Britain for
that much longer. General Weaver of the Services of Supply tried to minimize the difficulties too when he reflected
years afterwards: there *were*, he said, many 'flare-ups and
near riots' particularly in the early days, but the bulk of
these were 'minor in nature and extent', and 'never once
did they get out of hand'.[5] This was an assertion not supported by the facts.

The Office of the Inspector General of the US Army
carried out a special survey of racial incidents in Britain
during the three-month period from 19 November 1943 to
19 February 1944. Fifty-six were reported, an average of
just over four a week. Reflecting the movement of troops to
the pre-D-Day training areas, most of the offences, with
some exceptions, took place in the southern half of Britain.
There were some in Northern Ireland at Belfast and Lis-
burn, and in South Wales at Swansea and Carmarthen.
Other incidents happened in the Midlands at Oxford and
Coventry, but the bulk came from the south and south-
west of England where black troops were crowding in in

large numbers. Towns that witnessed disturbances here were Launceston, Brixham, Newton Abbot, Reading, Winchester (three in one day) and Basingstoke. The incidents were variously described as fights, assaults and 'riots' and took place in pubs, at dances and on railway stations.[6]

Typical of the affrays was one in the West Midlands. On 24 June 1944, a few weeks after the invasion of France, the Wolverhampton *Express & Star* reported a fight between black and white GIs at a popular dance hall, the Mirabelle ballroom, near what is today the zoo in Dudley. It spilled over into the street and according to the local paper 'scores of white and coloured Americans took part. The military police with revolvers came on the scene, and there was some shooting. The disturbance continued into the early hours'. Apart from the fact that altercations such as this had a vivid impact on young people at the time (the Dudley incident is now a folk memory), they illustrate just how much of a running sore the racial issue in Britain was. The investigations of the Inspector General's Department, the subsequent court procedures, the organization of fines and the arrangements that had to be made if confinement to barracks was part of the punishment, were all time-consuming processes, and whether there were private citizens involved or not the British police were always on the scene and produced reports for various government departments. All in all jim crow diverted energy from the main task of defeating Hitler. In addition to what were seen as these relatively minor disturbances, five major incidents in Britain which can be termed racial in origin stand out.

Detroit in Michigan grew rapidly in the 1920s as the lure of high wages in the automobile industry attracted southern blacks and whites into the area. By the early days of the war an increasing tension in the city was obvious as blacks complained about poor housing and their limited participation in lucrative war work, and their role in the Army. On the afternoon of Sunday 20 June 1943, with the temperature in the nineties, blacks poured out of their ghetto area, the ironically-named Paradise Valley, to picnic and cool off on Belle Isle in the Detroit river. Possibly 100,000 were there on that steamy day, mostly blacks but mingled with a few whites. Scuffles broke out and tempers were frayed as the exodus back to the city began. Rumours abounded, notably that a black woman and her baby had been murdered, and fighting broke out. It quickly fanned out into the city and became a full-scale riot. Disagreements among city and state officials meant that Federal troops weren't requested until 9.25 on the Monday evening. By that time the troubles were spent, leaving 25 blacks dead (17 shot by the police) and 9 whites. In the wake of Detroit other riots broke out in Texas, Massachusetts, Ohio and Harlem. Few would have anticipated the shock waves spreading 4,000 miles or so to northern England!

Some ninety-six hours or so after the problems began in Belle Isle, black Americans commandeered weapons and trucks from their quarters in Bamber Bridge in Lancashire, smashed through the gates and drove into town determined to open fire on all military vehicles and military police. News of the Detroit riot had quickly reached Britain.

On the evening in question, Thursday 24 June 1943, several black GIs had spent their time drinking at the Olde Hob Inn, a thatched pub, unusual for this area, not far from their barracks. Bamber Bridge had been the headquarters of the 1511th Quartermaster Truck Regiment for several months though the town itself had little to recommend it and many of the men preferred to spend their leisure time in Preston. Quite a few of these soldiers worked long, hard hours delivering weapons and ammunition by truck to American air bases all over the country. With the weather warm and sultry (though hardly matching Detroit's highs) some had decided on this occasion to drink nearer home. Doubtless the troubles back in the USA were on their minds.

At 10.00 p.m. the English pub-closing ritual began, to the jeers of the blacks and some local soldiers and civilians who were there. This attracted the attention of two white American military policemen, normally located in Preston, who happened to be driving by in their jeep. An attempt was made to arrest one black GI for being improperly dressed and one MP drew his gun when threatened by a black brandishing a bottle. After the occupants of the jeep beat a diplomatic retreat the vehicle returned with two more MPs. Arrests were again attempted this time while the black GIs were walking back along the quiet streets of terraced houses towards their base. Another scuffle took place and blood was drawn. An MP fired his pistol, hit one of the soldiers and there was further confusion and shouts of 'kill the goddam son of a bitch'. After several more shots were fired both sides withdrew, the blacks attempting to help their wounded.

Back at the camp rumour fed rumour: many blacks of the several hundred stationed there were shrieking, and stories of blacks being shot in the back increased the tension. Though some men had already gone back into town with arms, at about 11.30 things seemed to be getting calmer. This peace was shattered at midnight, however, when an improvised armoured car full of MPs screeched into the area with searchlights blazing and a machine-gun aloft. Ignoring all pleas the mutinous blacks broke into storerooms. Stealing weapons and ammunition, they smashed through the camp gates and careered into Bamber Bridge, firing at any military vehicles or personnel they saw. British civilians watched the activity with a mixture of awe and horror. The MPs set up a road block at the end of one street, and it was here that one black was shot, to die several days later. Trucks continued to chase around the streets until the early hours of Friday morning when the mutiny, as it was termed, ended.

Many of the weapons and several members of the battalion did not reappear for a few days. In addition to the dead GI, two other blacks and one white officer were shot and there were other injuries caused by bottles and fists. Over twenty men from the depot were eventually found guilty at two courts martial of charges ranging from assault, resisting arrest and illegal possession of rifles, to riot. Sentences of between three months and fifteen years were handed out, though on appeal these were reduced and most of the men were back on duty in about a year.[7]

Launceston is a pretty Cornish town on the edge of Bodmin
Moor with the port of Plymouth to its south and the seaside
resorts of Devon and Cornwall to the north. On Saturday
night, 25 September 1943, five black GIs from an ordnance
unit were told to return to camp by MPs when it was found
that they did not have passes, forcing them to miss the
local dance. They did not leave easily and one threatening-
ly told an MP: 'If you lay hands on me, you'll get what's in
my pocket'. The next night eighteen black soldiers entered
the lounge bar of a pub in the town. White soldiers were
drinking there too and the barman told the blacks that
they couldn't be served in that part of the house. These
blacks had not apparently been in Britain for long and
were loath to accept a practice by then common in many
public houses of landlords reserving separate areas for
black and white Americans. They left, reluctantly, only to
sneak back into town later having armed themselves with
tommy guns, rifles and bayonets. When they encountered
two MPs in a jeep in the town square they ignored calls to
disperse and opened fire, causing people to run in all direc-
tions. The two policemen were wounded in their legs and a
few weeks later fourteen black GIs faced a court martial in
Paignton in Devon, charged with mutiny and attempted
murder. After a three-day hearing all were sentenced to
death or life imprisonment. Some, according to Walter
White, were still serving their sentences two years later in
prisons in America.[8]

Preparations for the invasion of France in mid-1944 meant
that of necessity black and white Americans were forced
into closer contact, causing more vigorous competition for
recreational facilities and leading to a subsequent increase
in tension between the races. It is probably because it
happened so close to D-Day that an incident in Leicester
was not reported in the local press at all – to reveal the
names of the units to which the protagonists belonged

might have been helpful to the enemy.

Trouble between the races in Leicester was not new. At the beginning of February 1943 the Chief Constable there passed on complaints from the landlord of the Three Cranes pub about blacks bringing in young girls. In addition a white American from Kettering had been stabbed by a black based in Gaddesby. The Officer was concerned to point out, however, that the white troops were 'the cause of the trouble . . . they begin the taunting of the blacks'. He suggested that the black and white GIs should either have separate leave time in Leicester on the alternate-day system, or, failing that, whites should be told to use Northampton, further south, and Leicester or Nottingham should be designated 'black' towns.[9]

Though new troops were always coming and going in Britain during the war it was amazing how quickly the stories of black and white conflict could assume the status of folklore. Certainly black troops in Leicester had been dating local girls for some time when white paratroopers of the 82nd Airborne Division arrived in the area to train for the landings in France. When they saw black soldiers escorting white women to pubs and dances they made increasingly bitter taunts which eventually culminated in fights. For members of a black quartermaster aviation battalion working on aerodrome construction just outside Leicester this was the last straw. Since many of the young paratroopers were from the southern states clashes were almost inevitable. As at Bamber Bridge and Launceston the blacks commandeered weapons and a truck and the ensuing riot resulted in the death of an MP from the Airborne Division.[10]

Troubles of some sort between black and white troops in the Bristol area had been simmering for a long time. Part of the problem there was that the organization of the leave areas was complex, and seen by many blacks as discrimination. In addition Bristol was one of those areas where racist white Americans were busiest, and blacks were driven to using the least desirable pubs. John Keith of the

Colonial Office saw some of the problems for himself in the
summer of 1942. He'd been to visit the black Americans in
Liverpool and then in Bristol where the position was 'far
less satisfactory . . . giving rise to comments'. They were
said to be 'kept in barracks and only allowed out to be
marched to work on the pretext that they may interfere
with women'. Keith rightly felt that 'this confinement of
the troops was just the way to bring about undesirable
incidents'.[11] When blacks did step out of line they were
soon put right. A writer on the *Bristol Evening Post* saw
this at first hand in October 1942 when black GIs left a pub
rather worse for wear: 'As they were marshalled out and
told their carriage was waiting, each at the door received a
tap on the head from a very businesslike-looking trun-
cheon. They went quickly home probably unaware of the
cause of their sudden drowsiness. And I don't suppose there
was any subsequent "inquest" on the proceeding. They
have their own code of justice and who shall gainsay it?'[12]

July in Britain is high summer when the evenings are
long and light and 1944 was no exception with blackout
regulations not coming in force until just after 11.00 p.m.
Many of the black GIs in and around Bristol, however, had
other matters on their minds apart from the British weather. The big explosion there came late on Saturday 15 July,
but tension had begun to mount on the previous Monday,
and doubtless at the black American Red Cross Club
rumour was rife. Again, an aviation truck battalion was
involved. The lesson of Leicester had not yet been learned,
however, for these blacks were joined at their base, the
Miller Orphanage camp, on 10 July by white paratroop
replacements. The blacks claimed that two of their men
were beaten up without provocation. This was followed by
several incidents involving blacks and whites in Bristol
over the next few days. As usual the cause of the problem
was not difficult to find: the white paratroopers resented
the easy relations that had developed between the white
British girls in the town and the black soldiers.

On Thursday 13 July, the discontent spread. Men from
the 545th Port Company, based at Sea Mills Camp, tough
city blacks mainly from Detroit and New York, mutinied

by staying in their billets and refusing to turn out for reveille even when the Articles of War were read to them.

The eruption finally occurred on 15 July around Park and Great George Streets. A large number of black GIs had gathered there on that Saturday evening and brawling had broken out. Extra MPs were drafted in and some calm was restored. The black troops were then marched off to the Tram Centre where trucks were to take them back to their camps. This procedure in itself must have been an awesome sight for the onlooker: Great George Street comes down from Brandon Hill and runs into Park Street, one of the city's main arteries. Both streets slope quite steeply and the 'march' down to the Tram Centre about a quarter of a mile away (now simply called the Centre) may well have induced some panic in the GIs. Some of them had knives and while they were being disarmed a black soldier, who was stabbing an MP, was shot by another MP. Not surprisingly, a 'mob spirit' prevailed among the black GIs with MPs shooting people in the legs. Buses were drawn across some of the roads to confine the incident, while some of the wounded were dealt with by members of the St John Ambulance Brigade, who took the more seriously hurt off to Bristol Infirmary. The disturbance had involved 400 black and white troops and it had taken 120 military policemen and many arrests to bring the situation back under control. One black GI was killed and dozens may have been wounded. Bristol remained under military curfew for several days.[13]

At ten o'clock on the morning of Thursday 9 November 1944, one of the war's more bizarre chapters was about to unfold in a most unlikely location. A dartboard was still hanging on the wall of the mess room adjoining the barracks in Thatcham, near Newbury in Berkshire, where ten young black Americans were waiting with a mixture of apprehension and bewilderment for their court martial to begin. In the crowded, stuffy, makeshift courtroom they were about to face proceedings which could end with their executions. They listened quietly as the most serious of the charges, that of murder, was read to them. They were accused of killing three people, one of them the wife of a pub landlord, in an act of revenge which went dreadfully wrong.

The incident had begun exactly five weeks earlier to the day, and was all over in the space of about six hours. The men of the all-black 3247 Quartermaster Service Company had come from Devon on that Thursday, 5 October, to their new camp about a mile from Kingsclere, a village half-way between Newbury and Basingstoke in Britain's leafy south. They had arrived at their destination at about 4.30 in the afternoon, cleaned up their barracks and prepared their bunks. As was normal practice when they were on the move, each man had his weapon – a rifle or a carbine – and these were not taken away until about 10.45 that evening. After attending to their chores and eating, some of the men went into Kingsclere though no leave passes had been issued. They made their way to the Bolton Arms, one of several pubs in the village, where shortly after 7.00 p.m. they were approached by three or four American auxiliary military policemen. They were told that they had to return to camp because they had no passes and were improperly dressed. One soldier later claimed that an MP had cocked a rifle at him. An hour later they were on their way back to base in a truck and an earnest conversation began to develop about returning to get the MPs: 'We are going down there with our rifles', said one GI, while another argued that they should take the rifles away from the MPs and then beat them up.

At around 9.30 p.m. rural England took on the appearance of the Old West as ten black soldiers walked back into the village, loading their weapons as they went. They looked for the MPs first in the Bolton Arms, and then in another pub, the Swan Inn, before going on the the Crown Inn at about ten o'clock. Inside, in various rooms of the pub finishing off their drinks, were about eight or nine black GIs, probably also out without passes, a few locals and several MPs. One or two of the 'snowdrops' as the MPs were commonly called, left the pub and a single shot rang out, followed quickly by a volley of gunfire. In movie style everyone hit the floor. When the smoke had literally cleared one black GI lay dead in a pool of blood, shot in the head. The landlord's wife, Mrs Rose Napper, was lying in an inner room with a bullet wound in her jaw. She died in hospital in the early hours of the next morning. Outside, lying in a garden about 150 yards away, was the dead body of a black American MP, a bullet through his heart.

About forty people were packed into the cramped room as the court martial opened on that November morning. Apart from the defendants, the most interested spectators were the barrister representing the landlord of the Crown, and two senior officers from the Berkshire and Hampshire constabularies. As the day progressed the atmosphere grew more cloying and the air became thicker. Though smoking was not allowed while the trial was taking place everybody puffed away furiously during the short intervals. Two of the accused appeared to be asleep as 7.00 p.m. approached on the first day, one with his head in his hands.

The next morning was bright and sunny as the defence opened. That didn't take long for only one man elected to take the witness stand, while three of the others made short, unsworn statements. Ironically one of these said he wouldn't have been in the pub at all that evening if it hadn't been his birthday. It was thirty minutes before the military court reached its verdict and it was during this period that the gravity of it all seemed to hit some of the men, one of whom knelt and prayed with his Bible in his hand. Nine of the men were found guilty on all three counts – murder, riotous assembly and absence without leave – and despite having no previous convictions they were given life sentences with hard labour. The tenth man was found guilty of being AWOL. The trial had left as many questions as it provided answers. How and why had this hatred of MPs been generated in such a short time? Had the fact that at least one MP was black been of significance? Had the men's experience elsewhere in Britain led to this bitterness? Were any white officials reprimanded for sloppy weapons-storing procedures? The only known sequel to the affair was that a US colonel apologized to Harry Haig, the Regional Commissioner, for the company's behaviour, and the remainder of the men who had not been on trial were quickly dispatched overseas.[14]

It is obvious that several of these major incidents had, at least superficially, much in common. Insensitive and over-officious policing was the spark which ignited the large bonfire of deep-seated and bitter grievances. This is not surprising in view of the way in which many MPs were often selected. One policeman from Bay City, Michigan, who spent over thirty years in the force there, interrupted only by a tour of duty as an MP in wartime Britain, re-minisced years later about this period of his life:

> I don't know how the war was ever won, because they had no rhyme or reason why they selected a guy for an MP. When I was at Fort Custer, they was [sic] three guys ahead of me went in the air force like that, two of 'em in the infantry, and they come to me and said, 'You're MP'. The training they give us was just like a new sheriff goin' and gettin' a new bunch of deputies, trial and error. It had nothin' to do with police business. When we got our first assignment in Lon-don, I don't know how we ever made it. . . . The officers, they were dumber than we were.[15]

The calibre of some of the officers was an issue through-out in any case, particularly in Bristol and at Bamber Bridge, where according to an American Army report there was said to be some lack of control. White officers and enlisted men were alleged to have called blacks 'uncom-plimentary' names like 'jigaboos' and 'niggers'.[16] In addi-tion, lax weapons procedures, which could have been cor-rected by officers, allowed blacks to gain easy access to arms. Underpinning everything, however, and a direct cause of the troubles at Bristol and Leicester, was the woman problem – white soldiers forcefully exhibited their resentment at the association of black GIs and local girls. Added to this was the jim crow system itself. The necessity of cobbling together all-black units to comply with the policy of segregation led to morale problems such as those experienced by the 545th Port Company at Bristol. When its 210 members arrived in the United Kingdom, 125 were being treated for syphilis and before embarkation 26 replacements had to be culled from guardhouses near New York. When such soldiers were told that certain places were no-go areas for blacks, or heard stories of white soldiers smashing beer glasses used by blacks, it was clear that many situations had the potential for violence.

One of the other factors which contributed to tension was an ongoing cause for concern both in the US and Britain at this time: the role of the black radical newspapers. Publications like *The People's Voice*, in attempting to champion the interests of black soldiers would often indulge in aggressive speculation about the role of black Americans after the war; and they would not shrink from the delicate question 'Why should the coloured men fight the white man's battle?'

Whatever the reasons for the friction between the American soldiers in Britian, the report into the Bamber Bridge incident made it clear that the segregation which the United States authorities hoped would keep the lid on the problem failed to do so: 'Such enmity, bitterness, and difficulties as exist in the United States between the negro and white races were brought by both races to the United Kingdom'.[17] With reluctance, not only did the administrations on both sides of the Atlantic have to tend to the problems jim crow brought to Britain, but of necessity they also played host to visitors much less willing to keep the racial problem under wraps.

7
The Watchdogs: Jim Crow Under Close Scrutiny

Whilst accepting the inevitability of segregation in the US Army there were officers who within the limits open to them endeavoured to make jim crow in Britain as inconspicuous as possible. In addition there were those for whom the major racial incidents acted as a catalyst: it seems clear that the violence at Bamber Bridge, Launceston and elsewhere achieved some qualified results. Some Red Cross Clubs were thrown open to both races, though the one at Wellingborough in Northamptonshire seems to have been one of the few to experience a period of genuine integration. In addition Good Conduct Committees – black and white GIs from their separate units meeting together to discuss social arrangements – became *de rigueur*, though previously dismissed by high authority when canvassed by General Hartle in Northern Ireland. The biggest change was wrought by the VIII Air Force. The truckdrivers, ammunition dumpers and so on who formed its aviation support units suffered particularly from hard work and low morale. Consequently in 1943 they were formed into a Combat Support Wing in an attempt, which met with some success, to restore their pride.

Most importantly the US Army was driven to realize the enormous potential drain on the war effort which its racial problems could represent, forcing it to appoint individuals

and committees to keep an eye on the relationships between blacks and whites overseas. As a result Jim Crow's
temporary stay in Britain remained under close scrutiny.

The most important committee in Washington which
kept a watching brief on the racial situation in the Army
was the Advisory Committee on Negro Troop Policies. This
was established on 27 August 1942, and was commonly
called the McCloy Committee after its chief, John J.
McCloy, Assistant Secretary of War. Its brief was to look at
military problems relating to blacks, but the more effective
instrument for reporting on racial problems in Britain was
the Inspector General's Department of the Army, and its
investigations have been referred to elsewhere (see p. 107).

In the European Theatre one of the most controversial of
the Army's actions as far as the black media in the USA
were concerned was its utilization of Benjamin O. Davis.
Since his promotion to Brigadier General in October 1940
Davis was the highest ranking black in the American
armed services. Towards the end of September 1942 he
became a racial troubleshooter attached to the Inspector
General's Department.

Davis was a professional soldier of many years' standing.
He had seen service in the Spanish–American war, been on
Mexican border patrol and had served in Liberia. Light-
skinned and with greying hair, this distinguished-looking
black, easily recognizable in his later years by his metal-
framed spectacles, retired at the end of July 1941 after
more than forty years of service, but he returned to active
duty the next day. The growing problem of clashes between
black and white GIs in Britain, and in particular the death
of a black soldier in Antrim, Northern Ireland, persuaded
the Army to offer Davis a unique role. He was charged by
Eisenhower with conducting an investigation into racial
friction in Britain. Now 65 years old, Davis immediately
went with General J. C. Lee to the headquarters of the
Services of Supply in Cheltenham and got stuck into his
new job.

The problem for Davis, or more correctly for many of the
black organizations in America, was that his long career in
the Army made him an easy target for criticism. This

became more pronounced by 1942 after black pressure had failed to desegregate the Army in which Davis served. His dilemma was that the jim-crow army was official War Department policy and for him to have fought actively against that would have severely damaged his career. However, the evidence does show that Davis, though accepting a segregated army, tirelessly fought against discrimination in it. For many blacks, however, this was not enough. One black GI has remembered a visit that Davis paid to Fort Huachuca in Arizona: 'They felt he had not come down to hear about their problems but to give a biographical run-down on how he had made it and to tell us to turn the other cheek. After his visit the name of B. O. Davis, sen., was synonymous with "yes-sirism" and "Uncle Tomism" '.[1] Black newspapers in America, which had initially applauded Davis's promotion to the 'Black Cabinet', also became disillusioned with him. Lee Finkle, the historian of the black press, has argued that Davis and other leading racial advisers, with the exception of Judge Hastie, were almost universally considered

> tools of the administration to be used as 'buffers between the white people and the colored people'. Davis appeared to fit into this category of acting as a spokesman for the Army to ease tensions rather than speaking out strongly against racial discrimination within the service . . . his reports were not forceful enough for the black press. His public comments about black morale usually painted a picture more congenial to Army publicity drives than the realities of the situation as the black press perceived it.[2]

The fact that Davis later received a citation for his investigative work in the war and was highly commended by both Lee and Eisenhower further alienated black opinion. Even the none-too-liberal General Weaver respected Davis as a soldier, a patriot and a gentleman. On the other hand few could have realized what life was like for Davis in an army where black officers were as thin on the ground as five-legged mules. When he was stationed at Fort Riley in Kansas he and his wife used to make the obligatory social calls on brother officers at weekends when Davis knew that most of them had gone to the 'hop', the Saturday night dance on the base. In that way, evidently, they weren't put in the 'embarrassing' position of having to receive black people. Those who wanted to could return the call as Davis left his card. Lee witnessed Davis's humility also. After the invasion of France Davis would occasionally sit with Lee and other senior staff leaders at the same mess table at their Paris headquarters. This was until Davis excused himself and sat on his own, after he heard people say he had the place just because he was black.

Davis visited black troops in Scotland, Northern Ireland, and many parts of England, and spent some time in the company of British officers at Newbury in Berkshire. Again, however, Davis found himself at the centre of controversy. On 14 October 1942 *The Times* reported a speech he made in London when he acknowledged that some of the white GIs resented the British attitude to the blacks but, he continued, he'd had 'no complaint from coloured troops in Britain which would lead him to believe they were unhappy. From all the instructions he had seen there was no discrimination in the American Army between coloured and white troops. He felt that too much emphasis was being placed on colour'.

This viewpoint upset some black militants but within a month Davis had completed the task Eisenhower had given him and he presented his report on 25 October 1942.[3] Though it was marked 'secret', parts of it filtered through to black organizations in the United States, and it received a mixed reception. On 24 October, the day before publication, the *Baltimore Afro-American,* which had got wind of it, concluded that the report was 'Critical and objective'. The NAACP did not remain as sanguine. In one of their irregular but fairly frequent dialogues in December, Eleanor Roosevelt told Walter White that she thought Davis had done a good job in reducing racial tension. The NAACP, while not disagreeing with Mrs Roosevelt concerning the value of the investigation, thought more was needed. The League of Coloured Peoples in England, which had been optimistic about the situation, began to have second thoughts too. Its November *Newsletter* commented: 'Our experiences compel a non-acceptance of the statement

made by General Davis . . . that there is no colour bar
against the troops in this country'. The bitterest critic of
Davis was a correspondent of the *Nation*, a liberal American journal. Joseph Julian had himself spent two months
in England and he found it

> hard to reconcile General Davis's report with my own
> observations . . . or with what Negro soldiers told me. . . . The
> social difficulties mentioned by General Davis are not iso-
> lated cases and should not be considered of no concern to the
> army. . . . Perhaps General Davis did not get around as much
> as he should have, or perhaps he did not consider it wise to
> make an issue of the matter at this time. An ugly and
> dangerous situation does exist. . . . It is particularly shocking
> to observe the Jim Crow bacillus being injected into
> England.[4]

Given Davis's own starting point it is difficult to say the
opprobrium heaped on him was justified; hostile reactions
were due undoubtedly to his acceptance of segregation in
the Army. Davis believed that blacks and whites should
not have to mix: 'No white or colored soldier should be
required to violate any of his personal views as to social
relationship by being compelled to associate with anyone
undesirable to him'. Despite his inevitable support for the
prevailing racial situation Davis's report did contain a
frank assessment of the problem in Britain, and the
reasons for it. He believed that friction was caused by
white soldiers who were resentful of blacks mixing with
British people, particularly women. There was also a 'lack
of adequate officer control and supervision', and 'inefficien-
cy by small unit commanders in controlling their men'.
Davis recommended that more background material on the
American blacks and race relations should be given in
orientation courses for whites, and he offered to prepare
such materials. Further he suggested that both races be
reminded of their roles as Americans and the necessity of
working together. In areas of Britain where both black and
white soldiers were stationed, military policemen of both
races should work closely together. Davis concluded with a
potted history of the black American contribution to the
Army of the United States.

If some black critics were dismayed at Davis's role in the Army and his views on the black soldiers, their dismay would have greatly increased if they had been made aware of the reaction of the Army command to the few modest proposals that were contained in his report. The Inspector General, Major General Peterson sent it to the Chief of Staff on 24 December 1942 praising Davis's work and asking for it to be considered by the G1 Personnel Section. In fact the report was considered by the Personnel Section and by McCloy and Stimson, but all to no avail. Colonel P. B. Rogers of the London Base command, surveying the state of race relations in the United Kingdom in March 1943, noted that there had been numerous conflicts between black and white GIs, most of them caused by white soldiers from the South harassing blacks. With this General Davis would have heartily concurred but Eisenhower responded unenthusiastically to the report and no action was taken on it. Davis's views were not published.

Friction between black and white Americans got worse, not better, after December 1942, and even if Davis had been a much younger man keeping the lid on the problem would have been a colossal task for one individual. Davis remained on the active register until 1948 but his influence in Britain diminished after the completion of his investigation.

In view of the increasing seriousness of the troubles, particularly the Bamber Bridge incident, the Army decided in July 1943 that it needed special officers in the Services of Supply, V Corps and the VIII Air Force who could maintain closer supervision and control of black units. These senior men were to have the authority to issue on-the-spot orders and place more officers in areas where they were thought necessary. Appointed as the special officer to the SOS was George Murrel Alexander and for this purpose he was deemed an assistant deputy provost marshal. It is difficult to see what special qualification Alexander had for the job unless it was that he had spent considerable time in Virginia. He was born in that southern state, graduated from its Military Institute and then entered its National Guard. After various spells of duty, which included winning a Purple Heart in France in the Great War, he went back to the Virginia National Guard in 1920, there to stay until 1940. He was mustered into Federal Service with the Infantry early in 1941, working at Fort George G. Meade in Maryland until coming to Britain in the autumn of 1942, by this time a 53-year-old brigadier general.

Though the existence of the special officers doesn't seem to have been very well publicized within the American Army, Alexander had visited the majority of black units in England by the beginning of October 1943. He soon made it clear that no great changes were to be expected. He emphasized that no dance was to be attended by both black and white troops and urged the newer policies of overstrength in officers serving with black troops, and mixed MP groups. Since his appointment Launceston had seen trouble, but he felt that there was no justification for the view that the trouble was caused by white MPs harassing black soldiers. Again with Launceston in mind, where the troops had been for only a few days, he suggested that small black units be held in some kind of staging area until the officers in charge were satisfied with their discipline. He was a firm believer in separate leave areas though he realized that was not now possible in crowded Britain. All in all General Alexander was not going to rock any racial boat.

If the black pressure groups and individual black soldiers expected, and got, little improvement in the jim-crow army in Britain through official channels, many more hopes were pinned on the two most important unofficial visitors – Eleanor Roosevelt and Walter White. Even though their greatest achievements, along with people like Joe Louis and Lena Horne, were to boost black morale, that did not prevent them from incurring the wrath of the Army authorities.

Eleanor Roosevelt came to the White House in the 1930s fairly naive about racial issues but became increasingly politicized through her contacts with Walter White, Mary McLeod Bethune and other leading black figures. The First

Lady's relationship with White, particularly during the war years, was an important one. White would sign his letters to her 'cordially' and 'ever sincerely', and through this correspondence and personal meetings he kept the President's wife fully informed about what was happening to the black soldier during the war. White's alliance with Mrs Roosevelt was doubly important because the President did not over-concern himself with racial issues, while his advisers, according to a recent view, acted like a 'Palace Guard' with Press Secretary Stephen Early and Appointments Secretary Marvin McIntyre playing 'a major role in shielding the President on matters pertaining to blacks'. Both men, it has been argued, 'endeavored quite openly to diminish Eleanor Roosevelt's influence on racial policy and to frustrate her efforts to get the administration interested in the Negro's plight'. To these advisers meeting with blacks was 'missionary work'.[5] Certainly this statement has validity in relation to one attempt to acquaint the President with the black soldier situation. On 7 October 1942, Bishop Bray of Chicago complained to Roosevelt that attempts were being made in America and abroad by certain officers of the armed forces to 'foster, develop and spread racial doctrines founded upon prejudice and discrimination' and England was a 'concrete example' of where this was happening. McIntyre responded the next day by arguing that the complaints were too general, and in a memorandum said that the innocuous reply to the Bishop which he had prepared was a 'good "stock letter" for such cases'.[6]

In fact it is quite likely that the President was not embarrassed by his wife's views, especially when he could put them to political use. Eleanor's interest in racial matters would appease blacks but if it aroused the opposition of southern Democrats Franklin could always disown it as the wayward action of the 'missus'. Be that as it may, Eleanor's concern was deep and sincere; testimony to that are the letters branding her as a 'nigger-lover' and chiding her for her purported encouragement of Eleanor Clubs supposedly set up to liberate blacks from domestic service in the United States. In the war years Eleanor kept up a

bombardment of letters to her husband, to Stimson,
McCloy and anyone else in a high enough position in government to be able to influence racial matters.

It was Walter White who probably first drew Eleanor's
attention to the difficulties black soldiers would face overseas. The NAACP Secretary expressed his concern at the
exportation of American racial prejudice to India, where
black GIs arrived early in 1942, fearing that there would
be a repetition of the situation faced by blacks in France
during the Great War.

The British picture was brought directly to the attention of Mrs Roosevelt in a letter from Belfast in September 1942. A Mrs Kennedy, who said she had spent half her
life in America, had encountered black Americans in her
'backwater . . . this little Ireland'. The local population was
'unsophisticated' and 'old fashioned' and hence she was
afraid there might

> be trouble ahead – for the young girls will undoubtedly walk
> out with these [black] strangers in a way which will not
> surprise the local inhabitants who would wish to be friendly
> but may well infuriate your *own* troops. Many of the men
> stationed in these parts come from the Southern States and I
> really don't think there could be a more likely cause of
> trouble than seems possible here.

Surprisingly in view of the masses of mail she received
every day, Eleanor took the time to reply personally to this
letter. It was inevitable, she wrote, that black troops would
go to Ireland and

> also inevitable that they should be received over there in a
> perfectly natural way since they do not have the prejudices
> which have grown up in the South here. I think the possible
> reaction of some of our Southerners to what may happen
> there will have to be controlled by a little education, and it
> should be pointed out to them that different countries feel
> differently and that they cannot carry with them into other
> countries the attitude they have had at home.

Mrs Roosevelt sent copies of both her letter and Mrs
Kennedy's to Stimson with a note reiterating her own
view:

I think we will have to do a little educating among our
Southern white men and officers, emphasizing the fact that
every effort should be made to prevent marriages during this
period but that normal relationships with groups of people
who do not have the same feeling that they have about the
negro cannot be prevented.[7]

Even a statement as conservative as this must have given
the Secretary of War apoplexy, threatening as it did to
exacerbate the issue overseas. Stimson prepared a reply to
Mrs Roosevelt's letter saying the situation was being monitored: General Davis was there investigating the position
and so far it was not serious. The response was not sent
however as Stimson preferred to meet the First Lady personally. What changed his mind was that he had discovered that Eleanor was about to visit Britain and he feared
that she might do some damage there. Stimson noted this
in his diary on 2 October 1942 and revealed that he had
asked the President 'if he would not caution her on the
subject of making any comment as to the different treatment which Negroes received in the UK from what they
receive in the US. He was very much interested in this
whole subject and very sympathetic to our attitude and
told me he would pass the word on to Mrs Roosevelt'. Not
content with this Stimson also contacted the Army Chief of
Staff and in a secret message said tersely: 'Re: Negro situation in England. Mrs Roosevelt coming trip to UK and
request that she will not mention the US attitude towards
Negroes'.[8]

Lady Reading of the Women's Voluntary Service had
been urging Mrs Roosevelt to visit Britain for some time
and when the trip was approved the arrangements were
placed in her hands. Accompanying her on the tour was
Colonel Oveta Culp Hobby. She was an ambitious young
Texan, already sitting in that state's House of Representatives by the age of 21, who later became a newspaper
proprietress. When America joined the conflict she worked
first in public relations at the War Department, and then
was put in charge of the women's auxiliary forces and it
was in this role that she took part in the visit, which lasted
from 21 October to 17 November 1942.

The first leg of the journey was by flying boat to Northern Ireland – a 24-hour trip – but bad weather meant the party could not immediately proceed from there to London. She flew on the next day in a plane provided by Churchill but because of the uncertainty of the weather four special trains were laid on at different points in England with steam up awaiting her arrival. In fact she landed at Bristol and was met there by her special friend, John Winant, and Oliver Harvey, Eden's private secretary. From there the party went by train to Paddington in London where Eleanor received the red-carpet treatment, meeting the King and Queen and others including Lady Reading, Eisenhower and Eden. The first two nights were spent with the royal family at Buckingham Palace where Eleanor met the young Princess Elizabeth, the future Queen. Elizabeth, Mrs Roosevelt recorded in her account of the trip, was 'quite serious' though a child with a 'great deal of character and personality' who asked 'a number of questions about life in the United States and they were serious questions'. At one of the parties in the palace she met Ernest Bevin, the Minister of Labour, who told her about the Indian workers he had recruited. Continuing her whistle-stop tour she visited Chequers and met the Prime Minister's grandson, Winston. She found him a 'sweet boy'; just turned two he looked exactly like his grandfather – 'the resemblance was ridiculous'.[9]

Eleanor's reputation as an outrageous radical on racial issues preceded her to Britain. When Dowler's Notes were under discussion in the weeks before she arrived, Richard Law at the Foreign Office advocated acceptance of the US Army line in order to avoid complaint from her. Harvey recorded in his diary that he found the First Lady had 'a full share of the Roosevelt energy and bounce', but, he continued, she 'is a stormy petrel in American politics and outrages half America with her outspoken left-wing and far worse pro-negro opinions. She engaged a table from the White House at a smart Washington hotel for a party of six and arrived with five negresses! I call that grand'.[10] Those who expected great things in this area from her visit were disappointed. Though Walter White constantly reminded her of how black GIs resented their menial labouring jobs, Eleanor believed her prime objective in Britain was to raise morale not reform the Army.

Eleanor continued her busy social and political whirl. She lunched with Lady Astor and other women MPs, she stayed with Queen Mary at Beaufort Castle, and sang 'Keep right on to the end of the road' with Harry Lauder at a shipyard on the Clyde. She did manage to meet some black GIs. She visited them near Badminton, at Bristol with General Davis, at Cheetham Hill near Manchester, where she also saw 'Bevin's Bahama Boys', in Cheshire and at Maghull north of Liverpool where they were delighted to see her. However, her basic gradualism was expressed a year later in an article she wrote for a black journal. 'If I were a Negro,' it went, 'I would accept every advance that was made in the Army and Navy, though I would not try to bring these about more quickly than they were offered.'[11]

Stimson for one was greatly relieved that the danger had passed. He met Mrs Roosevelt a couple of days after her return to the US and heard that she 'was delighted with Lee's work among the colored; how he had solved the difficulties of that problem'. Of greater importance was her attitude: Stimson recorded in his diary that she was 'very temperate' with him on the subject of blacks. While the administration was expressing relief that Eleanor's trip had come off without incident, black leaders were disappointed. The reports from Britain clearly proved to them that the inherent racism of many white soldiers was being openly demonstrated, and this was a situation which cried out for remedial action. Mrs Roosevelt on the other hand, however gradually she might go down the liberal road, was still regarded by her peers as a dangerous maverick on the racial issue – there were enormous pressures on her to slow down. On the other hand the NAACP Secretary could not contain his frustration with her at times. The two disagreed, for example, when they discussed the role of General Davis who had recently completed his investigation into racial tensions in Britain. Eleanor and White met on Tuesday 1 December 1942, but White could not share the First

Lady's view that the black general had done well in his
efforts to lower the racial temperature in Britain.

The visit to Britain apart, Mrs Roosevelt's main role in
race relations was as a conduit – she was a direct pipeline
to authority, particularly to the President. This perception
of her was important to blacks both famous and 'humble'.
Early in November 1943 she received a long letter from
Roland Hayes. Hayes was a black lyric tenor who came up
from poverty in rural Georgia to fame on the concert halls
of the USA and Europe. Though he could sing in several
languages the black community revered him most for his
sensitive interpretations of spirituals. In 1943 the American Army invited him to Britain and asked him to be the
soloist at the Albert Hall in London with the 200-strong
black GI chorus. A recognition of both Hayes' popularity
with the black GIs and the fact that all was patently not
well in the Army came with an invitation from General
Devers and John Winant for the singer to stay on in Britain after the concert tour. He was given free rein to talk to
blacks everywhere in the country, in small or large groups,
with or without officers present. The thrust of what Hayes
discovered was echoed in a letter given to him in Bristol by
a black corporal. 'You wouldn't believe the lies' the whites
had told about the blacks, the letter read:

> They try to keep us out of all the 'pubs' and when they can't
> they fight us. The MP lock us up for anything and especially
> if they see us talking with any English women. They go in
> gangs and beat you up and then if our boys have to cut some
> of them to keep from getting hurt they say Negro soldiers are
> bad ... You [Hayes] are one of our leaders and if you want us
> to act proud you ought to tell some of the big shots you don't
> like this.

Hayes in turn felt that he 'would neglect a patriotic duty'
and fail in his 'loyalty' to the President and Mrs Roosevelt
if he did not bring this forward.

Eleanor passed Hayes' report to McCloy saying it de-
served 'real attention' as the blacks had 'something to gain
in the war', and she also sent a copy to Devers who had
initiated Hayes' involvement. Despite the evidence to the
contrary the General refused to believe that anything was

amiss in the ETO. Blacks were doing a 'splendid job', he wrote to Mrs Roosevelt, with 'no discrimination' and 'no favouritism', though he did promise that the matters raised by Hayes would receive his personal attention; but Devers was one more of those people who thought the President's wife at best a busybody.[12]

A year later, towards the end of November 1944, Mrs Roosevelt received a cable from a soldier in England. It was poorly written but with a direct message which she again dispatched straight to John McCloy:

> This is rather hard thing for me to do since it is my first time, but I am very much sure that you have read many similar. We are, my unit and I in a very dense [tense] situation, and I am hoping you can help us in some way. We were told that there was no serigation [sic] here in England, it isn't from the people, they are fine, only from our officers. We are receiving blurring rumors of reports they put out. We are forbidden any recreation that might cause us to mix as a whole with the people. We are a negro unit, I do hope you can help us in some way.[13]

The ordinary black GI, at least, continued to have faith in the First Lady.

Boxing champion Joe Louis was probably the most famous black personality to visit the GIs in Britain, but without a doubt the most powerful was Walter White. He had crossed swords with the British Government on several issues before America entered the war and his interest in jim crow overseas remained. Certainly a lot was expected of him – one black soldier's view was that White was 'what you might call an Assistant President of the United States in charge of colored people'.[14] Other reactions to him were in marked contrast to this. The British were at first a little nervous of him, perhaps understandably in view of previous contacts, while the American Army authorities, ever-polite and helpful while he was in Britain, seemed predetermined to ignore almost all of his many recommendations.

Walter Francis White was born in Atlanta, Georgia, in

1893. His father, a postman, was one-fourth black and his mother, a former teacher, one-sixteenth, still enough in legal terms to put him on the underprivileged side of the segregation line in many parts of the southern states. White understood what racism meant from an early age. During the Atlanta race riot of 1906 he remembered crouching in the dark with his father when a white mob approached their home. While working in the insurance business he helped to establish a branch of the NAACP in Atlanta and in 1918 moved to New York to work full-time for the organization. His skin colour, which a British official was later to describe as 'white as his name' and without 'a chemical trace of coloured blood',[15] allowed him to pose as a white reporter and probe lynching and race riots in America from a unique perspective. On these subjects he quickly became expert. In addition White had written two novels by 1926 and was one of the· leading figures in the Harlem Renaissance, the cultural awakening in black New York in the 1920s.

Having concerned himself with the problems of the black GIs overseas, particularly in Britain and Australia, from a distance for so long, White determined late in 1943 that he would see them at first hand. At the beginning of November the NAACP Secretary wrote to Eleanor Roosevelt outlining his plans. He had received personal security clearance from the head of the FBI, J. Edgar Hoover, and he explained that he was now trying to get accreditation as a war correspondent with a number of journals – *Life, Time* and the *The New York Post* among them. It was this that was giving him some difficulty and White wondered now whether a personal meeting with the President would speed up the paperwork. In this he was disappointed for the reply came back via the First Lady that the President did not want to be put in the position of approving some correspondents and not others.[16]

This proved only a temporary setback to White but of course he also had to get the British to allow him in. At some point in November, Lord Halifax, British Ambassador in America, met White in New York and White was also a guest at the British Embassy in Washington, DC.

White was a very courteous, sociable man and Halifax was
impressed. He told the Foreign Office in London of White's
plans, saying that he had found him 'sensible and friendly.
. . . it would be worth while to take some trouble with him'.
Eleanor again tried to hurry things along by writing to
Stimson at the beginning of December. By the middle of
the month he was able to say that everything had been
cleared and White arrived in England on 3 January 1944,
'to probe,' as he put it, 'the transplanting of racial emotions
and patterns from the Mississippi to the Midlands'.[17]

White's tour of Britain was arranged with the help of
General Alexander, the new coordinator of black troop
affairs, and was in two phases. Accompanying White on
the whole inspection was Captain Max Gilstrap, former
science editor of the *Christian Science Monitor* and now
associate editor of *Stars and Stripes*, the service newspaper. Gilstrap was temporarily relieved of these duties and he
and White travelled 1,700 miles through Britain in sixteen
days on a tour which encompassed the whole range of black
GI activity. They rode in jeeps, flew in a Fortress and
tramped miles and miles through winter mud to meet
black troops wherever they worked – on bulldozers and
cranes, in hospitals, kitchens, postal depots, weapons
rooms, laundries, supply rooms and under a camouflaged
tent where the 3010 Quartermaster Mobile Bakery Unit
were making 11,000 loaves a day. They held discussions in
Langport Detention Centre in the south-west and with the
923 Aviation Engineers who had a splendid big band in
East Anglia. In addition they met British civilians on the
streets, in the pubs and in their homes, and civic dignitaries like the Lord Mayor of Cambridge. White wanted to see
the trouble spots, and Launceston and Bamber Bridge were
both included in the itinerary.

At the end of the tour White returned to London to write
his report. Nevile Butler of the Foreign Office thought it
would be useful to arrange for him to have a few minutes
with Anthony Eden – to 'confirm Mr White in his good
opinion of this country', and to show the Roosevelts 'that
we have not neglected him'.[18] White had expressed the
desire at some point to meet Churchill and the King but

this was not fulfilled, partly because the British officials diverted his requests via the American Embassy where Winant and Herbert Agar appear to have thwarted him.

The NAACP Secretary presented his report to the War Department on 11 February 1944 and gave copies to Lee and Eisenhower.[19] The document was over twenty pages long and in it White made observations on the state of race relations in Britain and then detailed over a dozen ways in which the situation could be improved. He believed that the black soldiers had been well received though the spreading of derogatory stories by their white colleagues was affecting their morale to such an extent that the whites were now being seen as the 'enemy'. Part of the blame for this was put on the fact that there was now less indoctrination on racial matters on board the troop ships bound for the United Kingdom. White's recommendations were specific and detailed: he suggested the abolition of the 'off limits' system and 'odd and even' pass days; more black superior officers should be appointed and black combat units formed so that they could share the 'glamour' of war; rumours should be investigated; MP patrols should consist of blacks and whites; a Board of Review with at least one black lawyer should be established to investigate charges of excessive punishment of black troops; whites should not dictate racial policies in Britain; a senior black physician should be appointed to investigate blacks and VD; blacks should be allowed to lecture to British troops; more black entertainers should be sent to Britain; there should be less paternalism in memoranda (remember White had seen the Plank notes); refresher courses for blacks in the use of firearms should be set up; and finally American Red Cross Clubs should operate on a nonsegregated basis and indeed should be open to all nationalities.

In view of White's position an enquiry was obviously necessary, and two assistant Inspectors General – Colonel Day and Lieutenant Colonel Cocanougher – carried it out between 19 and 24 February 1944. Rarely can an Inspector General's report have been so dismissive of the charges it was set up to investigate, particularly when many of them had already been proved by previous investigations carried

out by members of the same department.[20] There were
concessions on two points: it was said the appointment of a
black lawyer to review court-martial decisions might raise
morale, that mixed MP patrols were being used and that
the Plank memorandum had been withdrawn; but point by
point White's charges were refuted:

> The specific allegations are considered to be satisfactorily
> explained, but those allegations which are general in nature
> and have the color of rumor, such as 'Personnel spreading
> vicious stories among the British,' are most difficult to trace
> and it is equally as difficult to determine their actual exist-
> ence. These stories probably do exist to a limited extent,
> accepting the statements of Negro soldiers who so state.
> While it appears that the morale of a few colored men might
> be somewhat impaired by such derogatory remarks of a few
> indiscreet white men, it is believed that the Negro troops as
> a whole are not affected and treat these remarks with uncon-
> cern as have been their instructions.

These conclusions flew in the face of the facts – rumours
and derogatory remarks had been one of the contributory
factors to the troubles at Bamber Bridge and Launceston.
It is difficult to believe that the constructive investigations
carried out by Haines emanated from the same department
as this one, but easy to understand in the light of such
complacency how some of the worst of the troubles at
Leicester and Bristol were yet to come. All in all the officers were of the opinion that the investigation had revealed
no

> serious condition in the racial situation that would tend to
> impede the war effort to any extent. Incidents do occur but
> they are for the most part minor in nature, and it is shown
> from the official records that in proportion to the number of
> troops now in the United Kingdom that the number of these
> incidents is decreasing constantly.

Furthermore, the IG report concluded, there was 'no evidence of discrimination against the colored troops'.

That White's charges were dismissed in such a near-
contemptuous manner is doubly surprising in that many of
them were corroborated in a report by Captain Gilstrap.

White, however, had presented his report directly to the War Department, whereas Gilstrap's went to a colonel in the public relations department of the European Theatre. The chances are that the two documents were never seen as two halves of one whole. It would have been difficult for IG officers to dismiss Gilstrap's conclusions lightly:

> Most of the difficulties resulting from the stationing of colored American soldiers in the British Isles is [sic] due to lack of uniformity in the treatment of white and colored soldiers both by the US Army and by British civilians. This is largely due to the failure of the US Army personnel in carrying out the Directives on this subject issued by the American High Command, and to a prejudiced minority of white soldiers, with a color bar mentality, who have made 'believers' out of the British.[21]

The reason why White's views were given such scant regard is not hard to find. If blacks had a difficult time in the 1940s those of mixed race sometimes faced even more prejudices, being regarded as the worst of both worlds. White, clearly a unique person in terms of ethnic origin, threw the whole thing into relief. This attitude is best summarized by this extract from a censored letter written by a white American airforce corporal at the time of White's visit:

> I have read about this negro White before (probably in *Time* or *Life* magazines who constantly plug the negro, with an eye to republican votes). It seems to me that he 'chose,' as you say, to be a negro and now he is trying to ease his inferiority complex by having negroes declared 'equal' with white people.[22]

Not knowing yet of the response to his report White stayed on in England and exchanged letters with Eleanor Roosevelt. In the middle of February 1944 he told her that though he'd found 'a great many things' which were 'disturbing' in Britain he was hopeful and full of praise for Lee, Ike and Winant.[23] Some time later in early April, Lee sent White a copy of the IG report with a covering letter attempting to sugar the pill. The General said the visit had been invaluable and Eisenhower was grateful for the many contributions White had made. In addition Lee said that he had instructed his staff 'to implement wherever possible your many fine suggestions'. Politely, however, White was snubbed. He was informed that in the ETO there was no 'Negro problem' but an 'American citizen problem' which was longstanding and the solution of this was 'evolution, not revolution'. Besides, the main task was to win the war.[24]

Despite this rebuff White told the First Lady that he remained hopeful and believed some recommendations had been effected. In early May 1944, White produced for the NAACP Board of Directors a report on what progress had been made in the ETO. There had been some slight headway on the question of blacks as combat troops, lectures to white troops on race relations, mixed MP patrols, and the provision of black entertainers overseas (Lena Horne was about to depart). In addition blacks were to receive more publicity in photographs and press releases. White significantly believed that the 'off limits' rule had been abolished and that this had been confirmed by the War Department, though no trace of any such order exists in the US Army files.[25]

White was not to remain this optimistic: in a speech in Chicago in July he told his audience that he wished 'it were possible for me to tell you truthfully that the alchemy of war and fighting to destroy Nazism had transformed the racial behavior of Americans in the armed services overseas. I cannot do so. We have merely transplanted to other lands the American pattern, both good and bad'. Reading this speech even Mrs Roosevelt had reservations about the hardening of White's attitude. 'I am always torn in my mind,' she wrote, 'as to whether the voicing of bitterness, and some of this speech is bitter of necessity, is going to help us solve our extremely difficult questions both in the present and the future.' White simply replied that he had not intended to be bitter but he only tried 'to tell the truth' as he saw it.[26]

How effective was the press, especially those black journals

with overseas' representatives, in airing the racial problems of the soldiers in the European Theatre? The answer
to the question lies in part with the official positions on
press censorship held by the British and American authorities.

In Britain theoretically the picture was quite clear: press
censorship, except for a brief interlude, was the province of
the Ministry of Information and its chief press censor, Rear
Admiral G. P. Thomson, whose 'blue pencil' was satirized
so well on the radio by comedian Jack Warner, later TV's
popular PC Dixon of Dock Green. Newspaper editors, like
all British citizens, were subject to Defence Regulations
and hence were prohibited from obtaining and publishing
information which might be useful to the enemy.[27] The
relations between black and white GIs in Britain and the
British reactions to the situation could well have been
construed as coming into that category, for it was a topic
that certainly could be, and was, exploited by Germany. In
addition, the Defence Notices listed subjects about which
the Ministry's advice was always to be sought, and it seems
that the black GIs soon became one of these. In the summer
of 1942 the Eastern Regional Commissioner in Cambridge
began to hear criticism from his fellow countrymen about
the attitude of white Americans to the blacks and was
anxious that such criticism should not be picked up by the
press. This sentiment was shared by others in both the
American and British camps and a joint policy emerged.
On 8 September 1942 a brief note 'on censorship for Censors' came from Commander Powell of the MOI and by
authority of US advisers. All references to black GIs 'calculated to inflame racial prejudice' in Britain or the USA, or
'characterising coloured troops as *labour* troops' had to be
referred to a duty assistant director, a senior censorship
official.[28]

Despite the strictures the British newspapers and journals at national and local level continued to report and
comment on the problems of black GIs. Often journalists
wrote about the courts martial of soldiers in great detail,
including in their reports all the evidence that was critical
of the US Army authorities. In essence newspaper cen-

sorship was a self-imposed system – no MOI officials would have had the time to review all material before publication. Hence papers felt free to express the view that the Americans should mend their racial ways in Britain and did so without pulling punches. In an article entitled 'Ways to smash the colour bar', in the Sunday *Reynolds News* of 26 September 1943, Tom Driberg suggested that the American authorities should explain to their troops that 'the colour bar is not one of *our* customs, and that they mustn't be shocked if we don't observe it,' a point of view already decisively rejected in private by the British Cabinet. Eight months later S. L. Solon, in the *News Chronicle* of 10 May 1944, argued that Britain's 'heritage of tolerance and liberalism' was being eroded. Many of the country's citizens were adopting the racist attitudes shown by white GIs to their compatriots simply, he contended, because 'their skins are brown'.

Ostensibly the early American attitude to censorship of racial issues was as flexible as the British. Eisenhower held his first press conference in England on 14 July 1942, and he later noted that until his arrival American headquarters had clamped down on stories of difficulties involving black and white troops.

> When I learned at the press conference that stories of this kind were on the censored list, I at once revoked the order and told the pressmen to write as they pleased – urging them only not to lose their perspective. To my astonishment, several reporters spoke up to ask me to retain the ban, giving me a number of arguments in support of their recommendation. They said that troublemakers would exaggerate the importance of the incidents and that the reports, taken up at home, could cause domestic dissension. I thanked them but stuck to my point, with the result that little real excitement was ever caused by ensuing stories.[29]

In fact Eisenhower's view was a little ingenuous; not everyone agreed with him about publicizing racial problems and some reporting certainly caused official headaches. Captain Butcher, Ike's aide, preferred more cautious advice to Raymond Daniell of the Association of American Correspondents in London, on 17 August 1942:

> News involving negroes is no more subject to censorship by
> military authorities than is any other type. This as I think
> everyone understands, does not mean that news which
> would tend to create and magnify racial difficulties within
> this command, and so operate adversely upon the effort to
> produce an efficient army, is above censorship. For example,
> if a story attempted to take an isolated case of friction be-
> tween white and colored soldiers and make it appear that
> this was typical, I would not only censor the whole story but
> would consider that it exhibited a far from cooperative atti-
> tude on the part of such [a] newsman.[30]

It was the black American newspapers which brought
special problems for both the American and British authorities. Newspapers aimed at a specific racial group within a
nation's citizenry were of course unknown in Britain, but
in the United States there were about 150 of them, and it
was their wide readership which created difficulties on
both sides of the Atlantic. For example, in 1944 it was
estimated that the black press had a circulation of over
1,600,000 with nearly half accounted for by sales of the top
five: the *Chicago Defender, Pittsburgh Courier, Norfolk
Journal and Guide, New York Amsterdam News, and Baltimore Afro-American.*

Initially the black press were critical of Britain as representing the worst of imperialism and the subjugation of
colonial peoples but as British treatment of black GIs began to be widely reported back in the USA this attitude
softened. So when Churchill parried Tom Driberg's questioning in Parliament late in September 1942, *Opportunity,* the journal of the National Urban League, reflected on
the state of race relations in Britain. In its January 1943
issue, using a boxing analogy, it argued that in round five
'Crow went down for a three count, but came back strong
and staggered Democracy (Churchill had no answer for
British discrimination)'.

The British Government was concerned about all American views on Britain, but there was particular anxiety
about black American perceptions. Of great significance,
therefore, was a proposal by Nevile Butler in 1942 that
special publicity be given to the British treatment of black

troops in the United Kingdom, stressing its divergence from the United States' line, in an attempt to win the approval of the black press. This flush of radicalism did not last long however. The plan was abandoned because of its potential political repercussions and one must assume (because the Foreign Office file has since been destroyed) that it would have annoyed many white Americans and in the climate of 1942 that was unacceptable.

As the war continued black papers became more and more delighted with the treatment of black GIs in Britain, and the liberal attitude of many British newspapers. Roi Ottley, a black writer who went overseas, even felt that it suggested 'the emergence of a new British policy on race'.[31] Some black journalists felt bold enough to question the British Government about its own troops. Michael Carter of the Afro-American newspapers asked Churchill eleven questions about blacks in the British Empire at the beginning of 1944. Among these were 'How many Negroes are in the British Armies? Do they operate in racially segregated units? May they become officers?' The letter was sent to the MOI for reply, who sent it in turn to the British Information Services in New York over two months later. As Walter White had discovered a couple of years earlier the British Government did not rush when answering such delicate matters![32]

For the American authorities the black newspapers presented a problem of different dimensions during the war. They were seen as either taking an anti-war stance, or as inflammatory, encouraging blacks to rebellion. Such was the concern that Archibald MacLeish of the Office of Facts and Figures, the forerunner of the OWI, called black editors together in early 1942 telling them to lay off the racial issue at least for the duration of the war. Military authorities were so concerned about this issue that G2, the Army Intelligence Section, suggested from time to time that certain black newspapers and journals be banned from Army posts. This did not become official policy but individual commanders did take such action on their own initiative. As with most racial difficulties in the Army, this problem surfaced in Britain. The Bamber Bridge incident was blamed in the official report partly on the *People's Voice*, a black journal. Publications like these, in attempting to champion the interests of black soldiers, would often indulge in aggressive speculation about the role of black Americans after the war; and they would not shrink from the delicate question of 'why should the coloured man fight the white man's battle?'

The *Chicago Defender*, the leading black newspaper, managed to raise hackles too when it reported the court martial which followed the Launceston affray in October 1943. Though it had sensational headlines, 'Pub Color Bar Results in Wild Shooting: Soldiers charge Military Cops Harass them in Town Bars', the piece was in fact fairly straight reporting. However, the *Defender* had already come to the notice of American military censors the previous July for articles about prejudice and what it called the 'shameful treatment' of black soldiers in Britain. The view of the examiner then was that journalism of this kind increased the difficulties of maintaining 'equable relations' between blacks and whites and caused a 'definite feeling of unrest among the colored troops'.[33]

Increasingly as the war went on many editors and publishers of black papers shared a willingness to cooperate with the authorities and began to check their stories more frequently with the Bureau of Public Relations or the Office of the Civilian Aide. To some, however, this was a sign of increasing censorship and papers published hints that they were not being allowed to tell the full story of racial troubles in Britain. As D-Day approached the system became even more rigorous and led to complaints such as that from the *Baltimore Afro-American* on 12 February 1944 that only 'sweet stories' were being approved and, as news of racial problems was being blocked, there was little further point in black war correspondents remaining in Britain.

The British Government's interest in the black American press was not the only evidence of its ongoing concern about the effect of the black GIs in Britain. Despite the earnest hopes of some officials that the deliberations and publications of 1942 had sewn up the racial problem as far as the British were concerned, the committees that were established by the Cabinet proved otherwise. Several of these had the subject of the black GIs on their agenda, and their comprehensive membership was a recognition by the Government that the problem had far-reaching implications.

Though there does not appear to have been a central committee coordinating its activities, the role of the British police was an interesting one. The policing of its troops was an American activity, indeed the Home Office had stated quite categorically from the start that Chief Constables were not to help establish the jim-crow system, but inevitably British police were drawn in. In the rural areas where blacks were located GIs took up most of the time of many 'bobbies' – they literally became official watchdogs.

Police authorities were asked to monitor race relations and conduct investigations, and the reports they produced were of great value to Home Intelligence, the Foreign Office's North American Department, and the Ministry of Information. As far as the black GIs were concerned Regional Police Headquarters were required to supply information under three headings: firstly, friction between white and black American troops; secondly, breaches of the peace caused by the fraternization of American troops (black and white) with British girls, and lastly, the particular association of black Americans with British women. Not all the reports sent to the ministries, of course, dealt with great philosophical and moral issues; one complaint about white British women associating with black soldiers was that they damaged growing crops!

Of the dozens of formal committees established during the war to control or monitor all aspects of life in Britain, four in particular spent some time looking at black American soldiers. The Anglo-American (Army) Relations Committee of August 1943 was charged with keeping an eye on relations between GIs and British troops and its members were drawn from the War Office and the American Army.

Looking at the relationships between the American

Forces and British *civilians* was the British-American
Liaison Board (BALB). Though its effectiveness was limited by its lateness (it was not established until early in
1944), its nominal members were powerful people. Representing the US Army, the War Office, The Foreign Office,
the American Embassy and the Ministry of Information
respectively were General J. C. Lee, Sir Ronald Adam,
Richard Law, John Winant and Brendan Bracken, all of
whom dealt almost daily with the ramifications of black
personnel in Britain. Janet Murrow, wife of the American
broadcaster, was one of the secretariat. Much of the
BALB's work was left to junior officials like Herbert Agar
of the US Embassy, and Alan Dudley of the Foreign Office,
but it did have much to do with black GIs. It commissioned
reports, investigated racial disturbances, looked at the
'brown baby problem' and sent information to the Foreign
Office and elsewhere. Inevitably in the light of the departments represented on it, BALB was essentially a conservative body, and never quite fulfilled the hopes that Walter
White, for one, had for it.

In terms of the post-war world and Britain's relationships with black members of its Empire, as well as its
association with America, two other committees were of
greater importance. Both were interested in the question of
how black Americans viewed Britain, and how this
affected the perceptions and outlook of black citizens of the
British Empire. A few politicians at least realized that
these issues might have some long-term significance.

A growing number of Colonial blacks came to Britain
during the war and consequently in August 1942 the
Advisory Committee for the Welfare of Colonial People in
the United Kingdom was established. It had wide terms of
reference, and doubtless looked at the question of black GIs
given that three of its members were Harold Moody of the
League of Coloured Peoples, J. L. Keith of the Colonial
Office and left-wing Labour MP Reginald Sorensen.

A few months later, near the end of 1942, anxiety about
American attitudes towards the British gave birth to the
Committee on American Opinion and the British Empire.
There was a growing fear in government circles that the

US would be a difficult and irritating ally after the war if it kept talking about colonial freedom. As Churchill reminded Roosevelt on several occasions, he was not fighting for the dissolution of the British Empire. The presence of the black GIs in Britain put the whole matter into sharp focus though whichever way the Government reacted to them was certain to upset some American interest groups.

As a result of these considerations the Director General of the Ministry of Information suggested a committee to monitor American opinion about the Empire, both favourable and hostile. Though it was not said in so many words the fact that the black press in America held strong views on this subject, and were also watching closely the treatment of black GIs in Britain, was doubtless at the back of some politicians' minds. Nevile Butler of the Foreign Office was not enamoured of the idea; he thought the committee a sop to prevent Wendell Willkie, the defeated presidential candidate of 1940, from becoming a rabid anti-imperialist.

The committee was chaired by Richard Law, MP, of the Foreign Office, and among the other members were Colonel Rowe of the War Office, and F. E. Evans of the Foreign Office, both of whom had attended the important Bolero meeting on black GIs in August 1942. Also on the committee were Sir George Gater of the Colonial Office, and Alan Dudley of the Foreign Office, two other men whose work brought them constantly up against the problem of race relations in Britain. It was significant that a large part of the first meeting of 30 December 1942 was spent discussing the presence in Britain of the black Americans. Two questions arose which were deemed vital to Anglo-American relations. Both Gater and Rowe thought that it might be instructive to tell the Americans to respect black *British* citizens, whatever they did about their own. Such a suggestion was a dead letter, however, having been deliberately omitted by the Cabinet a few months earlier for fear it might upset the Americans. The other issue was that white GIs 'were likely', according to Rowe, 'to be jealous of British good treatment of coloured troops'.[34]

As some observers had forecast, that likelihood quickly became a reality. Many of the British people gave practical

vent to their feeling that the black soldier was an underdog, protesting physically and verbally at the perceived
injustice he suffered at the hands of his white compatriots.
In short the attitude of the British public was probably the
most effective racial watchdog of the lot . . . and the one
that caused most concern to British and American authorities.

British citizens were often drawn into the disputes between black and white Americans by being in a pub or
restaurant at the wrong time, often with tragic results as
the Kingsclere incident showed. On other occasions the
British took part wittingly. At the height of the Bristol
incident, for example, civilians were encouraging the black
GIs to resist the military police when they were being
taken to the Tram Centre. At about the same time in
Bristol, and doubtless there were other cases elsewhere, a
28-year-old woman was fined £2. 10s. 0d. for behaving in a
disorderly manner, using obscene language and assaulting
an American military policeman. She was coming down
Brandon Hill with a black GI and, spotting an MP trying to
arrest three other blacks, she swore and struck him in the
chest. According to the British–American Liaison Board
civilians in the city were upset because MPs always
approached blacks with their truncheons in the attack
position, but never whites in this way. This was because,
the members of the Board were told, blacks were more
likely to attack MPs with knives.

There were other incidents too. In July 1943 a group of
MPs at Cosham, near Portsmouth, to the disgust of watching civilians, tried to disperse a group of black GIs after the
pubs had closed. A few weeks later there was a similar
occurrence at East Tytherley near Salisbury, an area
where blacks were based in several small towns and villages. Three white US officers and one ATS girl arrived at
a pub in a US Army car driven by a black GI. At closing
time one of the officers ordered the driver to hand over the
key and walk home. The soldier refused and there was a
scuffle, with the sympathies of the civilian onlookers again
entirely with the black American.

Despite General Eisenhower's early pronouncements

that it was no business of the US authorities how Britain treated the black GIs, the American authorities were resentful at what they saw as the 'spoiling of the negroes'. Part of the blame for the Bamber Bridge incident was laid on the host population according to the official report: 'A substantial portion of the British military and civil population treat the negro soldier on the basis of social equality. The white American soldier, on the other hand, treats the negro soldier exactly as he has treated him in the United States, refusing, in many instances, to recognize social equality, and frequently demanding segregation. This difference obviously created conflicts'. The Americans did not want to be rude to their hosts but what they were saying in a nutshell was that 'things wouldn't be so bad if the English didn't egg the Negro on!'[35]

After the Launceston and Bamber Bridge incidents there were questions about black GI behaviour and how much the British were involved. It was this kind of discussion which brought Winston Churchill back into the picture. Towards the end of October 1943 the Prime Minister received a visit from a relative, the Duke of Marlborough. Marlborough, John Albert Edward William Spencer-Churchill, went to see his cousin because he was disturbed at what he saw as the behaviour of the black troops in Britain. He considered it such an important issue that he felt duty-bound to bring it to the Prime Minister's attention. For part of 1942 Marlborough was the military liaison officer to the Regional Commander of the Southern Region and in this capacity no doubt had discussions with General Dowler, also in that area, and the Regional Commissioner, Harry Haig. Neither mentor was likely to have exercised a liberal influence on the Duke. Sometime in 1942 he became a liaison officer with the rank of Lieutenant Colonel, actually attached to the American forces, a post he held until the end of the war, and in August 1943 he became a member of the Anglo-American (Army) Relations Committee.

Much of Marlborough's concern was about the sexual angle of the black presence but, as a result of their conversation, the Prime Minister asked not only the Duke, but

P. J. Grigg, Secretary of State for War, a series of questions
about the black GIs. This he did either to play one adviser
off against the other or because Marlborough's position as
an impartial liaison officer would have been jeopardized if
he were seen to be blaming all Britain's ills on the black
GI. The net result, whatever the reason, was that Churchill stressed that the Duke's name was to be kept out of all
discussions on this issue.

Grigg had known the Prime Minister for some time,
working closely with him in the years 1924 to 1929 when
Churchill, who regarded him as one of Britain's finest civil
servants, was Chancellor of the Exchequer and Grigg was
the Principal Private Secretary. Translated from the post
of Permanent Under-Secretary at the War Office in 1939 to
that of Secretary of State for War by Churchill in February
1942, he fought and won the East Cardiff Parliamentary
seat as a Nationalist and retained it until 1945. He had a
reputation in the 1920s for being arrogant and intolerant
and certainly he was not popular with the Foreign Office
during the war. 'One might as well argue with a stone wall'
said Alexander Cadogan, the witty, urbane Permanent
Under-Secretary, in the middle of 1943. Grigg's views on
race were well-known in Whitehall too. Preparing a Commons' reply to a question about the black Americans,
Nevile Butler was wary of asking for the War Office line
because the Secretary of State 'might be tempted to get in a
jibe!'[36]

Sharing Marlborough's concerns and anxious to please
Churchill, Grigg's replies to the Prime Minister's questions
came the day after they were asked. The Secretary of State
for War was not quite so exercised as the Duke about black
behaviour (indeed both admitted that there had been few
complaints), as he was about the attitude of the locals. His
staff, he said, were 'much perturbed by the behaviour, on
occasions, of the British civil population, and in particular,
of some sections of the female population'. That Grigg's
views had hardened considerably on the issue became clear
from one of his conclusions:

> I expect that the British soldier who fears for the safety or
> faithfulness of his women-folk at home would not feel so

keenly as the BBC and the public at home appear to do in favour of a policy of no colour bar and complete equality of treatment of negro troops.

He argued that 'grave mischief' was being done to Anglo-American relations by these pro-black British sentiments. To solve that problem the country might have to face, he contended, the 'question of changing our attitude towards the colour question'.[37]

Both Churchill's informants seemed to be obsessed with the sexual issue. Though Marlborough conceded that there was no proof that it had been given to British women he reported that black troops possessed marijuana which taken 'in large quantities' could prove 'fatal'. 'If given to women,' he continued, 'it could excite their sexual desires either as a cigarette or ground up in food.'[38] Grigg discovered that black GIs committed fewer crimes proportionately than whites in relation to offences of dishonesty or drunkenness, but had twice as high a rate of sexual offences, and five times as high a rate in connection with crimes of violence. Ever simplistic the Secretary for War found a neat answer for this: 'The trouble is due,' he maintained, 'to the natural propensities of the coloured man rather than the effects of drink'![39]

Neither Grigg nor Marlborough seemed perturbed about another statistic. This was that in proportion to their numbers more blacks than whites were being held in detention in Britain, and that for similar offences blacks received longer and harsher sentences than their white compatriots. Though they had no access to this data, some Britons had the gut feeling that this was so, particularly in relation to the offence of rape. If there seemed a scant opportunity to influence the trials of black GIs in Britain when mass rebellion was involved, the pursuit of justice by British public opinion when individual black soldiers appeared to be on the receiving end of racial discrimination made it a very effective watchdog.

An extraordinary piece of legislation came into existence on Thursday 6 August 1942. This was the United States of

America (Visiting Forces) Act, and by it the British gave
the United States authorities exclusive criminal jurisdic-
tion over members of their armed forces. In short American
soldiers who committed criminal offences were to be tried
by American military tribunals according to United States
Law. The measure was passed through both Houses fairly
easily, too easily remarked the *Economist*, just as if 'it had
been providing drains for a municipality'. There was some
anti-Americanism expressed but ironically most debate
centred on whether American laws were severe enough. In
fact article 92 of the American military code specified that
rape carried a sentence of death or imprisonment for life.
From about 1943 it was this issue which gave the British
cause for concern: in particular the feeling grew that the
law was being applied much more rigorously to black GIs.

It seems likely that public consciousness about black
Americans and the law was raised by the particular case of
Joseph Ballot. Ballot was arrested for the alleged molesta-
tion of a girl in Portsmouth. His court martial revealed
that the girl had received injuries only to her face but that
neither the girl nor a policeman who was a critical witness
identified Ballot. He nevertheless received a life sentence
for rape. Although the sentence was later reduced to a
twenty-year term, a white sailor had just received only ten
years for a similar offence.

Though little change had been effected the airing of the
issue in public encouraged Members of Parliament to take
up the question of whether rape was a capital offence only
when committed by black GIs. It was raised several times
in 1944 with several Labour MPs to the fore – William
Leach, Rhys Davis, Francis Bowles, Dr Haden-Guest and
Richard Stokes – as well as Hugh Lawson, a young ex-
serviceman from the Common Wealth Party. The debates
on black Americans in the Commons were inconclusive but
they caused anxious behind-the-scenes activity at the British–American Liaison Board and drew comments from the
public. A Methodist minister from Cornwall implied that if
blacks were executed for rape when whites weren't, then
the USA was not a particularly valuable ally. He wanted
Eden to point out to Eisenhower what a terrible blow this

would be to Anglo-American friendship.

It was the Leroy Henry rape case in Bath (see pp. 1–4) which was arguably the most widely publicized and discussed single incident during the whole American presence in Britain. It is a case study of how the public, press and some politicians brought pressure to bear on a single issue and were instrumental in righting a wrong, though it was much to the chagrin of the US officials.

Henry was found guilty of rape at his trial on 25 May 1944, and it was the popular tabloid, the *Daily Mirror* that was responsible for bringing the case to the attention of a wider public. On 2 June the newspaper reported that it had received a large number of letters revealing unease, especially when there seemed such reasonable doubt about the guilt of a black man whose real crime may have been the colour of his skin.

Writing in his personal diary the next day, Cecil King, who was responsible for the *Mirror*'s political policy, was forthright about the case:

> This feeling is fairly common – that the negroes are nicer and better behaved than the ordinary Yank. So there is some indignation when negro soldiers are condemned to death for raping English girls. In the most recent case the evidence would certainly have resulted in an acquittal in an English court. In the far more numerous cases of rape or murder by white American soldiers, the punishment, if any, is of a wholly different order of severity.[40]

A few days later the Home Intelligence Report talked of growing public concern, particularly in the south-west. From that point matters proceeded apace. The NAACP cabled Eisenhower on 3 June requesting a stay of execution and an opportunity to review the court martial record in this case. Events began to take a more positive turn for Henry after the League of Coloured Peoples sent a diplomatically restrained plea to Eisenhower on 9 June. Eisenhower replied swiftly, aware of the controversy and publicity surrounding this case. He promised to investigate, and felt confident the verdict would be overturned. On 19 June came an announcement from the American military headquarters that Eisenhower had disapproved of the guilty verdict due to insufficient evidence. Henry was restored to normal duties soon after.

Though this decision was welcomed and Eisenhower himself was given credit for his swift action, the whole affair had wider implications. It had been responsible for bringing together a coalition of interests to act as a pressure group and this had earned the British renewed praise in some parts of black America. In addition, perhaps belatedly, it had made officials search diligently for the facts about blacks and their treatment in the US military courts.

The Henry episode closed on 24 June 1944 with the publication of another article in the *New Statesman* which Herbert Agar of the American Embassy had persuaded editor Kingsley Martin to include. 'It is often asserted,' it was argued, 'that in the American army in Britain only Negroes are sentenced to death or executed for rape. This is, I understand, quite untrue . . . If, as seems to be the case, the Army authorities here are in fact doing their best to obtain race equality within the American Army overseas, the sooner the facts are known the better for all parties'.

These facts, if known with any accuracy, were certainly never made public in Britain during the war. They would, if the figures for the whole of the ETO are a guide, have raised many eyebrows. One study revealed that by the time of victory over Japan in 1945 blacks constituted 8 per cent of the personnel in the European Theatre but 21 per cent of convicted American servicemen. Moreover 42 per cent of those convicted of sex crimes and 35 per cent of those convicted of certain crimes of violence were black GIs.

Black Americans had reason to be grateful to the press and public in Britain for keeping an eye on racial injustice in the war years. Despite all the adverse comments British affections remained pretty constant. While the behaviour of black troops often caused annoyance among Britons, the attitude of white Americans towards their black compatriots often caused downright anger. The problem of sex, however, was the one issue which nearly destroyed the whole balance.

8

'No Mother, No Father, No Uncle Sam': Sex and Brown Babies

The soft West Country accents of Leon York in Somerset and Jody Bryant in Dorset would indicate that both were natives of southern England; and so they are. Similarly, Abertillery's Ann Evans has the distinctive tones of a woman from South Wales, which is where she comes from. All three are black. Like the children of so many West Indian immigrants their speech and lifestyles vary little from their British neighbours, but Leon, Jody and Ann are members of an exclusive but little-known group. They are the most tangible legacy of the presence of GIs in Britain during the Second World War – their fathers were black Americans and their mothers were local white women.

Almost as soon as the black GIs stepped on to British soil many commentators knew that their sexual relations with white women would be the most volatile factor in their temporary stay. Children came quickly but solutions didn't: Britain was long on moralizing, short on answers.

Probably the most popular epithet about black and white Americans in wartime Britain was that they were 'overpaid, over-fed, over-sexed and over here'. It is this sexual dimension which provided the backdrop for almost all the concern expressed about the GIs on the home front, particularly the blacks. As their World War I experiences in France had shown, the fears of miscegenation, rape and venereal disease were paramount. These fears emerged again in Britain in the 1940s, though many were expressed implicitly rather than explicitly. Despite private and public pressures, however, British women did have sexual relations with the black Americans and even married some of them.

The near-universal hostility towards interracial sexual relations in Britain before and during the war varied only in the vehemence of its expression. It cut across all shades of political opinion and class to such an extent that it was accepted as a fact of life that needed little or no explanation. Thus Major General Dowler's Notes of August 1942 which led to Cabinet discussions in the following October did not spell out the difficulties, merely the solution. In the United States, he argued, the racial problem 'demands that the white man or woman does not intimately associate with the coloured man' and it was his view that the same situation should prevail in Britain. In varying degrees he was supported by Cripps, Grigg and Morrison in the debates of 1942.[1]

It is clear, then, that for whatever reason there was grave official anxiety about the possibility of sexual relations taking place between British women and black Americans. Hence, as we have seen, three solutions were put forward in an attempt to avoid what was perceived as a social evil: firstly there were attempts to stop blacks coming to Britain at all, or to limit their numbers if a total ban was not possible; secondly if they were of necessity to come it was suggested that they should be restricted to certain geographical areas of the country; finally it was argued that if black American female personnel could be brought to Britain to serve in various capacities the soldiers' sexual urges could be directed to women of their own race. All three policies were given serious consideration by British and American authorities but all three foundered.

Anthony Eden was most concerned about the presence of black soldiers in Britain, and it was he who was most energetic in trying to stop them coming. By September

1942 it was clear that this policy had failed. It was ironic therefore that it was the Foreign Secretary who found himself fielding questions on the sexual dimension of the black presence in the country. Amongst those who offered the most vitriolic advice to Eden was one of his Conservative Party colleagues, Maurice Petherick, the member for Penryn and Falmouth and a post-war high sheriff of Cornwall. Petherick was to claim later that many of his constituents felt as he did about the blacks. This may well have been true but it is certain that the first of the three letters[2] that he sent to the Foreign Secretary, on 16 August 1942, was the most circumspect of them. He wondered whether Eden had stood up to the Americans to try to stop the black soldiers coming in, an event which had 'alarmed and horrified' many people. He advanced several reasons for this course of action, all centred on the sexual issue.

1.   They will quite obviously consort with white girls and there will be a number of half-caste babies about when they have gone – a bad thing for any country.

2.   Not knowing that the girls who go with them are the lowest of the low it will give them a bad opinion of Englishwomen.

3.   It will upset the local populations when this occurs.

4.   It will frighten the men from these parts who are serving abroad as it did the French soldiers in the last war.

5.   Why not send them to other parts where they will be much more suitable – say the Solomon Islands or Egypt?

Petherick contacted the Foreign Office again in the middle of July 1943. He now wondered whether the Foreign Secretary could 'arrange with the American Government to send [the blacks] to North Africa, or to go and fertilize the Italians who are used to it anyhow?' Six months later, Petherick was still badgering Eden. In December 1943 he complained that considerable numbers of blacks had been sent to his own constituency, adding, 'I hope it was not deliberate'. The sexual worry was still to the fore: 'as in other parts of England women of the lowest order are consorting with the blackamoors. There is very strong feeling about this . . . Surely we are in a strong enough position to stand up to the USA . . . and tell them we will not have any more black troops here and ask them to send those we have to North Africa, where poor devils, they would be much more happy and warm'.

Unlike Petherick, most observers realized at an early stage that the black Americans would be in Britain for the duration of the war. Politicians reasoned therefore that if sexual contacts with the indigenous women were to cause the least anxiety, methods of controlling them would have to be found. Out of this came the suggestion that the incoming black troops should be based in port areas where the mixing of races and colours would be more acceptable. It seemed an easy answer to the problem and one which on the surface did not appear to be discriminatory, though in truth it was both impractical and naive.

The first reference to the plan seems to have been on 10 August 1942 when it was mentioned at a War Cabinet meeting. Brendan Bracken discussed the arrangements his Ministry was making to welcome the American troops, but in view of the difficulties associated with black GIs he reported that Eisenhower was going to segregate them in some areas. James P. Warburg of the US Information Services in Britain met Arthur Sulzberger of the *New York Times* in England in 1942, and found him a vigorous promoter of the special areas idea. Though Warburg did not agree with this he sent the suggestions, laced with discreet sexual references, on to Elmer Davis, his political boss in Washington:

> Colored troops should be moved out of rural areas and concentrated in ports like Liverpool . . . rural populations, which have had no experience with foreigners, let alone colored people, particularly the girls, do not know how to take the negroes and, as a matter of fact, are very much attracted by them . . . In the ports . . . where people are used to all kinds of foreigners, including negroes, there is not so much danger. Sulzberger seems to be very much afraid that if this is not done, nine months from now there will be a very serious problem.[3]

On his return to the US Sulzberger met Secretary Stimson, who had already been alerted to the racial difficulties in Britain by Eleanor Roosevelt. Apparently Stimson was warm to the idea, as was Franklin Roosevelt when he was acquainted with it at the beginning of October, and the Chief of Staff at SOS Headquarters whom Sulzberger also contacted. However, that appears to have been the end of the idea which was unrealistic in any case as black troops were needed all over Britain in many capacities. Moreover as the West Indian experience of racial difficulties in Liverpool showed, the corollary of the suggestion would have required white American troops to be placed well *outside* port areas to ensure racial harmony, and this was another logistical non-starter.

The third proposal for alleviating the prospective interracial sexual problem was given more serious consideration, and was made on several occasions during the war. This was to station black members of the Women's Army Auxiliary Corps (which became the Women's Army Corps, WAC, in the middle of 1943) in Britain, the idea being that if black soldiers had women of their own race to associate with, they would leave white women alone. Chaplain Edwin R. Carter, jun., who worked with the Services of Supply, stated more subtly the consequence of *not* having any black women in the European Theatre:

> Through no fault of his own the negro finds himself in an environment in which if he is to have any form of social life, other than that in his camp proper, it must be with members of the white race . . . There will be the gratification of the sexual urge in the life of the vast majority. The gratification of this urge can only be found, and will be found under the present conditions among members of the white race.[4]

Carter suggested that black women personnel be brought in from America to work as hostesses in service clubs, waitresses, stenographers and so on.

Many black soldiers would have liked more women of their own race in Britain. 'I am tired of this place', one soldier wrote home wearily. 'If I could see some colored girls I would feel better. I am sick of these fay broads they are no good but do [due] to nature I have to put up with them'. To a black master sergeant the lack of women of his own race seemed to be yet another blatant example of Army discrimination: 'one sees white nurses, white Waacs, white Red Cross workers,' he wrote, 'but no colored with the exception of three Red Cross workers during my ten months overseas'.[5] In fact some 130 black nurses and Red Cross women served in Britain, while there were 130,000 black GIs in the country.

Both British and American officials were confident in 1942 that black women would serve in Britain in some guise or other. Ronald Campbell cabled the Foreign Office from Washington on 12 August 1942 saying that ATS units were being organized 'largely in order to ease the situation by giving coloured troops women of [their] own race with whom they can associate'. John Winant reported to President Roosevelt that the 'question of Negro troops and the problems involved keeps cropping up. You are probably aware of General Eisenhower's recommendation to send a contingent of colored WAACS. I think this is a good idea'.[6]

In fact, Eisenhower went so far as to announce in London that WAACs would be sent to England for driving and secretarial work after completion of their training in Iowa.

President Roosevelt's intervention, however, firmly scotched any hopes of sending black servicewomen over. Breezily he told Winant that the dispatch of black WAAC units to England had been deferred for the present, that General Eisenhower had withdrawn his recommendation, and that the entire question was still being studied in the War Department.

Why was there a sudden change of heart? The answer certainly lies in Roosevelt's political need to protect his relations with the black establishment in the US. The black leaders had vigorously opposed sending black WAAC units to Britain. To the NAACP the idea that the black WAACs were being trained to entertain soldiers was abhorrent. Walter White, Judge Hastie, the civilian aide, and his assistant Truman Gibson had insisted that the women be permitted to serve in the capacities for which they had been recruited, and believed that to send over black women principally for the purpose of companionship would discredit the WAAC. Colonel Oveta Culp Hobby took their advice and rejected the requisition for black WAACs to be sent to the European Theatre.

There were others who advanced equally strong views against the employment of black women in Britain but for totally different reasons. Chaplain Horne, a black American based in Bristol (and seen by those in authority as somewhat radical), felt that to bring black women over for the companionship of black men was giving in to the segregation that was already being established in Britain. Still others had misgivings about the possibility of white men associating with black women.

The debate about black female personnel was a crucial one, but effectively all the discussions came to no avail. Though the ETO was the only theatre to employ black WAACs, this did not happen until early 1945 when the 6888th Central Postal Battalion, with about 800 women, came to Birmingham. Logistically, at least in terms of those who saw the women in a companionship role, the whole idea was impractical: how many women would have been needed to 'entertain' over 100,000 black GIs who were in Britain during the war?

It was evident by the end of 1942 that considerable numbers of black American troops were going to be used in Britain, and equally evident that unless this army was going to be extraordinarily celibate, sexual relations were going to take place between black men and white women. It was already manifest that such relations were anathema to many Britons as well as white Americans, so what advice on the sexual question, then, was offered by the authorities of the two allies?

Though, of course, all of its measures were secret the British Government adopted what may be termed overt and covert approaches to the question of black Americans and British women. In general terms it spent more time concerning itself with the reactions of the military, particularly the WAACs, to this issue. This may well have been because the debate was initiated by the Army and in any case more control could be exercised over service personnel. Civilians were not *directly* told how to behave towards the black Americans – such a policy could become dangerously public as some ministers realized – but there was advice to those in the armed forces. Dowler's words of caution on the sexual issue were echoed in the Cabinet's deliberations on 20 October 1942. What was said, bluntly, was that English women should stay away from black GIs. The intention was always clear, even when the language was more circumspect. Friendship with whites in Britain, wrote the journal *Current Affairs* on 5 December, would be new and unexpected because 'such contacts are not frequently made in his home country'. Hence 'great care should be exercised over here'.

Advice to civilians was of necessity more subtle, though here again constant checks were made on the situation. In September 1942 the Home Office warned all chief constables that difficulties might be caused by black soldiers associating both with other troops and with civilians, especially white women. As we have seen, one result of this directive was that police in the regions constantly monitored relations between the black GIs and British women. Some local police constabularies even contemplated prosecutions to prevent black soldiers and white women from mixing with one another.

These methods of warning off British girls from the black Americans were of course very limited and the covert approaches made by the Government on this issue are more interesting. On 12 August 1942, the important Bolero Committee devoted a special session to the black GIs. It was General Venning, the Quartermaster General to the Forces, who raised the sexual bogey. Venning argued that there were three difficulties which would arise if British women associated with black GIs. It appeared to present a no-win situation. In the first place there was concern about the repercussions on American opinion if

British women acted in a way 'which Americans by their up-bringing, could only regard as grossly immoral'. By contrast the effect on British opinion of 'the undemocratic American attitude to the colour problem' had to be considered. Lastly there was the 'effect on the morale of British soldiers if they heard reports that the white women at home were associating with coloured men'.

Someone, the minutes do not make clear who, then wondered whether 'an open statement on the danger of venereal disease' would deter British women from associating with the blacks. The Foreign Office representative said he would not countenance this move which progressive elements in the USA would regard as a slander on blacks, and apparently Eden had already said this to Grigg. The overt policy having been rejected, someone, and again the minutes of the meeting do not make it clear who it was, suggested a 'whispering campaign' along the same lines. Once more this met with a frosty response from F. E. Evans of the Foreign Office.[7]

Despite these decisions it is likely that a programme of rumour-spreading about the black GIs *was* started. A couple of weeks after the meeting John Keith of the Colonial Office reported that there had been a 'considerable whispering campaign emanating to some extent from Lady Reading's organization of the WVS against the association of white women with coloured men'. Moreover Keith's two impeccable sources were 'Judge' Parker, who had been at the Bolero meetings, and Gervase Huxley, both of them senior officials at the Ministry of Information.[8] These accounts were supported by Home Intelligence weekly reports. On 27 August 1942 came a story, naming the BBC as one originator of it, that the WVS had been told not to entertain black GIs in private houses 'owing to the prevalence among them of venereal disease'. In the middle of September reports came in that strong views had been expressed about 'certain leaders of women's opinion' because of a 'whispering campaign in favour of the colour bar'.[9] Certainly the establishment by the WVS of the segregated Silver Birch Clubs for black Americans later in the war was a logical extension of this covert operation.

From early 1944 a similar campaign, this time in local newspapers, was begun to deter British women from associating with black American soldiers. The method was to brand women who did seek out the company of blacks as collaborators, and again as with the VD campaign there appears to have been some official sanction for this policy. Usually the offences with which British girls were charged were trespassing on government property, or the breaking of curfew regulations, but no opportunities were missed to mention that black troops were in some way connected. A report came from Shropshire, for example, where there were considerable numbers of black Americans, that two girls were sent to prison for 'sleeping out without giving a good account of themselves'. A police reservist stated in court that the two girls were found with '12 coloured American troops'. Sometimes the coloured angle, though not of relevance to the offence, was part of the headline of newspaper stories. Thus when three Wolverhampton 15-year-olds were found guilty of trespass, the report in the *Wellington Journal and Shrewsbury News* of 30 September 1944 began, '3 young girls found in military hut, one with coloured man'. There was, by and large, general official approval for reporting of this nature – 'suitable but restrained publicity' for this kind of disciplinary action might allay the 'local inhabitants' apprehension' noted the British–American Liaison Board in May 1944.[10] Journalism in this vein continued.

The US Army's attitude to the prospect of its black soldiers having sexual relations with white British women provided another of the home front's nice ironies. In general the Army's advice to the soldiers was that interracial dating was bound to take place and they were to tolerate this. Thus while the British were cautioning citizens not to become too friendly with the blacks because that would not happen in the United States, and to defer to the American attitude, the American Army command was saying that black/white associations must be respected because they were going to happen in Britain!

Insofar as there was a basic instruction to American troops on the social issue it was Eisenhower's letter to General Lee of 5 September 1942 which said that everyone in the European Theatre must recognize that interracial relationships would take place on 'a basis mutually acceptable to the individuals concerned' and there must be no official attempt to curtail this. Lee was to ensure that this was transmitted to every officer in the theatre, and there is no doubt that many conscientious officers made sure the message, unpalatable to many though it was, went right down the line.[11] If black and white liaisons were tolerated in Britain, the Army authorities were anxious that this image should not be for export. Sometime in the second half of 1943 *Life* magazine showed pictures of black soldiers in London night clubs dancing with white girls. This was regarded as 'material . . . calculating to unduly inflame racial prejudice both overseas and in UNITED STATES [*sic*]'. The result was a War Department censorship regulation prohibiting the passing for any purposes of amateur photographs 'showing negro soldiers in poses of intimacy with white women or conveying "boy friend–girl friend" implications'. On 7 March 1945 because of the 'vigorous protest' in Europe Eisenhower requested that this ban be lifted for such photographs intended for the soldiers' personal use as opposed to those meant for publication.[12]

Despite all the prohibitions, white girls did go out with black soldiers, and these relationships had important repercussions. Arguably it was the most explosive aspect of the American presence, with four consequences all closely linked to each other. In the first place it was a major cause of the disturbances between black and white Americans, some of which resulted in deaths. Secondly, it affected British attitudes towards the blacks: most disliked the miscegenation they saw. Thirdly, females were largely blamed for 'chasing' the blacks and consequently British and white American opinions of British women were influenced. Lastly, there were several hundred illegitimate 'brown babies' born to English mothers, a problem which remained unsolved for some time in the post-war period.

The disturbances at Leicester and Bristol indicated that sexual rivalry was a major reason, if not *the* major reason, for the clashes between black and white Americans, and this scenario was repeated in varying degrees up and down the country. Black women being few in number, all GIs were competing for the favours of a finite number of white women in Britain. That this would cause trouble was obvious at an early stage in the American presence. Professor Gilbert Murray, an Oxford don and a member of the BBC's 'Brains Trust', reported at the end of June 1942 that American whites were 'taking a threatening attitude' towards the blacks and were talking of 'lynching any whom they find dancing with white girls'. Murray went on to note that an 'American colonel said in so many words that the great ambition of every one of these blacks was to rape a white woman!'[13]

The words of the white soldiers themselves shed some light on the depth of feeling. From Northern Ireland a quartermaster corporal forecast trouble:

> It seems that several outfits of colored troops preceded us over here and have succeeded pretty well in salting away the local feminine pulchritude . . . the girls really go for them in preference to the white boys, a fact that irks the boys no end, especially those of the outfit that come from the north. No doubt there will be some bloodshed in the near future.

Sheer gut response seems to have been the principal driving force of the white soldiers' outrage. 'I've seen nice looking English girls out with American Negro soldiers as black as the ace of spades', wrote a first lieutenant from Wellingborough. 'I have not only seen the Negro boys dancing with white girls, but we have actually seen them standing in doorways *kissing the girls goodnight*'.[14] On occasions white vehemence went hand in hand with popular mythology in an attempt to rationalize why the blacks got on so well with the locals: 'The lower classes of white girls . . . seem to prefer the coloured troops to white. "The good Lord was extra kind to the negro – so they say".' A member of a military police battalion in Liverpool did not mince words: 'Honey you should see how the "old women" like to go around with negroes here. Perhaps they like to go around with them because they have immense Penises.'[15]

British civilians were not immune to the rumours and reports of the sexual activity of the black GIs, especially in view of the likely principal stereotype about black people that was held in Britain at that time, namely that blacks were less sexually inhibited and capable of giving greater sexual satisfaction than white men. This attitude was typified by a civilian from Leamington Spa who felt in June 1944 that it was 'horrible to see the white girls running round with the blacks but they do say once a black never a white, don't they?' A local fellow in Somerset was even blunter. His view, when he witnessed girls looking into a black GI camp, was that these maids 'prick-mazed they be, prick-mazed'.[16]

In broad terms blacks were welcomed and liked in Britain during the war years. The one exception to this general pattern was when the sexual factor came to the fore. What is of interest, however, is that few people saw any intellectual gulf between their broad acceptance of blacks and their particular dislike of miscegenation. The implication is that separation between the races at the sexual level was the accepted norm of society and this could therefore be totally detached from the other aspects of black behaviour. The popular view was that blacks, especially in view of their part in the war effort, could be accepted by whites as brothers but never as spouses.

Concern about the racial problem continued in high places throughout the war. Harry Haig, the Southern Regional Commissioner, felt strongly enough about black troops and promiscuity to meet Herbert Morrison and Frank Newsam at the Home Office in November 1943 when he expressed anxiety that 'coloured troops were inclined to misconstrue ordinary politeness shown to them by English women'. The Home Secretary's response was to blame the American authorities who had considered it 'politically necessary that a reasonable proportion of coloured troops should be sent to this country'.[17] Comparable views emerged when Winston Churchill renewed his interest in the black Americans in the autumn of 1943. His correspondence with the Duke of Marlborough and James Grigg revealed concerns about VD, brown babies and rape. The War Minister reported to the Premier that some of the cases of association were because white women were sympathetic to the black soldiers but others were 'of a far more mundane and vicious nature' and called for measures 'more stringent than education'.[18]

It is important to remember at this point that white GIs were far more numerous in Britain than the blacks and that there was plenty of criticism of their sexual behaviour too; but most concern did settle on the black perspective of the problem. Home Intelligence reports verified this as did the Mass Observation survey of August 1943, which revealed that one in seven people disapproved of mixed marriages even though about 25 per cent of observers had become more friendly towards blacks, partly as a result of meeting American troops.

It was at this point that the British did a little more intellectual side-stepping, albeit unconsciously. Even the sternest critics thought the blacks in Britain were 'behaving well', were aware that there were few black women in Britain, and could see that some of the rape cases raised a lot of doubts. Almost as if to dissociate the blacks from charges of sexual extravagance and keep their records clean, the British now began to pin the responsibility for the sexual liaisons on to British women. They were only happening, was the implicit argument, because women of all ages were relentlessly pursuing the black GIs. The Ministry of Information reported 'furtive tales of sexual excesses . . . Young irresponsible girls from homes where there is little parental control are said to find coloured men tremendously fascinating and frequently accost them'.[19] Whether this was true was immaterial but clearly this attempt at understanding the situation rebounded to the blacks' disadvantage. Under pressure British girls began to drop their black boyfriends.

It is interesting here to turn from the general to the particular and return to the men of the black ordnance aviation company at Scout Dyke Army Base in the West Riding of Yorkshire. They did find at least their wine and women in Huddersfield and a discussion about this opened up in the local paper, the *Huddersfield Examiner*.[20] The correspondence would be quite remarkable even today but its frankness in times of war was refreshing at the very least. It is worth quoting at length because of the many issues related to the black American presence in Britain which were raised. The debate began on Monday 20 September 1943 after the publication of an article about the conduct of a 'small minority' of local girls. They were allegedly having sex with the black GIs – in shop doorways, quiet streets, open spaces and in vehicles drawn up alongside the pavements. After the investigation the reporter concluded that 'if blame is to be attached anywhere it should not be put on the shoulders of our coloured guests . . . the main responsibility lies with a small fraction of misguided young women in Huddersfield, some of them, I am sorry to say, nothing more than unscrupulous sponging "gold diggers" '. A Josephine Rickett rushed to the defence of her young Yorkshire contemporaries:

> The negro soldiers, though as a rule well-behaved, do whistle after our girls, stop them in the street, speak to them as they walk through the town, and invite them to go for drinks. Some (please note only some) of the girls tempted by the large quantity of money possessed by these negroes (as compared to our own troops) have agreed and gone for drinks with them. This, agreed, is not always the case but it could be that these girls are afraid of offending the negroes . . . they are taught in the church to treat the negroes exactly as they treat our own people. They are told to be friendly toward the negro soldier, and yet when they go out with them, they invoke a torrent of abuse from all quarters . . . If these [black] men are not strong enough to resist the wiles and temptations of mere children, then, they are not fit to fight for this country against the most desperate enemy she ever had.

One of the black GIs responded at length to the debate,

demonstrating just how alien a place he had found England. Half a crown, he admitted, was a cheap price for a double scotch and girls could be tempted by this, but it was the fact that the pubs seemed so central to all entertainment that puzzled this GI.

> We do not criticise your local 'pubs' for we happen to realize that is your life. Would it be asking too much of the local populace to realize that we are actually bored because it has nothing to offer? . . . we are a very small contingent of soldiers, thousands of miles from home, who have made . . . the best of our position and get what little pleasure that may be had in this locality . . . Please do not for a minute harbour the hallucination that we have no race pride, that we wouldn't glory in the possibility of spending our 'hard earned' finance on young ladies of our own race. It hasn't occurred to you that no-one will ever be able to fill the void that the absence of Negro girls has created . . . whistling at girls, offering them the opportunity of sharing a drink is not confined to the American Negro, but applied to men of all races, creeds or colours – yes, even the British Tommy . . . How many soldiers of any given race would resist the wiles and temptations of what is termed 'the camp follower' regardless of her age . . . who could not be regarded as an 'innocent virgin' or a typical English lady . . . you will find that just a 'cold shoulder' will relieve you of unwanted negro companionship. We, too, are a very reserved race.

At the beginning of the black American presence 'even the nicest type of female' enjoyed the company of black troops, wrote a British naval officer.[21] It was obvious that many young girls found the blacks fascinating, appreciating their attentiveness and good manners.

It is almost possible to pin-point exactly when the British ceased to view the black soldiers' relations with the local girls with equanimity. This change occurred about March or April 1943. During the last six months of 1942 favourable Home Intelligence reports on black GIs outnumbered the unfavourable ones by almost two to one. From mid-1943 to the end of 1944 this pattern was almost the exact reverse, with most of the unfavourable comments relating to sex. Colonel Rowe, the Liaison Officer at the War Office, felt as early as January 1943 that the tide of opinion was turning, helped along by the added pressure from white GIs, with the result that almost the whole weight of public opinion was now against those girls who continued to go with the black troops. The birth of the first brown babies in the spring of 1943 simply added fuel to a fire already well alight.

Added to the disapproval of British people, many white Americans too saw British women who dated blacks as prostitutes or people of loose morals, and not the least of the problems for the black GIs and their partners was that such judgements had very practical results. Whenever white GIs discovered girls who had consorted with blacks the girls were completely ostracized; and because whites could bring more pressure to bear on English girls, blacks were now in a 'catch-22' situation – cut off from normal relationships they were left to pay for their sex (with the attendant danger of venereal disease), or accept the favours of very young girls who often looked older than their years. Both alternatives merely served to bring them more condemnation from British citizens.

The problem of very young girls chasing the black American soldiers certainly was not easy to solve. Their behaviour was considered by many as quite brazen and disgusting, and beyond any measure of parental control. The issue gave the press some good headline opportunities. 'Midland Girls haunt coloured men's barracks' blared one provincial newspaper. The *Spectator* in August 1943 was more circumspect, though no less emphatic:

> There is no doubt that girls today are laying themselves out to attract these men, especially overseas troops, and coloured men in particular, who do not understand the fact that white girls are ready and anxious to give themselves, as they undoubtedly do, for money and to have a good time . . . frequently girls of thirteen and fourteen have attached themselves to coloured soldiers.[22]

Explanations are not hard to find. Family life was inevitably shattered by the war with so many males, fathers as well as husbands and fiancés, absent from home, and much routine industrial work to be done. One

38-year-old woman, in answer to Mass Observation, believed that the fascination for blacks came from 'unhappy little girls whose cramped lives at home and work seem to have driven them into a welter of sexual excitement'.[23]

Despite all the adverse publicity (or perhaps because of it) many girls remained faithful to the black Americans right to the end of the war. An incredible scene occurred at Bristol towards the end of August 1945 which must have underlined many of the fears that British citizens had experienced during the war. Hundreds of screaming girls aged 17 to 25 besieged the barracks where black soldiers were preparing to go back to the US, singing a Bing Crosby hit 'Don't Fence Me In'. Barriers were broken down and later the gates of the railway station were rushed. 'To hell with the US Army color bars! We want our colored sweethearts' was the cry, while one rain-soaked 18-year-old said 'We intend to give our sweeties a good send-off. And what's more, we intend going to America after them'.[24]

There was no question of the black soldiers being forgotten after their departure. After the war General Weaver recounted a rhetorical question put to him by an English prelate. 'How could you believe my dear cousins from overseas, that we will ever forget our magnificent amalgamation when we view the great crop of little brunettes you have left behind?'[25] In truth the real problem of the brown babies could not be dealt with so flippantly.

What then was the problem of the 'brown babies', or as they were sometimes called in the USA, the 'tan Yank' or 'wild oats' babies? Quite simply it was that most of the mixed-race children ('half-caste' was the more common contemporary term) not only had to cope with their illegitimacy but also with their colour – or their mothers did. The illegitimacy may well have been no problem for in many respects this was a 'normal' wartime feature, but the fact that the children had brown skins added an extra dimension to the situation. One estimate, for example, said there were over 20,000 babies born in Britain with *white* GI fathers but their absorption into society was much more straightforward. Harold Moody of the League of Coloured Peoples summed up the situation: 'When what public opinion regards as the taint of illegitimacy is added to the disadvantage of mixed race, the chances of the child's having a fair opportunity for development and service are much reduced'.[26]

The difficulties then were that many of the white mothers of the brown babies were already married to British husbands who were in many cases overseas oblivious to goings-on back home. For the single mothers the prospects of meeting men who would accept their brown offspring seemed remote. So what was to happen to these babies? Somerset was one of the counties which had large numbers of these children. Among them were Ann, Leon and Jody, and though their cases are not necessarily typical their experiences illustrate perfectly the hopes, aspirations and disappointments felt by those involved in the issue as it was carried forward through the 1940s into the 1950s.

Crucial to the debate on the future of the children was the question of whether the babies necessarily had to be illegitimate or whether any US soldier stationed in Britain, regardless of colour, was allowed under certain circumstances to marry a British white woman. There were certainly no written instructions about the prohibition of interracial marriages as any such document would have been political dynamite, but there is little doubt that there was opposition by the US military to such marriages. Like much of the European Theatre policy on racial matters, the implementation of marriage regulations was left to local American officers, certain of whom held strong views on the association of blacks and whites. General Weaver himself would have been a difficult man to face, to judge from his own published views:

> God created different races of mankind because he meant it to be so. He specifically forbade inter-marriage. Our Lord Jesus Christ preached the same tenet, the grounds for which were that such unions would make the blood of offspring

impure. It is a biological and historical fact that racial mongrelization results in the progeny acquiring the bad habits of both sides with very few of the good attributes of either.[27]

Journalist Ormus Davenport, himself an ex-GI, argued that official policy was often ignored in favour of a 'gentlemen's agreement' to forbid marriages. If a pregnancy was involved the soldier was quickly transferred, and even if there was not, the black soldier was given a serious talk by a superior officer and the girl was often 'counselled' by some Army authority or British welfare officer. Davenport contended in 1947 that not one GI bride 'going back to the US under the US government scheme is the wife of a Negro'.[28]

There was however one important legal barrier to interracial marriages. They were forbidden in about twenty states of the USA whether such marriages were contracted abroad or not. The Army authorities of course were very conscious that problems would certainly arise if the couples entered certain parts of America. Thus there were constant reminders through British channels, often in church diocesan magazines, that these mixed marriages were not legal in certain circumstances. Such warnings were reinforced by the American authorities from time to time throughout the war. *Time* magazine pointed out the difficulties and quoted one southern black who, when asked if he wanted to take his white wife to America, replied: 'Brother if I did I would have to leave her in New York when I went home'. Proof that the matter was not just of academic interest came in 1947 when Margaret Goosey, a Midlands girl, went to Virginia to marry Thomas Johnson, a black ex-GI she had met in England. Their marriage was in defiance of the local jim-crow laws and he was sent to the State Industrial Farm while the bride-to-be was gaoled and ultimately deported.[29]

It is not possible to estimate how many mixed marriages took place during the war years for, curiously, when the Department of State tried to obtain the numbers in a circular sent to diplomatic and consular offices in June 1945 no reply was forthcoming from Britain. In any event for most American soldiers in Britain, black and white, marriage was an academic issue and like many armies serving in foreign countries, particularly during wartime, no regulations or prohibitions could stop sexual relations or illegitimate babies.

The black Americans had not been in Britain very long before official fears were voiced at the prospect of mixed-race babies, fears echoed throughout the country in rather less diplomatic language. Herbert Morrison was the politician most concerned about the issue. His view that the babies would create a 'difficult social problem' was borne out by events of the later 1940s for it fell to the lot of his successors at the Home Office to wrestle with it. Earlier than this, in August 1942, Arthur Sulzberger of the *New York Times,* noticing that English girls were attracted to the black GIs, ruefully commented that 'nine months from now there will be a very serious problem'. It was at this same time too that Maurice Petherick reminded Eden that the half-caste babies evident when the black soldiers had gone would be 'a bad thing for any country'.[30] When Winston Churchill came back to the issue in October 1943 he appeared to be more concerned about the salacious aspects of the black presence. Enquiring about the numbers of brown illegitimate children he was told by the Duke of Marlborough that there were 34,875 black GIs in the country and about ten brown babies had been born. He quickly added though that it was 'quite conceivable that there are many others (which I know to be the case) which are on the way'.[31]

Official concern about the prospect of brown babies was quickly augmented by gossip, rumour and exaggeration from both sides of the Atlantic. At the time when the births of the first brown babies were anticipated a letter writer from North Wales in February 1943 crudely but succinctly put his finger on the essence of the post-war problem: 'Even horse racing is in the background and the bets these days are on expected babies whether they'll be black or white ... Won't Sgt. O ... get a shock if he comes home to a wee nigger'.[32]

Many of the social problems attendant on the war had to

wait for a solution for obvious reasons, but there was both
British and American concern about the plight of the
brown babies while the conflict was going on. Towards the
end of 1944 a conference specifically on this issue was
organized jointly by the National Council for the Unmarried Mother and her Child, and the Church of England
Moral Welfare Council. In addition a report from the
American Consulate in Manchester to the State Department, dated 12 January 1945, estimated that many of the
sixty illegitimate children in one institution were brown
babies, and a black American sergeant wanted to start a
fund for the future benefit of these children.[33]

The real difficulty was to find out accurately how many
babies with black American fathers had been born in
Britain. Magazines and newspapers after the war variously estimated that there were between 550 and 5,000,
though one American source in 1946 put the figure as high
as 20,000. (Numerically the number of babies with *white*
GI fathers – one estimate was 22,000 – was much larger
though that problem was much less visible.)

Without doubt the most careful investigation of the
situation in Britain in 1945 was carried out by Sylvia
McNeill for the League of Coloured Peoples. A Jamaican
schoolteacher, she began her work in July 1945 by writing
to the welfare officers of each county in England and
Wales, and she later made personal visits to some areas.
The LCP never claimed that the survey was complete for
some women were looking after their babies on their own,
while others evidently moved from district to district to
avoid identification. In all, the McNeill survey showed that
up to that time 553 brown babies had been born to 545
mothers, of whom 92 were married and 98 were unmarried.
The marital status of the remainder was unknown.

The counties reporting the largest numbers of brown
babies were those in the west of England where many
black troops had been stationed prior to D-Day: Gloucestershire 60, Cornwall 38, Hampshire 50, together with two
counties where the blacks had been concentrated in
support of the US airforce troops, Suffolk 34 and Lancashire 70. Somerset reported that 39 cases had arisen or

were being dealt with since September 1944 and among these were Ann, Leon and Jody who had all been taken into care by the spring of 1945. Nearby Devon reported 83 cases and when Sylvia McNeill went there in person county officials raised with her some of the important questions which were to occupy many people's thoughts as the difficulties surrounding the brown babies became clearer. Would there be special homes exclusively for these children? How could the kids get to the USA if their fathers wanted them? Would it be advisable for women to marry black Americans and live in America?

The LCP updated its figures from time to time as more information came to light. By 1947, 750 babies had come to its notice, and by December 1948 this figure had risen to 775. Another authoritative source of information was the black academic, John St Clair Drake. The publicity about the brown babies brought him to Britain in 1947 and 1948 to undertake research for his Chicago University Ph.D. He worked closely with the League of Coloured Peoples and he suggested later that there were some 2,000 illegitimate children of black American troops. The accurate figure was probably somewhere between 700 and 1,000 but certainly it was nowhere near the tens of thousands reported in the sensational press on both sides of the Atlantic during 1946 and 1947.

One thing that was equally certain was that in the short-term at least the solution to the problem lay in Britain and not the United States of America – Uncle Sam was not going to be much help. That this was so became clear in February 1945. Eleanor Roosevelt received a letter suggesting that some of the black English war babies could go to school in the US. 'What is the solution?' she asked the President, only to receive the curt response: 'I think this is a British problem – not American'.[34]

What then was the solution to this 'British problem'? As we have seen, marriage to the black father was not one of them. Those women who were already married did not have this option in any case, and the price of reconciliation with their husbands was often the abandonment of their brown babies. Similarly single girls thought their chances of marriage would greatly diminish if they kept their children. The brave ones who did often became social pariahs: 'I am shunned by the whole village', said one mother desperately, in a plea to *Time* magazine on 11 March 1946. 'The inspector for the National Society for the Prevention of Cruelty to Children has told my friend to keep her children away from my house . . . as didn't she know that I had two illegitimate coloured children? Is there anywhere I can go where my children will not get pushed around?' Many of the mothers were young girls for whom life must have been pretty unbearable. Some tried to hide their babies while one abandoned her 4½-month-old brown child in a public toilet at Shrewsbury. Many mothers gave up their babies and for these toddlers a statutory or voluntary children's home was where they were to spend their formative years.

It was clear too that in the early years there was no great scramble to adopt brown babies in Britain. In addition, the adoption agencies and homes were not very cooperative in their attitude. A report at the end of the war from the London Probation service stated quite categorically that no adoption society would consider a half-caste child.

Partly because of the problems at home the suggestion that the brown babies might be adopted in America began to find favour. In the autumn of 1945 it received the backing of a very important protagonist. W.E.B. Du Bois had been in Manchester in October attending the revived Pan-African Congress, where one of the debates had been about the plight of these mixed-race children. He suggested to the NAACP the next month that it might like to take up the matter, but his initiative came to nothing. At one point a plan devised by G. Daniels Ekarte, the black pastor-in-chief of the African Churches Mission in Liverpool held out promise for extensive fund-raising and adoption, but the plan foundered when some ill-judged publicity torpedoed the project. On 5 April 1947 the *Daily Mail* in London said that Britain was 'exporting' 5,000 'dusky problem babies' to America on a specially-chartered liner, and the story was picked up across the United States.[35]

Among right-wing circles in the US the prospect of importing brown babies was always viewed with disdain. Larry Asman, a disciple of Gerald K. Smith, the fundamentalist minister and ex-Huey Long organizer, had already in 1946 given congressmen a leaflet about the '20,000 Little Brown Bastards' who had been born in England and, according to one source, the Daughters of the American Revolution felt much the same.[36] This right-wing society had refused to let black contralto Marian Anderson sing in their Constitution Hall in Washington in 1939, and as a result of this Eleanor Roosevelt tendered her resignation. Not surprisingly Congressman John E. Rankin of Mississippi was equally indignant about the brown babies. In April 1947 Rankin was in his mid-60s. A lawyer by training, his particular brand of Americanism encompassed white supremacy, anti-Semitism, union baiting and hatred of things foreign. When he got wind early in the war that the American Red Cross was thinking of abandoning the 'black' and 'white' labels on blood reserved for transfusions he viewed it as an attempt by the 'crackpots, the Communists and parlor pinks . . . to mongrelize the nation'. His response to the brown baby issue was predictable. In the House he announced that he was 'unalterably opposed to bringing to this country a lot of illegitimate half-breed Negro children from England'. They were, he argued, 'the offspring of the scum of the British Isles'.[37]

Among the British too there were misgivings about the wisdom of encouraging the departure of the brown babies to the US. Chuter Ede, post-war Labour Home Secretary, had his doubts in view of the discrimination against blacks in many parts of America. Others felt uneasy at the notion that there was no room for mixed-race children in Britain. At a time when Britain was beginning the painful reappraisal of its imperial role one correspondent struck a very sore spot. How would Britain's colonial policy look, he enquired of the Foreign Office, if the country was 'unable to relieve, rehabilitate and educate a few thousand [coloured] children on our own doorsteps'?[38]

Apart from moral and ethical objections to the brown

babies being sent to America for adoption there were legal
hurdles too. An Adoption Act of 1939, which came into
effect in 1943, forbade the sending abroad of children
except to British subjects. Some of the black GIs wanted to
adopt their own offspring but putative fathers were not
deemed to be relatives in any case. In addition, in some
American states children offered for adoption had to have
been born in the US. The emigration of children was made
easier by the Children Act of 1948 but if children were too
young to make their own minds up about it (as all the GI
babies then were), the decision rested with the Home
Secretary. In 1948 Chuter Ede opposed this proposed
exodus.

While all these deliberations were going on Ann, Leon,
Jody and all the other babies in Somerset and elsewhere
were growing up. Arrangments had to be made for their
care. In the case of these three youngsters their early years
were to be spent at Holnicote House, a nursery run by the
county council near Minehead, a remote but beautiful part
of north Somerset. That they were there was due, in part,
to the county's reaction to a Ministry of Health directive at
the end of 1943 urging local authorities to give some
thought to the problem of the growing number of illegitimate children.
    At some point in 1944 or 1945 Somerset County Council
made a unique decision: to take into care all the brown
babies who came to its attention. Celia Bangham, the
Superintendent Health Visitor responsible for the county's
children, explained the policy to the Home Secretary at a
Home Office meeting in the middle of December 1945.
There were at that time 37 brown babies in Somerset's
nurseries, 27 of them born to married women. 'The local
authority', she explained, 'took the children when two
weeks old whether the mother was married or single in
order that she might be reconciled with her family and in
no case had they any subsequent enquiries from the
mother about the child's welfare'. The reason for this, Miss
Bangham argued, was that the children lacked parental

affection and their colour made adoption unlikely.[39] The cases of Ann, Leon and Jody were not typical but illustrated some of the difficulties that the children encountered.

Ann Evans (as she now is) was born in February 1945 to a mother who had one child and a husband overseas in the Army. She was taken into care at Holnicote about five weeks after her birth. Already in Holnicote was Leon York who was born in November 1944 and subsequently taken into care at ten weeks of age. They were soon joined by Jody Bryant (again as she now is) whose home circumstances were similar to Ann's. Leon's household had more than its share of problems without, as he has put it, 'a brown baby being plonked in the middle'. His mother was not married and she had two other children besides Leon. His mum's sister was also in the house (a single woman with three children) as well as a grown-up brother and a grandmother. And all these were living in a small country cottage with four rooms.

A general belief just after the war was that it would take people of quite exceptionally enlightened and courageous views to adopt brown babies. Ann Evans was one of the successes. She left Holnicote in October 1949 having been chosen by white parents after some publicity in the local newspaper. Her new home became Abertillery in South Wales where she instantly gained some elder brothers aged from 14 to 22. She was legally adopted in 1951. The explanation offered to her for her colour when she was about 6 or 7 was that she had been tanned in the sun, and anyway, she was told, 'God just made some of us different'.

Ignoring all the hurdles and despite some measure of achievement at home Miss Bangham pressed doggedly on with her attempts to find American homes for the brown babies. International interest in the plight of the babies raised her aspirations, particularly when *Newsweek* on 29 December 1947 carried an article on Britain's 'Brown Tiny Tims'. Ten of Holnicote's babies, including Leon, were featured, part of the total group of nineteen mixed-race

children there. The brown children, it was stated, were
being treated 'exactly like white children', with the people
of Minehead planning a big party for them on New Year's
Eve.

Soon after the start of the new year Eleanor Roosevelt
came back into the picture. In mid-February 1948 Celia
Bangham contacted an English relative of the former First
Lady to solicit help for the brown babies. Though this
attempt too was abortive there was great interest in the
Somerset children in Chicago where plans were made by
the Society for the Welfare of Brown British Babies for
twenty of them to be received by a prominent black
businessman before their adoption. Another eight were
lined up for California.

As the summer of 1948 progressed further world-wide
publicity occurred. On 28 August *Life* magazine featured
the children of Holnicote in an article entitled 'The babies
they left behind them'. Seven of the babies, including Ann
and Jody, beamed at the photographer. There were twenty
brown babies in the home altogether who were, according
to the article, 'happy and healthy . . . they feed the ducks,
hunt for tadpoles and play in the woods. Some are learning
to ride tricycles'. As yet, they had 'no consciousness of
being "different" '. As a result of this publicity eighty-five
applications for adoption were received from America with
each child being individually selected by prospective
parents, and many asking for the same one.

Jody was one of those already picked out for adoption by
a family in Cincinnati, Ohio, and, much to the annoyance
of social work agencies in America, enquiries were started
about the financial and domestic circumstances of the
prospective parents. The process was never completed but
Jody continued to receive cards, presents and clothes from
Ohio until she was about 13 years of age. In 1950 she was
fostered by a widow in Yeovil, Somerset, and it became
clear that her future lay in England.

For Leon adoption was not forthcoming. He spent all his
childhood and adolescence in institutions though he remembers many of the adults who cared for him with love
and affection. As Leon and Ann grew up both became

curious about their origins, and both were teased about being African by schoolmates, though Leon revelled in this exotica. When Ann went to secondary school in 1956 she met six other brown babies (the county of Monmouthshire recorded twenty-one in the McNeill survey) and one of these said that her real father was a 'coloured' GI. When told that this was true for her too, Ann felt some hostility to her parents, but only briefly.

In Somerset Leon remembers a chance remark he heard in his youth – 'Pity about you lot during the war'. When he changed schools at the age of 11 his official report noted that he was 'apprehensive about the boys . . . drawing attention to his colour . . . he has been self-conscious about his colour and anxious about his father's whereabouts'.

From the time of the birth of the first brown baby there was plenty of advice forthcoming about how the babies should be cared for, and the problems they would face. Not all this advice was offered in a serious vein. In April 1946 a magazine called *Courier* tried to forecast what the attitudes of the brown babies would be ten years hence in 1956. 'Ebony-skinned Franklin Winston Molasses, 14 year-old leader of the American Negro Youth in Britain Movement, today demanded recognition from the UNO Minorities Council. Molasses, a light-skinned youth with a markedly European cast of feature, led a deputation of 2000 twelve to fourteen-year-old piccaninnies down Whitehall'. Molasses, the 'report' continued, spoke 'in a soft voice that is a blend of the Deep South and Somerset burr' and declared 'our fathers were American. We demand the right to vote American, live American, and what is more important, eat American'.[40] The article was partly right about the mixture of accents the brown babies would have but few would claim to feel in any sense American. However, if the intention was to indicate that some of the children would have problems sorting out their own identity as they grew up, there is an element of truth in it.

Some of the brown babies have been successful in their attempts to trace the British halves of their parentage, but many mothers, aware that their brown children were the products of illicit relationships, maintain a metaphorical and physical distance from them. Leon is one exception: he has renewed his acquaintance with his mother, trying to nurture the family relationships he never had as a child.

Ann and Jody are both happily married to white men and have five children between them. For Jody the knowledge that she almost went to live in America as a youngster, and the stability of her own family seem to be identity enough. Ann, Leon and several other brown babies whose interest in their black GI origins has been aroused by media publicity want more. They are aware that what made them different in post-war Britain was their colour, and the last piece of the jigsaw completing their identities will, they believe, be found when they know about their fathers. Do they have half-brothers and sisters? Do they have uncles and aunts? What kind of relationships did their fathers and mothers have? The questions are many: the answers forty years on will not come easily.

9
The Black GI in Britain: Reflections and Results

The most tangible result of the presence of black soldiers in Britain during the war years was the brown babies. The most conspicuous evidence in the United States that American soldiers (white ones at least) had been overseas, were the thousands of GI brides who, after frustrating delays and seemingly endless red tape, crowded into the country to join their husbands. As we have seen, the presence of over 100,000 black soldiers in a country unaccustomed to racial problems occupied hours of official time at many levels and caused considerable consternation. Given all the excitement, passion and anger that had been generated by the temporary stay in Britain of over two million strange young men the immediate responses of the administrations on both sides of the Atlantic to this period were particularly muted. It was almost as if this interlude, important though it was, was best forgotten.

At the end of April 1945 the US Department of State asked the American Embassy in London for a report on the relations between the US troops and British citizens. The response, which took nine months to compose, was limp to say the least. 'The impact . . . on a nation of some forty million people obviously has been very great and the average Britisher's views of the United States and its citizens have been altered by the experience.'[1] The Ministry of

Information was hardly more forthcoming. The British people, it reported in October 1945, 'began to realise that though they spoke more or less the same language, the Americans really belonged to a different nation with different standards, customs, manners of approach, etc., etc.'[2]

In fact there was a whole series of questions which had already been raised as a result of the black GI experience in Britain. Would it lead to the end of segregation in the Army? What did black and white Americans think of Britain and had the experience brought them closer together? Was there likely to be any long-term effect on Britain's attitude to race? How were blacks going to react to a segregated America on their return home? More immediately American authorities had to react to a question frequently asked in Britain as soon as their troops arrived. Would the Axis powers use the jim-crow army as a propaganda weapon?

There were a number of people in Britain who charged that a segregated army was undemocratic and unfair to the black soldiers in it. Inevitably, and despite some censorship, the fights between black and white soldiers provided material of use to the Germans (while the Japanese exploited similar American racial problems in Australia). In short, these prejudices and discriminations were advertised all over the world. In part the American Army brought some of the problem on itself. The use of Joe Louis, for example, as a symbol of how blacks should see their stake in a war against a racist enemy raised their aspirations but was clearly inconsistent with the organization of an army divided on racial lines.

What upset many people in Britain was the aggressiveness with which some white Americans expressed their views on their black compatriots. In addition, because many nationalities were represented in Britain during the war years, the American colour problem had wider implications. It was an issue clearly impossible to contain among Americans. It was bound to, and did, spill over not just into British society but also into the many other foreign communities based in Britain during the war. As with Britons, many French, Czechs, Poles, Norwegians, Dutch,

Belgians and others experienced their first contacts with Americans in wartime Britain. For peoples unaccustomed to institutionalized colour prejudice, this dimension of wartime America was surprising, not to say disappointing, especially when their own social contacts with the black troops forced them into ugly confrontations with white Americans, which they could not grasp.

The wartime issue, born in Britain, was noticed on the Continent too. In September 1945, a Swiss newspaper, the Basle *Arbeiter Zeitung*, was blunt in its observations:

> When one reflects that these Americans, black and white, for years on two continents have fought against the racial theories of their opponents, it is very much to be regretted that at the end of the great misery which overwhelmed the world for years, soldiers of the United States are making such mistakes. The world has come to the conclusion that racial prejudice, the theory of superior and inferior human beings, must be completely destroyed; so it must be also with our American friends.

However, it was essentially the use of jim crow as an enemy propaganda tool which was potentially more damaging than its effect on allies or neutrals, and this was clear to both British and Americans. Germany used the black GI issue in its propaganda in two ways: the cruder material about blacks was an attempt to engender racial prejudice, but a subtler message was used to encourage the black soldier to desert. As the Germans extended their influence across northern France and the Low Countries they turned their attention to Britain and the Americans. In 1942 both approaches were used in their radio broadcasts. In September Lancer's Bremen magazine, broadcast from Calais, apparently referring to the presence of American troops in Germany after the First World War, remarked that 'The Germans know what it is like to have American Negroes quartered on them. May the English enjoy their turn of this doubtful pleasure'. In March 1943 the story was recounted on the German-controlled Luxembourg station of the English lady who offered to have American house-guests. She had remarked, however, that she did not want Jews, but the Jewish officer instead sent her four blacks. The story was probably apocryphal but was widely used in the British press and was picked up by the station: 'No doubt there are a number of British officers and men who would benefit by a weekend entertainment. It ought to be possible for competent military authorities to select them without including in their number either neg- roes, cat-burglars or Jews.'[3]

It is impossible to estimate how many people in Britain picked up these English language programmes; some may well have listened by accident for a Gallup Poll in January 1940 revealed that of the 65 per cent of the people who listened to foreign stations, 78 per cent tuned in to Berlin, Hamburg or Munich. Listeners would have been confused by the German approach however for in addition to the anti-black materials above, the Calais station would also urge that Roosevelt begin to fight for freedom from racial discrimination at home, and end jim crow in buses and restaurants.

Germany's printed propaganda – leaflets dropped from the air – was equally schizophrenic, and ranged in style from the crude, near-pornographic to the very subtle. In the former mould was a trick postcard dropped on Allied soldiers in the early days of the Normandy invasion. With the words 'white plays, black wins' it could be viewed from various angles and revealed a dead white soldier, and a black making love to a white woman, referring to black soldiers who were noncombatants and remained behind in England after the D-Day landings.[4]

Later, once blacks did get involved in combat duty, Ger- mans would address straightforwardly sentimental appeals to them to give up the war and return home to wives and children. On other occasions the messages had two themes – forget segregated America and come over to liberal Germany. Hence the black soldiers were urged to stop being 'cannon fodder in a rich man's war' because 'back home the colored man always had to do the dirty work'. By contrast 'the Germans give the colored man a square deal', with no segregation and no lynchings. Blacks were advised not to believe the 'nonsense about German prejudice against the colored man'.

It is not clear whether this propaganda had any effect on American soldiers. What is clear is that exposure to jim crow in Britain and other parts of the world had a great impact on individual black and white GIs. One of the surprises to members of the host population, reared on cinema images of the United States, was that Americans were not a homogeneous group. How familiar the visitors were with racial problems depended in part on whether they were from the north or the south, from rural or urban areas. Despite attempts to keep them apart, working in close proximity in Britain provided many Americans with their first introduction to people of a different racial group. The relations between white Americans and blacks was not just a tale of unremitting gloom though this aspect of it was less sensational a story than the frequently reported clashes.

Not all white GIs despised black people and it is evident that on a personal level they could get on very well.[5] Some whites after contacts with blacks began to respect them for their fighting qualities, particularly in the tank battalions in France. The black women personnel came in for grudging praise from some white soliders too: one comment was that they were 'all highly educated – and in spite of their color they are ladies. They stand out alongside the white Wacs in appearance of uniform and talk and actions'.[6]

On occasions letters were published from white soldiers who had experienced changes of heart on racial matters during the war. A Mississippi soldier wrote to *Yank* saying how he had hated blacks until he came into the Army but that 'Many Negro soldiers have died on the front for American soldiers who thought Jim Crow was right'. A letter in the *Fort Worth Star-Telegram* made this startling generalization: 'I am afraid that all race prejudice is gone from the boys who have fought this war, and it isn't going to be wise for any man, regardless of race, color, creed or profession, to try to abuse the colored people any more. The veterans of this war have learned that freedom means more than just freedom for the white man'.[7] Whether such confidence was justified is hard to say for there were few reliable opinion polls of veterans.

In similar vein some black GIs were optimistic about their relationships with whites. A technician in France in the spring of 1945 wrote with a euphoria which may have been induced by the imminence of the end of hostilities. He said there was no colour line among French or American soldiers, and blacks and whites of all ranks 'stay in the same hotels, eat at the same tables and buy each other drinks. I'll be so bold as to say, that even in New York the two races never get along as well as they do here'.[8]

Overseas service in Britain and elsewhere was influential in shaping the views of blacks on white people. Southern blacks, faced with the liberalism of their new environment and the opportunity to mingle with northern whites, found their own prejudices towards whites soften. Ironically, the northern urban blacks who faced official segregation for the first time during a military career spent in Britain emerged from the Army embittered by the experience.[9]

One aspect of the black presence overseas began to assume increasing importance as the war progressed. What would race relations be like in post-war America? Had the liberties enjoyed by the black GI in Britain, including to some extent the freedom to associate with white women, whetted his appetite for the same on demobilization? For blacks this represented a challenge, for many whites it was a threat – the 'spoilt nigger' theme was repeated with a vigour that was out of proportion perhaps to the numbers of those who endorsed it.

The question of the attitude the black soldier would adopt on his return to America was to the fore in British thinking right from the early days of the American presence. It was used as the justification for advocating coolness towards the black GIs, for England had been accused of encouraging 'uppity niggers' before. Just before the American revolution in 1776 the Countess of Huntingdon, who owned blacks in Georgia, encouraged a Christian Negro, David, to preach to his fellows. A Savannah merchant was sceptical of this as David had been in England before and 'the kind notice he has met with . . . will make him think too highly of himself'. David's preaching did indeed go beyond the spiritual and he was shipped back to England, with angry words going from the merchant to the Countess's agent:

> [David] is, if I am not mistaken, very proud, and very superficial, and conceited, and I must say it's a pity, that any of these People should ever put their feet in England, where they get totally spoiled and ruined both in Body and Soul, through a mistaken kind of compassion because they are black, while many of our own colour and Fellow Subjects, are starving through want and Neglect. We know these People better than you do.[10]

A century and a half later James Grigg, Secretary for War, would have nodded in approval. In September 1942 it was his view that the 'coloured troops themselves probably expect to be treated in this country as in the United States, and a markedly different treatment might well cause political difficulties at the end of the war'.[11] This became the official line and in counselling caution the Government argued that to treat blacks differently (that is as human beings) would embarrass the US authorities.

The Americans were equally nervous about the place of blacks in the post-war US. The prominent journalist Westbrook Pegler expressed fears that the end of the war might *not* bring changes for the black soldier: 'Now assuming that this boy comes back from the war to a victorious country, what status will he come back to? Will he be niggerized again and restricted to menial jobs, Jim-Crowed and driven back to the dreadful ghettoes of our cities or will he be treated as an American?'[12]

For many white American soldiers in Britain the answer to Pegler's rhetorical question was that the black's temporary freedom overseas would come to an end when he returned to America. In particular the blacks would certainly not win the freedom to associate with white women and this once again seemed to dominate discussions. American anger quickly emerged: a quartermaster soldier wrote home that he had seen 'nice looking white girls going with a coon. They think they are hot stuff. The girls are so dumb it's pitiful. Wait till Georgia gets those *educated* negroes back there again'. Another writer was disturbed when blacks danced with whites: 'What makes me livid is that the darn negro dare try it here when they know what would happen if they did it at home'. An airforce corporal saw no dilemma: 'we are not opposed to the negro "getting ahead in the world",' he argued, 'if he goes about it in the right way. We do object, however, to negro men sexing with white women . . . We're not fighting for that kind of "democracy". We could have it without fighting if we wanted it'.[13]

The Ministry of Information, as well as many white GIs, certainly believed that the British had spoilt the black Americans in the war, and this impression made its way to the United States. Stories of the 'uppity nigger' found a receptive audience there, and rumours abounded about police chiefs arming their forces heavily to counter the anticipated civil unrest. There was, too, evidence of increased Ku-Klux-Klan activities in the South by the autumn of 1946.

In fact far from being 'uppity', their experience of the rigid racial segregation established by their white compatriots in Britain totally demoralized many black soldiers. The road to civil rights, if this was typical, seemed to be a very long one indeed. Some black GIs did return home with a renewed vigour for the fight for full participation in education and employment, but many more expressed a desire to be demobilized in England or France . . . or anywhere but America.

Many simply sought re-enlistment in the Army – at least they knew where they stood there! But what of the Army? Did the jim-crow experience in Britain lead to changes? Early reports from the Army command revealed a deal of complacency. Black relations with civilians had been fine and major disturbances, it was reported, were few. Nevertheless John J. McCloy was amongst those who suggested that the Army might take an objective look at its future use of black troops.

In October 1945 Gerneral Alvan C. Gillem, jun., who had been in Europe as a corps commander in 1944, was asked to undertake this review. This he swiftly did though his bland report did not question the quota system or segregation. That it did not do so was due in part to the evidence he received from blacks. Walter White, who had seen jim crow in Britain at first hand, was unequivocal in his denunciation of segregation in the forces as expensive, inefficient and contributing to tension; but the two leading black officers, General B. Davis and his son, expressed anxieties lest integration in the Army be both compulsory and in advance of the same changes in American society.

The very notion that the Army might be contemplating some measure of integration was too much for one aspiring young politician. Robert C. Byrd from West Virginia, a Ku-Klux-Klan member in his youth, and much later the Democratic leader in the Senate, expressed his grave concern. He urged Theodore Bilbo, the extremist senator for Mississippi to exert any influence he could over General Eisenhower:

> I hope that our Army 'bigwigs' will not attempt to use the military as an instrument for experimenting with the race problem. Integration of the Negro into White regiments is the very thing for which the Negro intelligentsia is striving and such a move would serve only to lower the efficiency of the fighting units and the morale of the average white service man as well.
>
> I am a typical American, a southerner, and 27 years of age, and never in this world will I be convinced that race mixing in any field is good. All the social 'do-gooders,' the philanthropic 'greats' of this day, the reds and the pinks . . . the disciples of Eleanor . . . the pleas by Sinatra . . . can never alter my convictions on this question . . . but I am loyal to my country and know but reverence to her flag, BUT I shall never submit to fight beneath that banner with a negro by my side. Rather I should die a thousand times, and see old Glory trampled in the dirt never to rise again, than to see this beloved land of ours become degraded by race mongrels, a throw back to the blackest specimen from the wilds.[14]

The cold war with Russia made the segregated American Army too easy a propaganda target, and Harry Truman was determined to end this. By the middle of 1948 he pronounced that there should be equality of treatment and opportunity in the forces, and he clearly intended this to mean the end of segregation. However, it was the Korean

War in 1950, not events in Europe, which provided the catalyst. Pressure in Asia was seen as a prelude to communist pressure in Europe. Jim crow could not cope in 1951 with the increase in black troops from 9,000 to 27,000 in training courses in West Germany and segregation came to an end.

The attitude of the British to the black Americans in their midst *during* the war has been dealt with earlier, but there seems little doubt that by the middle of 1945 people had had enough of the conflict and were glad to see the Americans leave, seeing this as a step back towards peace conditions. If the regular polls carried out by Gallup and Mass Observation about feelings towards Americans are any measure, then the British had indeed lived with the imported racial problem long enough.

Nevertheless the black American experience was unique and it is possible to draw one or two conclusions from their presence in Britain. There is no doubt that blacks behaved in such a diverse way that some Britons believed what they wanted to believe. Some even shared the view of many American officers that the black GIs were pretty awful soldiers.

It was clear too that other people had advanced little beyong the traditional 'negro stereotype' of pre-war days. Cecil Roberts, another of that quasi-official group of writers who had worked for the British Information Services during the war, expressed uncomplicated views about blacks in 1946: 'The Negroes are a kind easy-going people,' he wrote. 'Soft-voiced, sensual, they shuffle through life with laughter always near the surface, and have a religious emotional nature easily exploited . . . I would call them a happy race. They sing, they laugh, they dance and they doze in a manner that rebukes the pushful over-organized white folk'.[15]

For most British people however the reaction to the black Americans who had spent several years in their midst was much more positive. The overriding feature of the experience was that those who had met them became better informed about the American racial situation and race in general – it was no longer an abstract concept. Many wanted more information about black people. Some realized that Britain's Empire contained many more black people than had ever been in the country during the war, and reactions to these GIs might have some significance for the country's imperial future. One important commentator was Eric John Dingwall, the co-author of the 1942 ABCA pamphlet on the black GIs. In 1946 he looked back on the wartime experiences of race:

> There is little doubt that with the coming of the American Negro troops many people found themselves in a position which forced them to take stock of the situation and decide for themselves what their attitude should be . . . there is little doubt that many people in Great Britain, especially those who came into close contact with the Negro troops, were awakened to a wider appreciation of a problem which up to that time few of them had ever considered seriously. . . . People began to realise that the questions of race and colour were not such as had merely an academic interest, but were closely bound up with moral and political problems of the first magnitude. They saw that here was something which was of interest not only to the United States.[16]

Both British and Americans thought that the war had presented an opportunity to get to know one another, and particularly to modify the stereotype of the blacks often seen in the movies. The British were genuinely anxious about the racial problem. Lacking the long American experience of familiarity with a mixture of racial and ethnic groups, they asked, perhaps naively, why everybody couldn't get along with each other. Young people were particularly eager to know more about black Americans, and the black GIs remained in British affections for several years after the war.

After 1947, however, much to the chagrin of some members of the Labour Government, many of the West Indians who had been in Britain during the war came back. Their permanence meant that race was no longer a temporary American problem – it was now a fully fledged British problem. Calypsos had arrived to stay, the black big bands had been just a musical interlude. Now the black people were buying houses next door to 'us', were queuing for 'our' jobs, and were dating 'our' sisters. It was no longer an academic debate.

One of the contemporary complaints about their service in Britain and elsewhere overseas was that the black GIs rarely featured in any publicity that didn't depict them in stereotypical roles or in a menial capacity – jazz-marching down the street or guarding chicken coops. Over forty years after the end of the Second World War the thirst of the public for this period remains unquenched – almost every avenue of conflict has been explored to provide dramatic material for novels, plays and films. Yet black Americans have almost as many complaints about the depiction of their role in the war today as they did at the time. With one or two notable exceptions it would be difficult looking at the popular arts to believe that a single black GI set foot on British soil between 1942 and 1945.

Apart from 'Choc'late Soldier' there were few other contemporary musical or poetic tributes to the black GI. Cartoons about the American soldiers abounded in *Punch, Lilliput* and other magazines, particularly from David Langdon and Carl Giles, but few were about blacks.

In the post-war years some references did sneak in. Nevil Shute's *The Chequer Board* in 1947 had a black American in wartime England as a central character. So too did *Deep are the Roots*, a play by Arnaud d'Usseau and James Gow. Staged in America in 1945 (and Britain in 1947), it featured a black GI who returned to his native South initially full of hope for race relations because he'd seen fairness and friendship in England.

More recent novels have touched on the theme of blacks in Europe as have, surprisingly, some war comics, not a genre noticeably attuned to realism. The great movie about blacks in wartime Britain has yet to be made. Norman Jewison successfully tackled the tensions felt by blacks in their American training in *A Soldier's Story*. John Schlesinger briefly explored the relationships between the black

GIs and their British hosts in *Yanks*, but the drama of Jim Crow in Britain has not been exploited to the full. Justice has not been done on television either. Perhaps typical was a major drama series, *We'll Meet Again*, made by Thames Television, one of Britain's premier commercial companies. Screened in 1982 it featured the professional and social activities of a white American airforce unit in wartime East Anglia. Black service troops would have been an integral part of such a scene but not a single one was shown or even mentioned!

For many people the years 1942 to 1945 are now a nostalgic period – the Glenn Miller years when only pleasant memories are evoked. Americans in Britain and particularly the blacks, are remembered for their largesse, their grins and their music. Britons' acquaintanceship with the blacks ought to have been of enormous help when they came to cope with dismembering the Empire, and receiving some of their fellow citizens from the former Colonies into their own communities. Considering that those new black arrivals soon became an 'influx' and then very quickly a 'problem', the wartime experience of the British does not appear to have prepared them in any significant way for the new era in their country's history.

Notes

The full sources of all the notes, where they are located and their particular categories, can be found in the Bibliography.

Chapter 1 Prologue: The Great War – Black Americans in Europe

1. Quoted in Jack D. Foner, *Blacks and the Military in American History* (New York 1974), p. 111. This is a very useful survey and the source of most of the statistics in this chapter.
2. John J. Pershing, *My Experiences in the World War* (London 1931), p. 261.
3. Arthur E. Barbeau and Florette Henri, *The Unknown Soldiers: Black American Troops in World War I* (Philadelphia 1974), p. 110. This work is indispensable to an understanding of the black soldier in France.
4. Franklin D. Roosevelt to Elmer Davis, 17 June 1942, OF 93, Franklin D. Roosevelt Library, Hyde Park, New York.
5. Major General Ulio to commanding generals, 23 June 1942. Operations Division decimal file 1942–5, RG 165, National Archives, Washington, DC.
6. Addie W. Hunton and Kathryn Johnson, *Two Colored Women with the American Expeditionary Forces* (New York 1920), pp. 182–3.
7. Barbeau and Henri, p. 142.
8. In *The Messenger*, William N. Colson, an ex-officer in the 367th Infantry wrote several articles on blacks and their service in World War I: 'Propaganda and the American Negro Soldier' (July 1919), pp. 24–5; 'An analysis of Negro patriotism' (August 1919), pp. 23–5; 'The

social experience of the Negro soldier abroad' (October 1919), pp. 26–7. This quote from 'Propaganda and the American Negro Soldier', p. 25.

9. Quoted in Barbeau and Henri, p. 133.

10. Hunton and Johnson, p. 185.

11. *Crisis*, vol. 18, no. 1 (May 1919), pp. 16–17; see also Emmett J. Scott, *The American Negro in the World War* (Chicago 1919; rpt New York 1969), pp. 442–3.

12. Hunton and Johnson, pp. 189, 186; see also Scott, p. 442.

13. Quoted in Barbeau and Henri, p. 142.

14. *Crisis*, vol. 18, no. 2 (June 1919), p. 172.

15. Colson, 'An analysis of Negro patriotism', p. 25.

16. *Crisis*, vol. 18 no. 1 (May 1919), p. 16.

17. Colson, 'The social experience of the Negro soldier abroad', p. 27.

18. Quoted in Stephen Graham, *Children of the Slaves* (London 1920), p. 279.

19. Quoted in David M. Kennedy, *Over Here: The First World War and American Society* (New York 1982), p. 187.

20. Quoted in Foner, p. 124.

21. Graham, p. 159.

22. *ibid.*, p. 159.

23. Quoted in Barbeau and Henri, p. 175.

24. Quoted in Foner, pp. 124–5.

25. Colson, 'Propaganda and the American Negro soldier', p. 25.

26. *Crisis*, vol. 18, no. 1 (May 1919), p. 16.

27. Quoted in Graham, p. 69.

28. Graham, p. 248.

29. Lawrence Levine, *Black Culture and Black Consciousness: Afro-American Folk Thought from Slavery to Freedom* (New York 1978), p. 341.

30. Quoted in *Crisis*, vol. 17, no. 5 (March 1919), p. 222. The leaflets were dropped near St-Dié and Raon-l'Étape on 3 September 1918. At the same time German propaganda could be anti-black. In the film *Honte noire* (Black Shame) black soldiers were depicted as rapists.

31. History of the operations of Base Section no. 3, vol. 3, p. 195, entry 2473, RG 120, NA.

32. Pershing, pp. 390, 394–5.

33. *The Times*, 13 June 1919.

34. Colson, 'An analysis of Negro patriotism', p. 24.

35. Major General Strong, ACS G2, to ACS Operations Division. Memorandum, 'Utilisation of Negro troops in friendly foreign territory', 17 June 1942, decimal file 1942–5, RG 165, NA.

36. *Crisis*, vol. 49, no. 120 (October 1942), p. 311.

Chapter 2 The Early War Years: First Encounters

1. For a full discussion of blacks in the American Army between the wars, and in the early years of World War II, see Ulysses Lee, *The*

United States Army in World War II: The Employment of Negro Troops, Special Studies (Washington, DC, 1966), particularly pp. 21–87, 136–78; A. Russell Buchanan, *Black Americans in World War II* (Santa Barbara 1977). pp. 59–70; Jack D. Foner, *Blacks and the Military in American History* (New York 1974), pp. 127–43; Alan M. Osur, *Blacks in the Army Air Forces during World War II* (Washington 1977), pp. 1–19.

2. James MacGregor Burns, *Roosevelt: The Soldier of Freedom 1940–1945* (New York 1970), p. 266. Another view is that it was Roosevelt's approach tọ 'bury racial problems as deeply as possible – a mixture of blindness, patchwork compromise, and faith that good public relations could gloss over prior errors' (Harvard Sitkoff, 'Racial militancy and interracial violence in the Second World War', *Journal of American History*, vol. 58, December 1971, p. 670).

3. Henry Stimson, *Diary*, 13, 24 January 1942. Microfilm edition.

4. Draft letters, Roosevelt to Spingarn, 28 September, 1 October 1943, with notes: PPF 133.6, Franklin D. Roosevelt Library, Hyde Park, New York.

5. Walter White, *A Man Called White* (London 1949), pp. 186–7.

6. Lee, pp. 75–6 has a copy of the statement. White's comment is in *A Man Called White*, p. 187.

7. A. Philip Randolph, 'Why should we march?', *Survey Graphic*, November 1942, reprinted in *Annals of America*, vol. 16 (1940–9), (Chicago 1968), pp. 124–6.

8. Quoted in Lee, pp. 137–8.

9. Forrest C. Pogue, *George C. Marshall: Ordeal and Hope 1939–1942* (London 1968), p. 96.

10. Stimson, 21 February 1945.

11. Quoted in Lee, pp. 140–1.

12. McCloy to Hastie, 2 July 1942, file 291.2, RG 107, National Archives, Washington, DC.

13. Fernando Henriques, 'The colour bar in the West Indies', *New Statesman*, 18 November 1944, pp. 334–5.

14. White to Churchill (with copy to Cordell Hull) 841-4016/5, RG 59, NA. The letter was acknowledged on 17 November, and 'receiving careful attention' said the British Embassy in Washington on 21 November. Foreign Office deliberations are in file FO 371/30665, Public Record Office, Kew, London. Churchill's reply (of 27 March 1942!) was published in *Crisis*, vol. 49, no. 6 (June 1942), pp. 196–7.

15. Eisenhower to Chief of Staff, 'The colored troop problem', 25 March 1942, file 291.21, RG 165, NA.

16. Major General Strong, ACS G-2, for Chief of Staff, 3 June 1942, OPD 291·21, RG 165, NA.

17. White to Churchill, 26 September 1941, 841-4016, RG 59, NA.

18. *ibid.*

19. *Crisis*, vol. 49, no. 6 (June 1942), pp. 196–7.

20. Foreign Office memorandum, piece A531, in FO 371/30644, PRO.

21. *ibid.*, A1855 and A2171.

22. *ibid.*, A2788.

23. The Foreign Office memoranda are dated 18 February 1942, A1638 and 28 February 1942, A1774. Halifax to Foreign Office 22 February 1942 is A1744, all in FO 371/30665, PRO.

24. *Pittsburgh Courier*, 24 June 1939, has the Schuyler comment. It is quoted in Lee Finkle, *Forum for Protest: The Black Press During World War II* (Cranbury, New Jersey 1975), p. 197. Finkle devotes pp. 191–200 to the Black Press in Britain. Other quotes are from here. See also Richard M. Dalfiume, 'The forgotten years of the Negro revolution', *Journal of American History*, vol. 55 (1968–9), p. 93.

25. Harold Moody, *The Colour Bar*, pamphlet (London 1944), p. 4; K. L. Little, *The Relations of White People and Coloured People in Great Britain*, pamphlet (Malvern 1946), p. 2; Little, 'A note on colour prejudice amongst the English middle class', *Man*, vol. 3 (September–October 1943), pp. 104–7.

26. Peter Noble, *The Negro in Films* (London 1949), p. 8.

27. FO 371/4460, AN 3040, PRO.

28. There is a copy of the report 'America', 17 February 1944 (headed 'confidential'), in file INF 1/292, attached to Home Intelligence weekly report no. 175, PRO.

29. File report 1095, 13 February 1942; file report 1569, 22 January 1943 (quote is on p. iv), Mass Observation Archives, University of Sussex, Brighton.

30. Butcher to Major General Surles, Bureau of Public Relations, Washington, 10 September 1942, box no.1, Butcher Papers, Eisenhower Library, Abilene, Kansas.

31. Kenneth Little, letter to *New Statesman*, 29 April 1942, p. 141.

32. Dr Harold Moody, letter *New Statesman*, 5 September 1942, p. 158.

Chapter 3 Attitudes and Anxieties: Jim Crow and the British Government

1. Quoted in Winston S. Churchill, *The Second World War*, vol. iii (London 1950), p. 483.

2. Mrs Horace Fry to Grace Tully, 4 June 1942, OF 93, Franklin D. Roosevelt Library, Hyde Park, New York.

3. *Parliamentary Debates* (Lords), vol. 124, cols. 70–1, 73, 29 July 1942.

4. *Parliamentary Debates* (Commons), vol. 383, cols. 670–1, 29 September 1942.

5. *Pittsburgh Courier*, 10 October 1942; 'Black and white', *Time*, 19 October 1942, p. 32; *Baltimore Afro-American*, 24 October 1942.

6. John Harvey (ed.), *The War Diaries of Oliver Harvey 1941–1945* (London 1978), 21 July 1942, p. 141.

7. Campbell to Foreign Office, telegram 4086, 12 August 1942, FO 954/30A, Public Record Office, Kew, London.

8. Hopkins to Marshall, 19 August 1942; Marshall to Hopkins, 21 August 1942; Hopkins to Campbell, 22 August 1942; Hopkins Papers, FDRL.

9. Warburg to Davis, 1 September 1942, 291.2, RG 107, National Archives, Washington, DC.

10. Winant to Roosevelt, telegram 4705, 22 August 1942, RG 59, NA.

11. Foreign Office to Washington, 1 September 1942, FO 954/29, folio 540 PRO; file closed until 1993.

12. Roosevelt to Winant, 10 September 1942, President's Secretary's file; diplomatic: John G. Winant, FDRL.

13. Note by J. C. Donnelly FO, 16 November 1943, FO 371/34126, A10199, PRO.

14. NAACP telegram, FO 371/30680, A11660; Malcolm memorandum, 28 December 1942, FO 371/30680, A11093, PRO.

15. Grigg memorandum, 'United States coloured troops in the United Kingdom [n.d. probably 7 September 1942], PREM 4/26/9, PRO. Grigg wrote two papers on the subject; the other was dated 3 October 1942; WP(42)441, CAB 66/29, PRO.

16. The preamble was telephoned to the Colonial Office on 29 August 1942, CO 876/14; the 'Notes on relations with coloured troops' (Dowler's Notes), 7 August 1942, are annexed to WP(42)441, CAB 66/29, PRO.

17. Young to Cranborne, 26 August 1942, CO 876/14, PRO.

18. *Parliamentary Debates* (Commons) vol. 383, cols. 670–1, 29 September 1942.

19. Denis Argent, panel directive, June 1943, Mass Observation Archives, University of Sussex, Brighton.

20. There is a copy of the minutes in CO 876/14, PRO, marked 'Most Secret'. All quotations are from this document.

21. There is a copy of the memorandum attached to WP(42)456 in CAB 66/29, PRO.

22. Keith to Cranborne, 12 September 1942, CO 876/14, PRO.

23. All the Foreign Office comments were made between 1 and 12 October 1942, and are in FO 371/30680, A 9731, PRO.

24. The full citations of the papers, all of which are in CAB 66/29, PRO are: Cranborne, 2 October 1942, WP(42)442; Simon, 9 October 1942, WP(42)455; Morrison, 10 October 1942, WP(42)456; Bracken, 12 October 1942, WP(42)459; Cripps, 12 October 1942, WP(42)460. No further references are made.

25. Quoted in David Dilks (ed.), *The Diaries of Sir Alexander Cadogan 1938–1945* (London 1971), p. 483. The preceding Cadogan comment is also from here.

26. Cabinet conclusions, 13 October 1942, CAB 65/28, PRO.

27. Cripps memorandum, and notes (Appendix A), 17 October 1942, CAB 66/30, PRO.

28. Grigg memorandum, 7 September 1942, PREM 4/26/9, PRO.

29. Cabinet conclusions, 13 October 1942, CAB 65/28, PRO.

30. Constantine to Watson, 12 January 1943, CO 876/15, PRO.

31. Rogers to CG ETO, 11 March 1943, 291.2 1943, RG 332 NA, Suitland.
32. *Welcome to Britain*, British Film Institute, London.
33. Letter from W. J. Elmslie, January 1943, BCC Archives.
34. *Spiritual Issues of the War*, no. 239 (1 June 1944), p. 2.
35. Phyllis Bentley, *Here is America* (London 1942), pp. 8, 14 and 39.
36. Maurice Colbourne, *America and Britain: A Mutual Introduction, with special reference to the British Empire* (London 1943), pp. 160–2.
37. Hilary St George Saunders, *Pioneers! O Pioneers!* (London 1944), pp. 84, 164.
38. J. L Hodson, *Home Front* (London 1944), pp. 187, 201.
39. J. L. Hodson, *And Yet I Like America* (London 1945), pp. 51, 116 and 276–7.
40. Quoted in Norman Longmate, *The GIs: The Americans in Britain 1942–1945* (London 1975), p. 61.

Chapter 4   Jim Crow in Britain: The US Army and Racial Segregation

1. The report of the investigation (carried out 1–3 October 1942) is 11042/72, 13 October 1942, IG VIII Air Force Service Command, RG 332, National Archives, Suitland.
2. Quoted in Phillip McGuire, *Taps for a Jim Crow Army* (Santa Barbara 1983), p. 67.
3. R. G. Hersey, AG to CG Field Forces, 14 February 1942, AG 332-97, RG 332, NA, Washington, DC.
4. Captain Harry C. Butcher, *Three Years with Eisenhower. His Personal Diary* (London 1946), pp. 16–17.
5. Fred Meyer for Eisenhower, to CG SOS ETOUSA, 16 July 1942, Adm. Hist. 218, RG 332, NA.
6. Colonel Landon, for Lee, to Base Section COs, 7 August 1942, Adm. Hist. 218, RG 332, NA.
7. Unpublished material on General Lee was obtained from Morris McGregor at US Army Department of History, Washington, DC.
8. Lee to Plank, 28 September 1942, AG 291.2 ETO 1942–3, RG 332, NA(S).
9. Carter, 'The racial problem in Britain', 25 August 1942, AG 291.2, RG 332, NA(S).
10. Montgomery to Lee, 5 August 1942, AG 332.999, RG 332, NA(S).
11. Elbert L. Harris, 'Social activities of the Negro soldier in England', *Negro History Bulletin*, vol. 11, no. 7 (April 1948), pp. 152–66.
12. Dahlquist ACS to Newsam, 3 September 1942, Adm. Hist. 218, RG 332, NA.
13. Eisenhower to Lee, 5 September 1942, Adm. Hist. 218, RG 332, NA.
14. Charles Higham and Roy Moseley, *A Biography of Merle Oberon* (Sevenoaks 1983), p. 103.

15. Devers to CG SOS ETOUSA, 25 October 1943, Adm. Hist. 218, RG 332, NA.

16. Oliver Haines, 'Inter-racial relations: Liverpool-Manchester area', 18 December 1943, AG 291.2, RG 332, NA(S).

17. Oliver Haines, 'Inter-racial relations: Ipswich', 21 November 1943, 250.1, RG 332, NA(S).

18. Gibson to Assistant Secretary of War, 17 December 1943, with attachments, 291.2, RG 107, NA.

19. Joe Louis (with Edna and Art Rust, jun.), *Joe Louis: My Life* (Brighton 1978), p. 186.

20. *Birmingham City Council Proceedings*, General Purposes Committee, 15 May 1945, p. 440, Birmingham Reference Library.

21. Report, 'Inter-racial relations', 250.1, entry 11042, 1943, RG 332 NA(S).

22. Quoted in James MacGregor Burns, *Roosevelt: The Soldier of Freedom 1940–1945* (New York 1970), p. 472.

23. Censorship report, 'Inter-racial relations', 1–15 April 1945, Adm. Hist. 58, RG 332, NA(S).

24. Quoted in Kenneth P. Werrell, 'Mutiny at Army Air Force Station 569: Bamber Bridge, England, June 1943', *Aerospace Historian*, vol. 22, no. 4 (Winter 1945), p. 206.

25. Section 4(d), report on 'Negro troops in Theatres', 8 October 1943, WDCSA 291.21, RG 165, NA.

26. Plank, 'Leadership of colored troops', 15 July 1943, AG 291.2, RG 332, NA(S).

27. Plank to Lee, 28 October 1943, AG 291.2, RG 332, NA(S).

28. David Lampe, 'Over-paid, over-sexed, over here', *Sunday Times Magazine*, 4 December 1964, p. 25.

29. Fisk for Eisenhower, to CGs and COs, 9 April 1944, Special Staff A-G files 291.2, RG 331, NA.

30. 'Command of Negro troops', War Department pamphlet WD 20-6, 29 February 1944.

31. Roi Ottley, 'Dixie invades Britain', *Negro Digest*, vol. iii, no. 1 (November 1944), p. 7.

32. Timuel Black, quoted in Studs Terkel, *The Good War* (London 1984), p. 279.

Chapter 5 Novelty to Familiarity: The Home Front

1. Quoted in Paul Addison, *The Road to 1945: British Politics and the Second World War* (pbk; London 1977), p. 147.

2. Army mail censorship report no. 59, 11–25 January 1943, FO 371/34123, A787, Public Record Office, Kew, London.

3. *Observer*, 8 April 1979.

4. Choc'late Soldier from the USA' by Elton Box, Sonny Cox and Lewis Ilda, published 1944 by Dash Music Company, London; reproduced here by courtesy of Campbell Connelly & Company, London.

5. Darvall MOI to Foreign Office, 22 January 1943, with survey of 16 December 1942, FO 371/35114, A852, PRO.

6. S. Orwell and I. Angus (eds.), *The Collected Essays, Journalism and Letters of George Orwell* (London 1968), vol. ii, p. 280, vol. iii, pp. 54, 128. The first and third comments were originally in *Partisan Review*, the second in *Tribune*.

7. The raw material is Panel Directive, June 1943, the report is file report 1885, Mass Observation Archive, University of Sussex, Brighton.

8. These comments from: raw material for file report 1569, box: America 1941–6, MO; extract from regional weekly Intelligence, 2–9 March 1943, FO 371/34123, A 1609; and 'British public feeling', FO 371/44601, AN 3040, PRO; postal and telegraph censorship report, 'Opinion on American troops in Britain', July 1943, FO 371/34126, A6922, PRO; Army mail censorship report on US troops, no. 92, 26 May–10 June 1944, FO 371/38625, AN 2452, PRO; 'British public feeling', FO 371/44601, AN 3040, PRO; raw material for file report 1569, MO Archives; Panel Directive, June 1943, MO.

9. 'British public feeling about America', in Haggard to Broadmead, 27 September 1945, FO 371/44601, AN 3040, PRO.

10. George W. Goodman, 'The Englishman meets the Negro', *Common Ground*, vol. v, no. 1 (Autumn 1944), p. 7.

11. Robin Cruickshank of the MOI, quoted in Walter White, *A Rising Wind* (New York 1945), p. 57.

12. Army mail censorship reports no. 62, 26 February–10 March 1943, FO 371/34124, A2391 and no. 91, 11 May–25 May 1944, FO 371/38624, AN 2231, PRO.

13. 'Black and white', *Time*, 19 October 1942, p. 34.

14. Roi Ottley, 'Dixie invades Britain', *Negro Digest*, vol. iii, no. 1 (November 1944), p. 8.

15. Donald Attwater, 'Black and white in England', *The Commonweal*, vol. xli, no. 12 (5 January 1945).

16. Eric Dingwall, *Racial Pride and Prejudice* (London 1946), pp. 61, 121–2.

17. Report, 'Investigation and action in Westonbirt', FO 954/30B, Avon Papers, PRO.

18. Inspector General's report, 'Investigation at Depot Q-104, Ditchingham Hall', 3 December 1943, entry 11042, box 72, RG 332, National Archives, Suitland.

19. 1st Ind. Hq., USFET Main, 1 October 1945, AG 291.2, RG 331, NA, Washington, DC.

20. Walter White, *A Rising Wind* (New York 1945), pp. 53–5.

21. Captain Shile [?] memorandum, 24 July 1942, AG 291.2, ETO 1942–3, RG 332, NA(S).

22. Carter, 'Racial problem in Britain', 25 August 1942, AG 291.2, ETO 1942–3, RG 332, NA(S).

23. The three quotes by US servicemen from: morale report, 1–15 September 1942, APO 887, Adm. Hist. 58, RG 332, NA(S); special

report, 'Colored troops', 16–31 August 1943, 1 September 1943, ASW 291.2, RG 107, NA; morale report 15–31 August 1943, APO 871, 353.8, RG 107, NA.

24. George Orwell, 'As I please', *Tribune*, 26 May 1944.

25. All comments are in: 'A preliminary report on attitudes of Negro soldiers in ETO', report ETO-B2, 7 February 1944, attitude reports, RG 330, NA.

26. Quotes from black US servicemen: morale reports (colored troops), 16–31 August, APO 887, 291.2 RG 107, NA, and 1–15 September 1942, APO 831, 291.2, RG 332, NA(S).

27. Ralph Ellison in Dorothy Sterling (ed.), *I Have Seen War* (New York 1960), pp. 103–10; Ellison to the author, 20 March 1977.

28. White to War Department, 11 February 1944, file: Staff WW Battlefront Tour, Recs. to WD, NAACP Papers, Library of Congress, Washington, DC.

Chapter 6 Dixie Invades Britain: The Racial Violence

1. Inspector General's report: 'Inter-racial relations in Oxford – Chipping Norton', 18 November 1943, 250.1, RG 332, National Archives, Suitland.

2. Captain Susie J. Thurman, AUS(WAC), Historical Section, 29 May 1944 on Negro morale report 16–30 April 1944, Adm. Hist. 218, RG 332, NA, Washington, DC.

3. Read, OSS to Black, G2 Intelligence, 28 July 1942, 5940 GB file, RG 165, NA(S).

4. Morale report 1–15 September 1942, APO 813 Belfast, 291.2, RG 332, NA(S).

5. William Weaver, *Yankee Doodle Dandy* (Ann Arbor 1958), pp. 217, 220.

6. Report, 'Investigations of racial relations in the United Kingdom', 11080/73, 291.2, RG 332, NA(S).

7. Reports of the incident are in Major Mills to CG VIII AF, 26 June 1943, and Miller to CG ETO, 13 July 1943, both in 519.765-1 at the Albert F. Simpson Historical Research Centre, Maxwell Air Force Base, Alabama; IG report 17 July 1943, 11080, 333.5, RG 332, NA(S). The incident has been fully examined by Kenneth P. Werrell in two articles: 'Mutiny at Army Air Force Station 569; Bamber Bridge, England', *Aerospace Historian*, December 1975, and 'The mutiny at Bamber Bridge', *After the Battle* (nd).

8. IG reports of this incident are by Captain Thrift, 29 September 1943, and by Lieutenant Colonel Plunkett, 7 October 1943, in AG 333.5, ETOUSA Report no. 3, 1943, RG 332, NA(S). See also White, *Rising Wind*, pp. 52–3, and *Chicago Defender*, 23 October 1943.

9. Chief Constable Cole to Acting Inspector of Constabulary, North Midlands Regional Office, 4 February 1943, 250.1, 1943, RG 332, NA(S).

10. Memorandum from General Henry Arnold, October 1945, to War Department, Arnold Papers, Library of Congress, Washington, DC; 'When top brass had to calm troops', *Leicester Mercury*, 9 December 1982.
11. Keith to Jeffries, 31 July 1942, CO 876/14, Public Record Office, Kew, London.
12. *Bristol Evening Post*, 28 October 1942.
13. *Bristol Evening Post*, 17 July 1944; minutes of British-American Liaison Board (BALB), 21 July 1944, FO 371/38511, AN 3007, PRO; Deputy Theater Provost Marshal to Deputy Theater Commander, 20 July 1944, OASW 204, RG 107, NA.
14. The Kingsclere incident was reported in the national press but full coverage of the trial is in *Newbury Weekly News*, 16 November 1944. For apology see regional commissioners' reports for quarter ending 31 December 1944, FO 371/44601, AN 421, PRO.
15. Quoted in Studs Terkel, *The Good War* (London 1985), p. 387.
16. Miller to CG ETO, 13 July 1943, 5198.765-1, AFSHRC, Alabama.
17. *ibid.*

Chapter 7 The Watchdogs: Jim Crow Under Close Scrutiny

1. Quoted in Mary Penick Motley, *The Invisible Soldier* (Detroit 1975), p. 180.
2. Lee Finkle,*Forum for Protest: the Black Press During World War II* (Cranbury, New Jersey 1975), p. 156.
3. B. O. Davis to CG ETOUSA, 'Survey concerning friction between colored and white troops', 25 October 1942, 291.2, RG 332, National Archives, Suitland, and a slightly different version for the Inspector General's Department, 24 December 1942, 255-291.2, RG 107, NA, Washington, DC.
4. Joseph Julian, 'Jim Crow Goes Abroad', *The Nation*, 5 December 1942, p. 610.
5. Harvard Sitkoff, *New Deal for Blacks* (New York 1979), pp. 42–3, 317. See pp. 58–66 for an assessment of Mrs Roosevelt's involvement in racial matters.
6. Bray to Roosevelt, 7 October 1942; Roosevelt to Bray, 8 October 1942; McIntyre memorandum, 8 October 1942, OF 93, Franklin D. Roosevelt Library, Hyde Park, New York.
7. Mrs Kennedy to Mrs Roosevelt, 10 September 1942; Mrs Roosevelt to Mrs Kennedy, 2 October 1942; Mrs Roosevelt to Stimson, 22 September 1942, personal letters, ER Papers, FDRL.
8. Stimson to Mrs Roosevelt, 16 October 1942 (but not sent), with attached memorandum, 23 October 1942, 291.2, RG 107, NA, Washington, DC. Stimson, *Diary*, 2 October 1942; Stimson to Chief of Staff, 2 October 1942, 291.2, RG 107, NA.
9. The record of the the visit is in file 190.3, Trip to England, ER Papers, FDRL.

10. John Harvey (ed.), *The War Diaries of Oliver Harvey 1941–1945* (London 1978), 23 October 1942, p. 171.

11. Quoted in Joseph P. Lash, *Eleanor Roosevelt* (pbk; New York 1971), p. 869.

12. Hayes to Mrs Roosevelt (with enclosure of corporal's letter), 8 November 1943 (sent on to Roosevelt, 23 November), OF 93, FDRL; Mrs Roosevelt to McCloy, 23 November 1943, 291.2, RG 107; Devers to Mrs Roosevelt, with comment sheet, 22 December 1943, AG Central 291.2, RG 332, NA(S).

13. Pt. William Johnson to Mrs Roosevelt, 13 November 1944, 291.2, RG 107, NA.

14. Gilstrap report, 'Tour of Mr Walter White in the ETO', to Colonel Lawrence, PRO ETO, 11 February 1944, 291.2, RG 332, NA(S).

15. Cruickshank to Butler, 18 January 1944, FO 371/38699, AN 269, Public Record Office, Kew, London.

16. White to Mrs Roosevelt, 1 November 1943; Mrs Roosevelt to White, 3 November 1943; ER Papers, FDRL.

17. Halifax to Foreign Office, 21 November 1943, FO 37138699, AN 666, PRO; Point 6, Gibson memorandum to ASW, 17 December 1943, 291.2, RG 107, NA; Walter White, *A Rising Wind* (New York 1945), p. 13.

18. Cruickshank and Malcolm, FO, 11 February 1944; Butler minute, 12 February 1944, FO 371/38699, AN 587, PRO.

19. 'Observations and recommendations of Walter White on racial relations in the ETO', 11 February 1944, OASW 204, RG 107, NA. Digests of his report and recommendations also appear in a file: White's battlefront tour 1944, in NAACP Papers, Library of Congress, Washington, DC. See also *Crisis*, vol. 51, no. 6 (June 1944), pp. 98–9.

20. Inspector General's report, 'Investigations of racial relations in the UK', to CG ETOUSA, 27 February 1944, Staff: White's battlefront tour, recs. to WD, NAACP Papers, LC.

21. Gilstrap report, 'Tour of . . . White', RG 332, NA(S).

22. Morale special report, 1–15 March 1944, Adm. Hist. 218, RG 332, NA.

23. White to Mrs Roosevelt, 13 February 1944 and 23 February 1944, ER Papers, FDRL.

24. Lee to White (with enclosures), 3 April 1944, personal letters, ER Papers, FDRL.

25. White to Mrs Roosevelt, 25 April 1944, ER Papers; White to NAACP board, 8 May 1944 (with copy to Mrs Roosevelt, 15 May 1944), ER Papers, FDRL.

26. White to Mrs Roosevelt, 19 July 1944 (with Chicago speech); Mrs Roosevelt to White, 3 August 1944; White to Mrs Roosevelt 10(?) August 1944, ER Papers, FDRL.

27. On the wartime press see Angus Calder, *The People's War 1939–1945* (London 1969), pp. 581–6, and on press censorship Admiral G. P. Thomson, *Blue Pencil Admiral* (London 1947), *passim*.

28. Notes on censorship J217, no. 240, 8 September 1942, Adm. Hist. 58 RG 332, NA(S).

29. Dwight D. Eisenhower, *Crusade in Europe* (London 1948), pp. 66–7.

30. Butcher to Raymond Daniell, 17 August 1942, box no. 1, Butcher Papers, Eisenhower Library, Kansas.

31. Roi Ottley, *Inside Black America* (London 1948), p. 248.

32. Michael Carter to Churchill, 28 January 1944, FO 371/38633, A 1013, A 1426, PRO.

33. On the earlier incident see censorship report, 24 September 1943, ASW 291.2, RG 107, NA. On the Launceston incident (when a reporter, David Orro, was recalled to the States) see correspondence between Gibson, McCloy and Surles, between 25 October and 4 November 1943, 291.2, RG 107, NA.

34. Minutes, FO 371/34086, A 78, PRO.

35. Major Miller to CGT ETO, 13 July 1943, 519.765-1, Albert F. Simpson Historical Research Center, Maxwell Air Force Base, Alabama.

36. David Dilks (ed.), *The Diaries of Sir Alexander Cadogan 1938–1945* (London 1971), 15 July 1943, p. 530; Butler note, 24 February 1944, FO 371/38623, AN 587, PRO.

37. Grigg to Churchill, 21 October 1943, PREM 4/26/9, PRO.

38. Marlborough to Churchill, 18 November 1943, PREM 4/26/9 PRO.

39. Grigg to Churchill, 2 December 1943, PREM, 4/26/9, PRO.

40. William Armstrong (ed.), *Cecil H. King: With Malice Toward None; A War Diary* (London 1970), p. 255.

Chapter 8 'No Mother No Father, No Uncle Sam': Sex and Brown Babies

1. References to Dowler's Notes and Cabinet debates of 1942 are in Chapter 3. To avoid unnecessary repetition only new references are cited here.

2. Petherick to Eden' 16 August 1942, FO 954/30A, folio 153/4; 17 July 1943, FO 954/30A, folio 132; 4 December 1943, FO 954/30A, folio 204, Public Record Office, Kew, London.

3. Warburg to Elmer Davis, 1 September 1942, 291.2, RG 107, National Archives, Washington, DC.

4. Carter memorandum, 'The racial problem in Britain', 25 August 1942, AG 291.2, HQ SOS ETO 1942–3, RG 332, NA, Suitland.

5. Morale report, 1–15 September 1942, APO 813, 291.2, 1943; censorship report, 'Inter-racial relations', 16–30 June 1945, Adm. Hist. 212; censorship report, 16–30 September 1944, Adm. Hist. 58, all in RG 332, NA(S).

6. Campbell to FO, telegram 4086, 12 August 1942, FO 954/30A, folio 151, PRO; Winant to FDR, telegram 4705, 22 August 1942, 740.0011, RG 59, NA.

7. Bolero Combined Committee (London), 12 August 1942, CO 876/14, PRO.

8. Keith to Wyndham, 28 August 1942, CO 876/14, PRO.

9. Home Intelligence weekly reports, nos. 99 and 102, 27 August 1942 and 17 September 1942, INF 1/292, PRO.

10. British-American Liaison Board progress report, 26 May 1944 sent by Agar to Winant, 1 August 1944, RG 84, NA(S).

11. Eisenhower to Lee, 5 September 1942, Adm. Hist. 218, RG 332, NA.

12. Eisenhower to Surles, AGWAR, 7 March 1945, S-81213, 291.2, RG 331, NA.

13. Murray to Miss Richards, 24 June 1942, CO 876/14, PRO.

14. Morale report, 1–15 September 1942, APO 813, RG 332, NA(S); special report (Colored troops), 16–31 August 1943; 291.2, RG 107, NA (the emphasis is in the original).

15. US censored mail, 1–20 September 1943, FO 371/34126, A 9114.

16. Army mail censorship reort, no. 93, 11–25 June 1944, FO 371/38625, AN 2646, PRO; 'prick-mazed' is quoted in Susan Briggs, *Keep Smiling Through: The Home Front 1939–45* (London 1975), p. 133.

17. Haig report, 6 September 1943, FO 371/34126, A 10199: report of a conference, 23 November 1943, FO 371/34126, A 11600, both in PRO.

18. Grigg to Churchill, 21 October 1943, PREM 4/26/9, PRO.

19. MOI report, 'British public feeling about America', June 1943, FO 371/44601, AN 3040, PRO.

20. *Huddersfield Examiner*, 20 September, 28 September, 29 September, 8 October 1943.

21. *The Nation*, 31 October 1942, p. 459.

22. Wolverhampton *Express & Star*, 28 April 1943; *Spectator*, 6 August 1943.

23. Raw material for file report 1569, 22 January 1943, Mass Observation Archive, University of Sussex, Brighton.

24. *Sunday Pictorial*, 26 August 1945; *Pittsburgh Courier*, 1 September 1945,.

25. William Weaver, *Yankee Doodle Dandy* (Ann Arbor 1958), p. 220.

26. Harold Moody, 'Anglo-American coloured children', *The World's Children*, March 1946, p. 44.

27. Weaver, p. 365.

28. Ormus Davenport,'US race prejudice dooms 1000 British babies', *Reynolds News*, 9 February 1947.

29. There is a note of the Goosey case in J. A. Rogers, *Nature Knows No Color-Line* (New York 1952), pp. 151–2.

30. Morrison memorandum, 13 October 1942, CAB 66/29, PRO; Sulzberger quoted in Warburg to Davis, OWI, 1 September 1942, 291.2, RG 107, NA; Petherick to Eden, 16 August 1942, FO 954/30A, folio 153/4, PRO.

31. Marlborough to Churchill, 21 October 1943, PREM 4/26/9, PRO.

32. Postal censorship report no. 38, letter of 17 February 1943, FO 371/34124, A 3468, PRO.

33. No records of this conference have been traced; the sergeant's concern is in American Consulate, Manchester, to State, 12 January 1945, confidential file 1945–1949, RG 59, NA.

34. Sarah G. Moyse to Eleanor Roosevelt, 25 February 1945; Eleanor Roosevelt to FDR, 9 March 1945; FDR to Eleanor Roosevelt, 12 March 1945, box 10, OF 93, FDRL.

35. On Ekarte see Alfred Eris, 'Britain's mulatto "GI" babies', *Liberty*, 7 December 1946 (pagination not clear) and FO 371/61016, AN 97, PRO.

36. 'Britain's brown babies', *Ebony*, November 1946, p. 19; Ras Makonnen, *Pan-Africanism from Within* (London 1973), pp. 143–4.

37. *Congressional Record* (House), 23 April 1947, vol. 93, pt. 3, p. 3861.

38. Ede's comments came at Home Office meeting, 13 December 1945, FO 371/51617, AN 3/3/45, PRO; the colonial comment is Siggins to FO, 18 July 1947, FO 371/61020, PRO.

39. The meeting which Miss Bangham attended was on 13 December 1945, FO 371/51617, AN 3/3/45, PRO.

40. *Courier: Picturing Today*, vol. 6, no. 1 (April 1946). This is a special insert forming pages 125–36, but numbered 1–12. This article is on page 12.

Chapter 9 The Black GI in Britain: Reflections and Results

1. W. J. Gallman, London Embassy to State, Despatch 27253, 5 December 1942, file 822, RG 84, National Archives, Suitland.

2. A History of the American Forces Liaison Division 1942–5, INF 1/327B, Public Record Office, Kew, London.

3. Transcripts of Axis broadcasts mentioned are in BBC Written Archives Centre, Caversham, Berkshire.

4. The propaganda leaflets mentioned are in the collection of R. G. Auckland, St Alban's, Hertfordshire.

5. Pete Grafton, *You, You and You! The People out of Step with World War II* (London 1981), pp. 97–9.

6. Censorship report 16–30 April 1945, Adm Hist. 58, RG 332, NA(S).

7. Quoted in *Southern Frontier*, vol. vi, no. 9 (September 1945).

8. Censorship report, 16–31 May 1945, Adm. Hist. 212, RG 332, NA(S).

9. Harry W. Roberts, 'The impact of military service upon the racial attitudes Negro servicemen in World War II', *Social Problems*, vol. i, October 1953, pp. 65–9, and 'Prior-service attitudes towards whites of 219 Negro veterans', *Journal of Negro Education*, October 1953, pp. 455–65.

10. Winthrop Jordan, *White over Black: American Attitudes Toward the Negro* (Baltimore 1969), pp. 209–10.

11. Grigg memorandum, September 1942, PREM 4/26/9, PRO.

12. Quoted in *Crisis*, vol. 49, no. 8 (August 1942), p. 247.

13. Morale report (Coloured troops), 1–15 September 1942, APO 813, 291.2, RG 332, NA(S); A 6922, FO 371/34126, PRO; the airforce corporal's comment is in Negro morale extracts, Base Censor Office, no. 1 APO 813, 1–15 March 1944, RG 332, NA, Washington, DC.

14. Byrd to Bilbo, 11 December 1945, decimal file 1944–5, RG 165, NA.

15. Cecil Roberts, *And So to America* (London 1946), pp. 216–17.

16. Eric John Dingwall, *Racial Pride and Prejudice* (London 1946), pp. 3–4.

A Select Bibliography

Manuscript and Archive Sources

United States of America

Albert F. Simpson Historical Research Center, Maxwell Air Force Base, Alabama
Army Air Force Records.

Columbia University, New York
John Foster Dulles: report of 21 October 1942 for Institute of Pacific Relations on his trip to England 28 June–25 July 1942.

Centre of Military History, US Army, Washington, DC
Transcripts of Lee Nichols' interviews with Generals Lee and Almond.

Eisenhower Library, Abilene, Kansas
Harry Butcher Papers.

Franklin D. Roosevelt Library, Hyde Park, New York State
Eleanor Roosevelt Papers.
Harry Hopkins Papers.
President's Secretary's File (PSF).
President's Official File (OF).
President's Personal File (PPF).
Miscellaneous Papers.

Library of Congress, Manuscript Division, Washington, DC

General Henry Arnold Papers.
General Ira Eaker Papers.
NAACP Papers.
General Carl Spaatz Papers.
Arthur Barnett Spingarn Papers.

National Archives, Washington, DC, and Suitland Records Center, Maryland
Record Groups:

RG 59	Department of State
RG 84	Foreign Service Posts
RG 102	Children's Bureau Records
RG 107	Office of Secretary of War
RG 120	American Expeditionary Forces 1917–23
RG 160	Army Service Forces
RG 165	War Department, General and Special Staff
RG 330	Secretary of Defense
RG 331	Allied Operational and Occupation HQ
RG 332	Theatres of War, US, World War II

United States Army Military History Institute, Carlisle Barracks, Pennsylvania
Briefs of testimonies compiled by Captain Pease for Gillem Committee.

Britain

Auckland Collection, St Alban's, Hertfordshire
Private collection of Axis propaganda leaflets.

British Broadcasting Corporation, Written Archives Centre, Caversham Park, Reading
Daily digest of Axis radio broadcasts.

Church House, London
Church of England Moral Welfare Council: Executive and Finance Committee Minutes.

Greater London Record Office, London
Records of Family Welfare Association.

London School of Economics
Hugh Dalton diary.

Public Record Office, Kew, London

CAB   War Cabinet Papers
CO   Colonial Office Papers
FO   Foreign Office and Avon Papers
HO   Home Office Papers
INF   Ministry of Information Papers
LAB   Ministry of Labour Papers
PREM Prime Minister's Papers
WO   War Office Papers

Selly Oak Colleges, Birmingham
Records of British Council of Churches:
Department of International Friendship.
Executive Committee Minutes.

Taunton, Somerset
Records of committees and sub-committees of Somerset County
Council.

University of Keele, Staffordshire (or any large public or uni-
versity library)
Parliamentary Debates for House of Commons and House of
Lords (Hansard)

University of Sussex, Brighton
Mass Observation Archive (MO).

University of Warwick, Near Coventry
Papers of National Campaign for Abolition of Death Penalty.

Published Material

Books

Addison, Paul, *The Road to 1945: British Politics and The Second
World War* (London 1977).
Ambrose, Stephen, *The Supreme Commander. The War Years of
General Dwight D. Eisenhower* (London 1971).
Armstrong, William (ed.), *Cecil King. With Malice Toward None:
A War Diary* (London 1970).
Banton, Michael, *The Coloured Quarter: Negro Immigrants in an
English City* (London 1955).
Barbeau, Arthur E. and Henri, Florette, *The Unknown Soldiers:
Black American Troops in World War I* (Philadelphia 1974).

Blum, John Morton, *V Was for Victory: Politics and American Culture during World War II* (New York 1976).

Buchanan, A. Russell, *Black Americans in World War II* (Oxford 1977).

Burns, James MacGregor, *Roosevelt: The Soldier of Freedom 1940–1945* (New York 1970).

Butcher, Capt. Harry C., *Three Years with Eisenhower: His Personal Diary* (London 1946).

Byers, Jean, *A Study of the Negro in Military Service* (Washington 1947, 1950).

Calder, Angus, *The People's War 1939–1945* (London 1969).

Chandler, Alfred D., jun. (ed.), *The Papers of Dwight David Eisenhower: The War Years*, 5 vols., (Baltimore and London 1970).

Colbourne, Maurice, *America and Britain: A Mutual Introduction* (London 1943).

Constantine, Learie, *Colour Bar* (London 1954).

Craven, Wesley Frank and Cate, James Lea (eds.), *The Army Air Forces in World War II* (Chicago 1948–58).

Dalfiume, Richard M., *Desegregation of the US Armed Forces: Fighting on Two Fronts 1939–1953* (Columbia, Missouri, 1969).

Davie, Maurice R., *Negroes in American Society* (London 1949).

Davis, John P. (ed.), *American Negro Reference Book* (New Jersey 1966).

Dilks, David (ed.), *The Diaries of Sir Alexander Cadogan 1938–1945* (London 1971).

Dingwall, Eric John, *Racial Pride and Prejudice* (London 1946).

D'Usseau, Arnaud and Gow, James, *Deep are the Roots* (New York 1946).

Eisenhower, Dwight D., *Crusade in Europe* (London 1948).

Ellison, Ralph, 'In a strange country', in Sterling, Dorothy (ed.), *I Have Seen War* (New York 1960).

Ferguson, Sheila and Fitzgerald, Hilde, *Studies in the Social Services* (London 1954).

Finkle, Lee, *Forum for Protest: The Black Press During World War II* (Cranbury, New Jersey, 1975).

Foner, Jack D., *Blacks and the Military in American History* (New York 1974).

Foot, Paul, *Immigration and Race in British Politics* (Harmondsworth 1965).

Fryer, Peter, *Staying Power: The History of Black People in Britain* (London 1984).

Furr, Arthur, *Democracy's Negroes: A Book of Facts Concerning the Activities of Negroes in World War II* (Boston 1947).

Gallup, George H. (ed.), *The Gallup International Public Opinion Polls, Great Britain 1937–1975*, 2 vols, (New York 1976).

Glass, Ruth, *Newcomers: The West Indians in London* (London 1960).

Grafton, Pete, *You, You and You! The People Out of Step With World War II* (London 1981).

Graham, Stephen, *Children of the Slaves* (London 1920).

Graves, Charles, *Women in Green: The Story of the WVS* (London 1948).

Hachey, Thomas (ed.), *Confidential Dispatches: Analyses of America by the British Ambassador 1939–1945* (Evanston 1974).

Halsey, Margaret, *Color Blind* (New York 1946).

Harvey, John (ed.), *The War Diaries of Oliver Harvey 1941–1945* (London 1978).

Hodson, James Lansdale, *Home Front* (London 1944).

——— *And Yet I Like America* (London 1945).

Howat, Gerald, *Learie Constantine* (London 1975, 1977).

Hunton, Addie and Johnson, Kathryn, *Two Colored Women with the American Expeditionary Forces* (New York 1921).

Irving, David, *The War Between the Generals* (Harmondsworth 1982).

Jackson, Stanley, *An Indiscreet Guide to Soho* (London 1946).

Jordan, Alexander B. (ed.), *I Can Tell the World* (Ipswich 1943–4).

Karsten, Peter, *Soldiers and Society: The Effects of Military Service and War on American Life* (Westport, Conn., 1978).

Kellog, Charles Flint, *NAACP: A History of the National Association for the Advancement of Colored People*, vol. 1, 1909–1920 (Baltimore 1967).

Langdon-Davis, John, *American Close-up: The Portrait of An Ally* (London 1943).

Lash, Joseph, *Eleanor and Franklin* (London 1972).

Lee, Ulysses, *The United States Army in World War II: The Employment of Negro Troops* (Washington, DC, 1966).

Levine, Lawrence, *Black Culture and Black Consciousness: Afro-American Folk Thought from Slavery to Freedom* (New York 1978).

Little, Kenneth, *Negroes in Britain: A Study of Race Relations in English Society* (London 1948).

Logan, Rayford (ed.), *What the Negro Wants* (Chapel Hill, North Carolina, 1944).

Longmate, Norman, *How We Lived Then* (London 1971, 1973).

——— *The GIs: The Americans in Britain 1942–1945* (London 1975).

McGuire, Phillip, *Taps for a Jim Crow Army: Letters from Black Soldiers in World War II* (Santa Barbara 1983).

McLaine, Ian, *Ministry of Morale: Home Front Morale and the Ministry of Information in World War II* (London 1979).

McWilliams, Carey, *Brothers Under the Skin* (Boston 1943).

Mandelbaum, David C., *Soldier Groups and Negro Soldiers* (Berkeley 1952).

Menefee, Selden, *Assignment USA* (London 1944).

Moskos, Charles C., jun., *The American Enlisted Man: The Rank and File in Today's Military* (New York 1970).

Mosley, Leonard, *Backs to the Wall: London Under Fire 1939–1945* (London 1971).

Motley, Mary Penick, *The Invisible Soldier* (Detroit 1975).

Mullen, Robert W., *Blacks in America's Wars: The Shift in Attitudes from the Revolutionary War to Vietnam* (New York 1973).

Murray, Florence (ed.), *Negro Handbook* (New York 1947).

Nalty, Bernard C., *Strength for the Fight: A History of Black Americans in the Military* (New York 1986).

Nichols, Lee, *Breakthrough on the Color Front* (New York 1958).

Noble, Peter, *The Negro in Films* (London 1949).

Odum, Howard W., *Race and Rumors of Race* (Chapel Hill, North Carolina, 1943).

Orwell, Sonia and Angus, Ian (eds.), *The Collected Essays, Journalism and Letters of George Orwell*, vols 2 and 3 (London 1968).

Ottley, Roi, *Inside Black America* (London 1948).

Patterson, Sheila, *Dark Strangers: A Study of West Indians in London* (Harmondsworth 1965).

Perrett, Geoffrey, *Days of Sadness, Years of Triumph: The American People 1939–1945* (Baltimore 1974).

Pershing, John J., *My Experiences in the World War* (London 1931).

Pogue, Forrest C., *George C. Marshall: Ordeal and Hope 1939–1942* (London 1968).

Polenberg, Richard, *War and Society: The United States 1941–1945* (Philadelphia 1972).

Richmond, Anthony, *Colour Prejudice in Britain* (London 1954).

———— *The Colour Problem* (Harmondsworth 1955).

Roberts, Cecil, *And So To America* (London 1946).

Rogers, Joel, *Nature Knows No Color-Line* (New York 1952).

Rudwick, Elliott M., *W. E. Du Bois; A Study in Minority Group Leadership* (Oxford 1960).

Saunders, Hilary St George, *Pioneers O Pioneers!* (London 1944).

Schoenfeld, Seymour J., *The Negro in the Armed Forces* (Washington, DC, 1945).

Scobie, Edward, *Black Britannia: A History of Blacks in Britain* (Chicago 1972).

Scott, Emmett J., *American Negro in the World War* (Chicago 1919; New York 1969).

Shute, Nevil, *The Chequer Board* (London 1947).

Silvera, John D., *The Negro in World War II* (Baton Rouge 1946).

Sitkoff, Harvard, *New Deal for Blacks: The Emergence of Civil Rights as a National Issue. vol. 1, The Depression Decade* (New York 1979).

Smithies, Edward, *Crime in Wartime: A Social History of Crime in World War II* (London 1982).

Stewart Ollie *et al.*, *This Is Our War* (Baltimore 1945).

Stillman, Richard, *Integration of the Negro in the US Armed Forces* (New York 1968).

Stimson, Henry L., and Bundy, McGeorge, *On Active Service in Peace and War* (New York 1947).

Stouffer, Samuel *et al.*, *Studies in Social Psychology in World War II, vol. 1: The American Soldier — Adjustment during Army Life* (Princeton 1949).

Terkel, Studs, *The Good War* (London 1985).

Terry, Wallace, *Bloods: An Oral History of the Vietnam War by Black Veterans* (New York 1984).

Thorne, Christopher, *Allies of a Kind* (London 1978).

Treadwell, Mattie E., *The Woman's Army Corps: Special Studies* (Washington 1954).

Osur, Alan, *Blacks in the Army Air Forces During World War II* (Washington 1977).

Vaughan, David A., *Negro Victory: The Life Story of Dr Harold Moody* (London 1950).

Walvin, James, *Black and White: The Negro and English Society 1555–1945* (London 1973).

Weaver, William G., *Yankee Doodle Dandy* (Ann Arbor 1958).

White A. C. T., *The Story of Army Education 1643–1963* (London 1963).

White, Walter, *A Rising Wind* (New York 1945).

—— *A Man Called White* (London 1949).

Whitney W. D., *Who Are the Americans?* (London 1941, 1942).

Wilson, Ruth, *Jim Crow Joins Up* (New York 1941).

Wimperis, Virginia, *The Unmarried Mother and her Child* (London 1960).

Wynn, Neil, *The Afro-American and the Second World War* (London 1976).

Pamphlets and reports

Dr Barnardo's, *Racial Integration and Barnardo's*, report of a working party (London 1966).

Fisher, Lettice, *Twenty-one Years and After: A Short History of the National Council for the Unmarried Mother and Her Child* (London 1946).

Little, K. L., *Relations of White People and Coloured People in Great Britain* (Malvern 1946).

MacNeice, Louis, *Meet the US Army* (London 1943).

McNeill, Sylvia, *Report of a Survey of the Illegitimate Children Born in Britain of English Mothers and of Fathers Who Are Mostly American Coloured Servicemen* (London 1946).

Moody, Harold, *Colour Bar* (London 1944, 1945).

———— *Christianity and Race Relations* (London(?) 1943).

National Council for Unmarried Mother and Her Child, *Reports 1943–1944, 1944–1946* (London).

Padmore, George (ed.), *History of Pan-African Congress of 1945* (London 1947, 1963).

Styler, W. E., *What About Race? WEA Topics for Discussion No. 2* (London 1944).

Watson, Arnold, *West Indian Workers in Britain* (London 1942).

Newspapers

Whole series

Baltimore Afro-American	1942–8
Bridgnorth Journal	1942–5
Bristol Evening Post	1942–3
Express & Star (Wolverhampton)	1942–4
Ludlow Advertiser	1943–5
Shrewsbury Chronicle	1942–5
The Times	1942–7
Wellington Journal and Shrewsbury News	1942–5
Whitchurch Herald	1943–5

Specific articles in other newspapers

'Hint tan-yank baby deal a fund raising hoax', *Chicago Defender*, 3 May 1947.

'Britain "Exports" 5000 babies', *Daily Mail*, 5 April 1947.

Bedford, Ronald, 'The colour-barred babies', *Daily Mirror*, 22 July 1947.

Hinton, Harold, 'Klan in the South keeps under cover', *New York Times*, 1 September 1947.

Solon, S. L., 'Because their skins are brown', *News Chronicle*, 8 May 1944.

Driberg, Tom, 'Ways to smash the colour bar', *Reynolds News*, 26 September 1942.

Davenport, Ormus, 'US race prejudice dooms 1000 British babies', *Reynolds News*, 9 February 1947.

————— 'Half-caste GI babies lead restless lives', *Reynolds News*, 16 February 1947.

————— 'They want these half-caste babies', *Reynolds News*, 2 March 1947.

Bracken, Brendan, 'Colour bar must go', *Sunday Express*, 20 September 1942.

'Vicar's wife insults our allies', *Sunday Pictorial*, 6 September 1942.

'All this happened in England yesterday', *Sunday Pictorial*, 26 August 1945.

'The twenty "black" babies of Porlock', *Sunday Pictorial*, 25 July 1947.

Marquis of Donegall, 'Negro soldiers find Britons are cordial', *Sunday Dispatch*, 5 March 1944.

Weekly magazines

Whole series

Economist	1942–5
New Statesman	1942–5
Picture Post	1942–8
Spectator	1942–5
Spiritual Issues of the War	1942–5
Time and Tide	1943–4

Specific articles in other magazines

Attwater, Donald, 'Black and white in England', *The Commonweal*, vol. xli, no. 12, 5 January 1945.

'The babies they left behind them', *Life*, 23 August 1948.

'The black buffaloes', *Newsweek*, 8 June 1970.

'Black and white', *Time*, 19 October 1944.

'Brown Tiny Tims', *Newsweek*, 29 December 1947.

'These coloured intruders', *John Bull*, 26 January 1946.

Eris, Alfred, 'Britain's mulatto "G.I." babies', *Liberty*, 7 December 1946.

'Is There Anywhere', *Time*, 11 March 1946.
Julian, Joseph, 'Jim Crow goes abroad', *Nation*, vol. 155, 5 December 1942.
Lampe, David, 'Over-paid, over-sexed, over here', *Sunday Times Magazine*, 4 December 1966.
'Report on the GI', *Time*, 30 October 1944.
'Report on Negroes', *Newsweek*, 2 March 1944.
Reynolds, Quentin, ' . . . Finished 33 miles singing', *Illustrated*, 26 September 1942.
'Their father was a Negro', *Newsweek*, 11 March 1946.
'The trial of a Negro', *Tribune*, 9 June 1944.
'Unhappy soldier', *Time*, 10 July 1944.

Journals

Whole series

Army Quarterly	1942–6
Civil Liberty	1940–5
Common Sense	1942–5
The Crisis	1940–52
Current Affairs	1942–5
Documentary News Letter	1942–5
Ebony	1945–50
Interracial Review	1942–5
Messenger	1919
Monthly Summary of Events and Trends in Race Relations	1943–5
Negro Digest	1942–5
Newsletter	1940–50
Opportunity	1942–5
The Outpost	1942–4
Southern Frontier	1942–5
Survey Graphic	1942–5
Transatlantic	1943–5

Specific articles in other journals

Dalfiume, Richard M., 'The "forgotten years" of the Negro revolution', *Journal of American History*, June 1968.
Drake, St Clair, 'The "colour problem" in Britain: a study in social definitions', *Sociological Review*, vol. 3, 1955.
'G.I. kids cry for self rule', *Courier: Picturing Today*, vol. 6, no. 1, April 1946.

Glaser, Daniel, 'The sentiments of American soldiers towards Europeans', *American Journal of Sociology*, March 1946.

Goodman, George, 'The Englishman meets the Negro', *Common Ground*, vol. v, no. 1, Autumn 1944.

Hachey, Thomas, 'Document: Jim Crow with a British accent', *Journal of Negro History*, January 1974.

————— 'Walter White and the American Negro soldier in World War II: a diplomatic dilemma for Britain', *Phylon*, vol. xxxix, no. 3, September 1978.

Hall E. T., jun., 'Race prejudice and Negro-White relations in the Army', *American Journal of Sociology*, March 1947.

Landes, Ruth, 'Summary of a survey on Negro-White relationships in Britain', *Man*, vol. lii, September 1952.

Little, K. L., 'A note on colour prejudice amongst the English middle classes', *Man,* vol. iii, September–October 1943.

MacDonald, Roderick J., 'Dr. Harold Arundel Moody and the League of Coloured Peoples. A retrospective view', *Race*, vol. xiv, January 1973.

McNeil, Edwin C., 'United States Army courts-martial in Britain', *Law Quarterly Review*, vol. 60, October 1944.

McGuire, Phillip, 'Judge Hastie, World War II and army racism', *Journal of Negro History*, October 1977.

Moody, Harold, 'Anglo-American coloured children', *The World's Children*, March 1946.

Moskos, Charles C., jun., 'Racial integration in the armed forces', *American Journal of Sociology*, September 1966.

————— 'Success story: blacks in the Army', *The Atlantic Monthly*, May 1986.

Roberts, Harry W., 'Prior-service attitudes towards whites of 219 Negro veterans', *Journal of Negro Education*, October 1953.

————— 'The impact of military service upon the racial attitudes of Negro servicemen in World War II', *Social Problems*, October 1953.

Sitkoff, Harvard, 'Racial militancy and interracial violence in the Second World War', *Journal of American History*, December 1971.

Smith, Graham, 'Jim Crow on the home front', *New Community*, Winter 1980.

Terry, Wallace, 'Bringing the war home', *The Black Scholar*, November 1970.

Thorne, Christopher, 'Britain and the black GIs: racial issues and Anglo-American relations in 1942', *New Community*, Summer 1974.

Weil, Frank E. G. 'The Negro in the armed forces', *Social Forces*, October 1947.

Werrell, Kenneth P., 'Mutiny at Army Air Force Station 569: Bamber Bridge, England', *Aerospace Historian*, December 1975.

White, Milton, 'Self-determination for black soldiers', *The Black Scholar*, November 1970.

Wynn, Neil A., 'The impact of the Second World War on the American Negro', *Journal of Contemporary History*, vol. 6, no. 2, 1971.

Unpublished and miscellaneous material

Drake, St Clair, 'Value systems, social structure and race relations in the British Isles' (unpublished Ph.D. thesis, University of Chicago, 1954).

Murphy, Michael, 'British views of the American racial minorities 1917–1945, with special reference to travel literature' (unpublished M.Phil. thesis, Nottingham University 1974).

Stimson, Henry, *Diary*, Microfilm Edition.

Correspondence of author, including letters from:
  Ralph Ellison
  J. L. Keith
  City of Birmingham Public Relations Section (visit of black WAACs 1981).

Interviews with, and personal material from:
  Leon York
  Ann Evans
  Jody Bryant

INDEX